T0214108

Lecture Notes in Computer Science 12329

More information about this series at http://www.springer.com/series/7412

Islem Rekik · Ehsan Adeli · Sang Hyun Park ·
Maria del C. Valdés Hernández (Eds.)

Predictive Intelligence in Medicine

Third International Workshop, PRIME 2020
Held in Conjunction with MICCAI 2020
Lima, Peru, October 8, 2020
Proceedings

 Springer

Editors
Islem Rekik (iD)
Istanbul Technical University
Istanbul, Turkey

Ehsan Adeli (iD)
Stanford University
Stanford, CA, USA

Sang Hyun Park (iD)
Daegu Gyeongbuk Institute of Science
and Technology
Daegu, Korea (Republic of)

Maria del C. Valdés Hernández (iD)
The University of Edinburgh
Edinburgh, UK

ISSN 0302-9743 ISSN 1611-3349 (electronic)
Lecture Notes in Computer Science
ISBN 978-3-030-59353-7 ISBN 978-3-030-59354-4 (eBook)
https://doi.org/10.1007/978-3-030-59354-4

LNCS Sublibrary: SL6 – Image Processing, Computer Vision, Pattern Recognition, and Graphics

This Springer imprint is published by the registered company Springer Nature Switzerland AG
The registered company address is: Gewerbestrasse 11, 6330 Cham, Switzerland

Preface

It would constitute a stunning progress in medicine if, in a few years, we contribute to engineering a predictive intelligence, able to predict missing clinical data with high precision. Given the outburst of big and complex medical data with multiple modalities (e.g., structural magnetic resonance imaging (MRI) and resting function MRI (rsfMRI)) and multiple acquisition timepoints (e.g., longitudinal data), more intelligent predictive models are needed to improve diagnosis of a wide spectrum of diseases and disorders while leveraging minimal medical data. Basically, the predictive intelligence in medicine (PRIME) workshop primarily aims to diagnose in the earliest stage using minimal clinically non-invasive data. For instance, PRIME would constitute a breakthrough in early neurological disorder diagnosis as it would allow accurate early diagnosis using multimodal MRI data (e.g., diffusion and functional MRIs) and follow-up observations all predicted from only T1-weighted MRI acquired at baseline time point.

Existing computer-aided diagnosis methods can be divided into two main categories: (1) analytical methods and (2) predictive methods. While analytical methods aim to efficiently analyze, represent, and interpret data (static or longitudinal), predictive methods leverage the data currently available to predict observations at later time points (i.e., forecasting the future) or predicting observations at earlier time points (i.e., predicting the past for missing data completion). For instance, a method which only focuses on classifying patients with mild cognitive impairment (MCI) and patients with Alzheimer's disease (AD) is an analytical method, while a method which predicts if a subject diagnosed with MCI will remain stable or convert to AD over time is a predictive method. Similar examples can be established for various neurodegenerative or neuropsychiatric disorders, degenerative arthritis, or in cancer studies, in which the disease/disorder develops over time.

Following the success of the first two editions of PRIME MICCAI in 2018 and 2019, the third edition of PRIME 2020 aims to drive the field of 'high-precision predictive medicine,' where late medical observations are predicted with high precision, while providing explanation via machine and deep learning and statistically, mathematically, or physically-based models of healthy, disordered development and aging. Despite the terrific progress that analytical methods have made in the last 20 years in medical image segmentation, registration, or other related applications, and efficient predictive intelligent models and methods are somewhat lagging behind. As such predictive intelligence develops and improves – and this is likely to do so exponentially in the coming years – it will have far-reaching consequences for the development of new treatment procedures and novel technologies. These predictive models will begin to shed light on one of the most complex healthcare and medical challenges we have ever encountered, and, in doing so, change our basic understanding of who we are.

What are the key challenges we aim to address?

The main aim of PRIME MICCAI is to propel the advent of predictive models in a broad sense, with application to medical data. The workshop accepted 8 to 12-page papers describing new cutting-edge predictive models and methods that solve challenging problems in the medical field. We envision that the PRIME workshop will become a nest for high-precision predictive medicine, one that is set to transform multiple fields of healthcare technologies in unprecedented ways. Topics of interests for the workshop included, but were not limited to, predictive methods dedicated to the following topics:

- Modeling and predicting disease development or evolution from a limited number of observations
- Computer-aided prognostic methods (e.g., for brain diseases, prostate cancer, cervical cancer, dementia, acute disease, neurodevelopmental disorders)
- Forecasting disease or cancer progression over time
- Predicting low-dimensional data (e.g., behavioral scores, clinical outcome, age, gender)
- Predicting the evolution or development of high-dimensional data (e.g., shapes, graphs, images, patches, abstract features, learned features)
- Predicting high-resolution data from low-resolution data
- Prediction methods using 2D, 2D+t, 3D, 3D+t, ND, and ND+t data
- Predicting data of one image modality from a different modality (e.g., data synthesis)
- Predicting lesion evolution
- Predicting missing data (e.g., data imputation or data completion problems)
- Predicting clinical outcome from medical data (e.g., genomic, imagining data, etc.)

Key Highlights

This workshop mediated ideas from both machine learning and mathematical/statistical/physical modeling research directions in the hope of providing a deeper understanding of the foundations of predictive intelligence developed for medicine, as well as an understanding of where we currently stand and what we aspire to achieve through this field. PRIME MICCAI 2020 featured a single-track workshop with keynote speakers with deep expertise in high-precision predictive medicine using machine learning and other modeling approaches – which are believe to stand in opposition. PRIME 2020 ran virtually and keynote talks were live streamed this year due to the COVID-19 pandemic. Pre-recorded videos of accepted papers and keynote presentations were posted on the PRIME web page[1]. Eventually, this will increase the outreach of PRIME publications to a broader audience while steering a wide spectrum of MICCAI publications from being 'only analytical' to being 'jointly analytical and predictive.'

We received a total of 20 submissions. All papers underwent a rigorous double-blinded review process by at least 2 members (mostly 3 members) of the

---

[1] http://basira-lab.com/prime-miccai-2020/.

Program Committee composed of 27 well-known research experts in the field. The selection of the papers was based on technical merit, significance of results, and relevance and clarity of presentation. Based on the reviewing scores and critiques, all but one of the PRIME submissions were scored highly by reviewers, i.e., all had an average score of above the acceptance threshold.

Diversity and **inclusion** was one of main focuses of PRIME MICCAI workshop. This year we were able to have a gender-balanced Organizing Committee. We also promoted gender balance and geographic diversity in the Program Committee. The authors of the accepted PRIME papers were affiliated with institutions in the four continents: Africa, Europe, America, and Asia. We have also provided two PRIME awards to register the papers of talented minority students in low research and developing countries (both were from Africa). The eligibility criteria of the PRIME award were included in the CMT submission system. We will strive to continue this initiative in the upcoming years and see a similar trend in other conferences and workshops.

August 2020   Islem Rekik
                                                      Ehsan Adeli
                                                   Sang Hyun Park
                                       Maria del C. Valdés Hernández

Organization

Chairs

Islem Rekik	Istanbul Technical University, Turkey
Ehsan Adeli	Stanford University, USA
Sang Hyun Park	DGIST, South Korea
Maria Valdes Hernandez	The University of Edinburgh, UK

Program Committee

Alaa Bessadok	University of Sousse, Tunisia
Amir Alansary	Imperial College London, UK
Baiying Lei	Shenzhen University, China
Benjamin S. Aribisala	Lagos State University, Nigeria
Changqing Zhang	Tianjin University, China
Dong Hye Ye	Marquette University, USA
Duygu Sarikaya	University of Rennes 1, France
Guorong Wu	The University of North Carolina at Chapel Hill, USA
Febrian Rachmadi	RIKEN, Japan
Heung-Il Suk	Korea University, South Korea
Ilwoo Lyu	Vanderbilt University, USA
Jaeil Kim	Kyungpook National University, South Korea
Jon Krause	Google, USA
Lichi Zhang	Shanghai Jiao Tong University, China
Manhua Liu	Shanghai Jiao Tong University, China
Mayssa Soussia	The University of North Carolina at Chapel Hill, USA
Minjeong Kim	The University of North Carolina at Greensboro, USA
Pew-Thian Yap	University of North Carolina at Chapel Hill, USA
Qian Wang	Shanghai Jiao Tong University, China
Qingyu Zhao	Stanford University, USA
Seung Yeon Shin	National Institutes of Health, USA
Seyed Mostafa Kia	Donders Institute, The Netherlands
Ulas Bagci	University of Central Florida, USA
Victor Gonzalez	Universidad de León, Spain
Xiaohuan Cao	United Imaging Intelligence, China
Yu Zhang	Stanford University, USA
Yue Gao	Tsinghua University, China
Ziga Spiclin	University of Ljubljana, Slovenia

Contents

Context-Aware Synergetic Multiplex Network for Multi-organ Segmentation of Cervical Cancer MRI

Nesrine Bnouni[1,2], Islem Rekik[2(✉)] (iD), Mohamed Salah Rhim[3], and Najoua Essoukri Ben Amara[1]

[1] LATIS-Laboratory of Advanced Technology and Intelligent Systems, Université de Sousse, Ecole Nationale d'Ingénieurs de Sousse, 4023 Sousse, Tunisia
[2] BASIRA Lab, Faculty of Computer and Informatics, Istanbul Technical University, Istanbul, Turkey
irekik@itu.edu.tr
[3] Department of Gynecology Obstetrics, Faculty of Medicine of Monastir, Monastir, Tunisia
http://basira-lab.com

Abstract. Generative Adversarial Networks (GANs) have increasingly broken records in solving challenging medical image analyses problems such as medical image de-noising, segmentation, detection, classification or reconstruction. However, to the best of our knowledge, they have not been used for female pelvic multi-organ segmentation. Accurate segmentation of uterine cervical cancer (UCC) organs (i.e., bladder, vagina and tumor) from magnetic resonance imaging (MRI) is crucial for effective UCC staging. However, it is a highly challenging task due to 1) noisy MR images, 2) *within-subject* large variability in structure and intensity of UCC organs, and 3) *across-subject* variability. More importantly, there have been very limited works on how to aggregate different interactions across MRI views using GANs for multi-organ segmentation while providing context information. In this work, we propose a novel synergetic multiplex network (SMN) using multi-stage deep learning architecture based on cycle-GAN to segment pelvic multi-organ using complementary multi-view MRI, introducing three major contributions in multi-organ segmentation literature: (1) Modeling the interactions across data views using a novel multiplex architecture composed of multiple layers. Each SMN layer nests a cascade of *view-specific* context-aware cycle-GANs and synergistically communicates context information to other paralleled view-specific layers via multiplex coupling links. (2) SMN captures shared and complementary information between different views to segment UCC in different MRI views. (3) It enforces the spatial consistency between neighboring pixels within the same tissue for UCC segmentation. Specifically, in a gradual and deep manner, the proposed method improves the segmentation results by iteratively providing more refined context information from other views to train the next segmentation cycle-GAN in the SMN layer. We evaluated our SMN framework using 15 T2w-MR sequences with axial and sagittal views. We show that SMN is robust for the UCC segmentation task by significantly ($p < 0.05$) outperforming comparison segmentation methods.

© Springer Nature Switzerland AG 2020
I. Rekik et al. (Eds.): PRIME 2020, LNCS 12329, pp. 1–11, 2020.
https://doi.org/10.1007/978-3-030-59354-4_1

1   Introduction

Uterine Cervical Cancer (UCC) is one of the common cancer among women, the fourth most frequently diagnosed cancer and the fourth leading cause of cancer death in women with an estimated 570,000 cases and 311,000 deaths in 2018 worldwide [1]. The clinical stage of UCC is based on the prognostic factors such as the tumor volume and the nodal status. Magnetic Resonance Imaging (MRI) is the preferred imaging modality as it is able to assess soft tissue details allowing better identifying tumor. Specifically, MRI mostly helps in the evaluation of tumor extension to the body of uterus, vagina, parametrium, urinary bladder wall, and rectal wall. Additionally, to stage UCC, accurate segmentation of three pelvic organs is required. Multi-organ segmentation would help in speeding up the diagnosis and treatment processes. However, accurate segmentation of three UCC organs might be limited by three challenges. *First*, MR images are quite noisy. As shown in (Fig. 1), the contrast among tumor, bladder, and vagina is somewhat low. These three organs are also similar to their neighboring tissues and might overlap in advanced stages which further complicates their identification. *Second*, the manual delineation of pelvic organs is time-consuming and prone to inter-observer and intra-observer variabilities even for experienced clinicians. *Third*, UCC organs have large anatomical variations and are all deformable soft tissues, and thus both shape and appearance of these three organs can have high variations across different patients (Fig. 1). Hence, developing automated multi-organ segmentation tools with good-quality accuracy and robustness would be of great assistance in patient staging and diagnosis for clinicians.

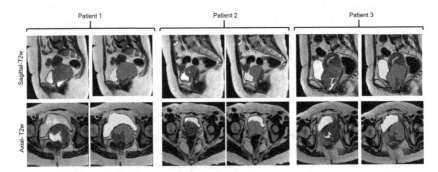

Fig. 1. *MR images of female pelvic regions in three typical patients.* Red: tumor. Yellow: bladder. Green: vagina. (Color figure online)

Related works on male pelvic multi-organ segmentation leveraged machine learning techniques for automated tissue labeling using Computed Tomography (CT) and MRI data. For instance, advanced multi-organ segmentation approaches such as male pelvic multi-organs using deep learning methods were proposed in [2,3]. In [2], a two-stage distinctive curve guided Fully Convolutional Network (FCN) was proposed to tackle the challenging pelvic CT segmentation problem. In [3] used the U-Net to delineate the prostate, bladder, and rectum. More recently, generative adversarial networks (GANs) [4] have shown their excellent performance particularly for medical image segmentation tasks thanks to their unique ability to mimic data distributions and the possibility to bridge the gap between learning and synthesis. Particularly, in tasks where the joint segmentation of multiple organs is desired, GANs have broken records [5–8]. Recently, cycle-GAN [9] was used to learn the relationship between a source domain and target one by adding a second generator that interprets the target image generating from the first generator back into the source domain. Cycle-GAN was successfully applied to MR-to-CT synthesis [10]. [11] used cycle-GAN with an identity loss in the denoising of cardiac CT. [12] used cycle-GAN for unsupervised domain adaptation of medical image segmentation. In another work, [12] improved cycle-GAN with a novel semantic-aware loss by embedding a nested adversarial learning in semantic label space. In [13], cycle-GAN model was used for image-to-image translation of T1- and T2-weighted MR images, by comparing generated synthetic MR images to ground truth images.

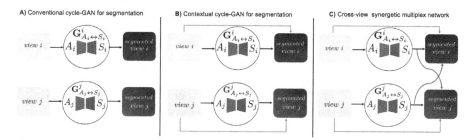

Fig. 2. *The core idea of the proposed cross-view synergetic multiplex network using cross-layer coupling links and context information links in comparison with its ablated version (B) and a conventional ensemble translator method (A) for multi-organ segmentation of uterine cervical cancer using multi-view imaging.*

However, recent surveys on GANs [4] and their application to multi-organ segmentation [8] point to a big gap in GAN literature, where the theory of *ensemble learning* and *adversarial learning* have barely intersected and most likely overlooked *multi-view* ensemble learning architectures. In fact, most deep learning based methods chain deep learners (e.g.., CNN) [8], where each learner benefits from the training of its antecedent learner in the chain by passing its outputted segmentation map without any appearance-aware context (Fig. 2A). However, in such setting, learners do not communicate across data views. By constantly feeding the original source image to each learner in the cascade, one provides contextual information enforcing spatial consistency in the target segmentation map, however remains view-independent (Fig. 2A). Another work [14] proposed a dynamic multiscale CNN forest for cervical cancer segmentation;

however, this cannot also handle multi-view datasets. To address these limitations, we propose a novel *synergetic multiplex network* (SMN) using multi-stage deep learning architecture based on cycle-GAN to segment pelvic multi-organ using complementary MRI views while introducing three major contributions in multi-organ segmentation and UCC staging: (1) Modeling the interactions across data views using a novel multiplex architecture composed of multiple layers. Each SMN layer nests a cascade of *view-specific* context-aware cycle-GANs and synergistically communicates context information to other paralleled view-specific layers via multiplex coupling links. (2) SMN captures shared and complementary information between different views. (3) Our SMN enforces spatial consistency between neighboring pixels within the same tissue for UCC segmentation. Specifically, in a gradual and deep manner, the proposed method improves the segmentation results by iteratively providing more refined context information from other views to train the next segmentation cycle-GAN in the SMN layer. The novel aspects of our work as listed below:

1. We design a novel ensemble learning framework with Cycle-GAN as a base classifier.
2. We draw inspiration from the multiplex network architecture to introduce a novel ensemble learning strategy based on cycle-GAN. Our synergetic multiplex network (SMN) is composed of multiple layers with interactions across data views. Each SMN layer nests a cascade of view-specific context-aware cycle-GANs and synergistically communicates context information to other paralleled layers via multiplex coupling links.
3. Our SMN is generic and can nest any segmentation deep learning architecture such as SegNet [15] or UNet [16]. In this paper we chose Cycle-GAN as a proof-of-concept for the boosting capacity of our SMN.

2   Proposed Context-Aware Synergetic Multiplex Network for Multi-organ Segmentation

Problem Statement. Synergetic learning is a class of ensemble learning problems where the goal is to learn how to model interactions between a set of learners to eventually boost the performance of learning system. However, for tasks handling multi-view datasets, where each sample is represented by different views, conventional ensemble learning architecture such as cascading view-specific learners (Fig. 2A) fail to capture cross-view interactions. Inspired from the multiplex architecture [17,18], we present a new *shifted* formalization of the multiplex network to build a synergetic learning network, where each node nests a cycle-GAN, shifted cross-view coupling links are introduced, and context information links are added (Fig. 2C). Using the designed SMN, we learn a set of synergetic and more refined mappings from the input view-specific image to its output segmentation map.

Cycle-GAN Overview. For each data view i, we learn a cycle-GAN to translate the MR appearance image A_i in domain $\mathcal{A}_i$ into a multi-label segmentation map S_i in domain $\mathcal{S}_i$. The core concept of cycle-GAN [9] lies in learning a bidirectional mapping from appearance to segmentation images and vice versa, where a cycle consistency loss is added to limit the number of possible solution mappings and avoid mode collapse. Specifically, we aim to learn two mappings $G_{\mathcal{A}_i \to \mathcal{S}_i} : \mathcal{A}_i \longrightarrow \mathcal{S}_i$ and $G_{\mathcal{S}_i \to \mathcal{A}_i} : \mathcal{S}_i \longrightarrow \mathcal{A}_i$. Notice that the model learns both mappings, however, in the testing stage, we only test the generator $G_{\mathcal{A}_i \to \mathcal{S}_i}$. Cycle-GAN is formalized as an adversarial learning problem, where a first discriminator $D_{\mathcal{A}_i}$ aims to differentiate between images A_i and translated images $G_{\mathcal{S}_i \to \mathcal{A}_i}(S_i)$ and a second discriminator $D_{\mathcal{S}_i}$ discriminates between S_i and $G_{\mathcal{A}_i \to \mathcal{S}_i}(A_i)$, respectively. For each view, adversarial loss from domain $\mathcal{A}_i$ to $\mathcal{S}_i$ is defined as follows:

$$\mathcal{L}_{GAN}(G_{\mathcal{A}_i \to S_i}, D_{\mathcal{S}_i}, A, S) = \mathbb{E}_{S_i}[log D_{S_i}(S_i)] + \mathbb{E}_{A_i}[log(1 - D_{S_i}(G_{\mathcal{A}_i \to S_i}(A_i)))] \qquad (1)$$

where $G_{\mathcal{A}_i \to \mathcal{S}_i}$ generates $G_{\mathcal{A}_i \to \mathcal{S}_i}(A_i)$ images similar to images from domain $\mathcal{S}_i$. On the other hand, $G_{\mathcal{A}_i \to \mathcal{S}_i}$ aims to overcome its adversary $\mathcal{S}_i$ by maximizing the following function:

$$\min_{G_{\mathcal{A}_i \to \mathcal{S}_i}} \max_{D_{\mathcal{S}_i}} L_{GAN}(G_{\mathcal{A}_i \to \mathcal{S}_i}, D_{\mathcal{S}_i}, \mathcal{A}, \mathcal{S}) \qquad (2)$$

As both learned translation functions should be cycle-consistent, i.e., for each appearance image A_i from domain $\mathcal{A}_i$, the image translation cycle should be able to reverse A_i back to the original image $A_i \longrightarrow G_{\mathcal{A}_i \to \mathcal{S}_i}$ generates $G_{\mathcal{A}_i \to \mathcal{S}_i}(A_i) \longrightarrow G_{\mathcal{S}_i \to \mathcal{A}_i}(G_{\mathcal{A}_i \to \mathcal{S}_i}(A_i)) \simeq A_i$ using a cycle consistency loss:

$$\mathcal{L}_{cyc}(G_{\mathcal{A}_i \to \mathcal{S}_i}, G_{\mathcal{S}_i \to \mathcal{A}_i}) = \mathbb{E}_{A_i}[||G_{\mathcal{S}_i \to \mathcal{A}_i}(G_{\mathcal{A}_i \to \mathcal{B}_i}(A_i)) - A_i||_1] \qquad (3)$$
$$+ \mathbb{E}_{S_i}[||G_{\mathcal{A}_i \to \mathcal{S}_i}(G_{\mathcal{S}_i \to \mathcal{A}_i}(S_i)) - S_i||_1],$$

where $||\cdots||_1$ denotes L_1 norm. Hence, our full objective for a single cycle-GAN in view i is defined as (Fig. 2C):

$$G_{\mathcal{A}_i \leftrightarrow \mathcal{S}_i} = \underset{G_{\mathcal{A}_i \to \mathcal{S}_i}, G_{\mathcal{S}_i \to \mathcal{A}_i}}{\text{argmin}} \underset{D_{\mathcal{A}_i}, D_{\mathcal{S}_i}}{\text{argmax}} \mathcal{L}(G_{\mathcal{A}_i \to \mathcal{S}_i}, G_{\mathcal{S}_i \to \mathcal{A}_i}, D_{\mathcal{A}_i}, D_{\mathcal{S}_i}) \qquad (4)$$

$$= \mathcal{L}_{GAN}(G_{\mathcal{A}_i \to \mathcal{S}_i}, D_{\mathcal{S}_i}, A, S) + \mathcal{L}_{GAN}(G_{\mathcal{S}_i \to \mathcal{A}_i}, D_{\mathcal{A}_i}, S, A) + \lambda \mathcal{L}_{cyc}(G_{\mathcal{A}_i \to \mathcal{S}_i}, G_{\mathcal{S}_i \to \mathcal{A}_i}) \qquad (5)$$

where λ regulates the relative influence of the cycle consistency loss.

Synergetic Multiplex Network. Multiplex networks have been proposed as a means to capture high level complexity in interaction networks [17,18]. In this paper, we propose an synergetic learning model capitalizing on the multiplex network, which is conventionally defined as a triplet $\mathbb{M} = < V, \mathbb{E}, C >$ where V denotes a set of nodes, $\mathbb{E} = \{E_1, \ldots, E_n\}$ represents a set of n types of edges linking pairs of nodes in V. $C = \{(v, v, i, j)\} : v \in V, i, j \in [1, n], l \neq k$ is a set of coupling links connecting a node v to itself across different layers i and j.

Typically, multiplex networks have ordinal couplings, where a node in one layer is connected to itself in adjacent layers, whereas multiplexes with categorical couplings comprise nodes that are connected to themselves in each other layer [17]. Since the core idea of ensemble learning lies in communicating the learning of a baseline learner to another learner, we adapt the multiplex architecture to our goal by proposing three alterations: (i) *shifted* cross-layer links where a node in one layer is connected to its precedent node in another way, (ii) each node has a shifted connection to its precedent nodes across all layers, thereby enforcing a *one-to-many* couplings across other layers, and (iii) *context information links* are added to all within-layer nodes in the multiplex for all layers (Fig. 3).

SMN Within-View Learning. Specifically, given view-specific layer i in $\mathbb{M}$, the kth cycle-GAN $\mathbf{G}_{A_i^k}^{i,k} \leftrightarrow S_i^k$ translates an appearance image A_i^k into a segmentation map S_i^k. Within each layer, each $\mathbf{G}_{A_i^k}^{i,k} \leftrightarrow S_i^k$ communicates its output segmentation map to the next $\mathbf{G}_{A_i^{k+1}}^{i,k+1} \leftrightarrow S_i^{k+1}$ node in the layer providing a more refined semantic contextual information for conditioning its learning. Notice that a cycle-GAN can map a set of input of appearance images to any random permutation of segmentation images in the target domain, where any of the learned mappings $\mathbf{G}_{A_i^k}^{i,k} \to S_i^k$ can randomly match the distribution of domain $\mathcal{S}$. This might produce mappings that fail to map an input image A_i^k to an accurate segmentation map S_i^k. To narrow down the space of possible solution mappings to learn in order to map A_i^k onto S_i^k, we argue that providing semantic and appearance context information passed on as segmentation image from the previous node and appearance source view-specific image to each node, respectively, should progressively improve the learned mappings between consecutive nodes in the layer (Fig. 3).

SMN Cross-View Learning. More importantly, as we aim to segment an input image in different views, each $\mathbf{G}_{A_i^k}^{i,k} \leftrightarrow S_i^k$ in view i also inputs the segmentation maps outputted by its antecedent learners $\mathbf{G}_{A_j^{k-1}}^{j,k-1} \leftrightarrow S_j^{k-1}$ in other views $j \neq i$ via cross-layer coupling links in $\mathbb{M}$ (Fig. 3). Our SMN promotes a mutual synergetic learning between its view-specific layers, so the jointly learned segmentation mappings can benefit from each another in each layer. Notice that our SMN has not only a static context transfer where the same appearance context information is fed to all nodes in the multiplex falling in the same layer, but also a dynamic deep transfer across nodes in one layer and between layers (Fig. 3). Such setup allows a joint within-layer and cross-layer synergetic learning to produce multi-organ segmentation maps in different views.

3   Results and Discussion

Dataset and Parameter Setting. We evaluated the proposed segmentation and classification framework using 15 clinical pelvic T2w UCC MR database with different stages collected from a gynecologic oncology referral center, acquired

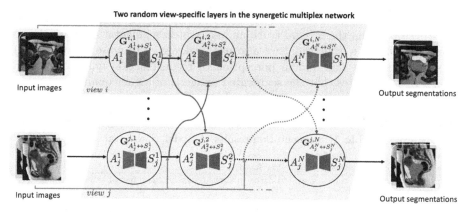

Fig. 3. *Pipeline of the proposed synergetic multiplex network using multi-view MRI for multi-organ uterine cervical cancer segmentation.* For $k > 1$, the kth cycle-GAN $\mathbf{G}^{i,k}_{A^k_i \leftrightarrow S^k_i}$ in the view-specific layer i is trained using (i) the segmentation map outputted by its antecedent translator $\mathbf{G}^{i,k-1}_{A^{k-1}_i \leftrightarrow S^{k-1}_i}$ in the layer, (ii) the segmentation maps outputted by all other cross-view antecedent translators $\mathbf{G}^{j,k-1}_{A^{k-1}_j \leftrightarrow S^{k-1}_j}$, where $j \neq i$ (i.e., cross-layer coupling links), and (iii) the context appearance source image in view i. (i.e., context coupling links). Our SMN enforces within-layer and cross-view synergetic learning and produces segmentation maps of each view.

between January 2016 and December 2017 diagnosed with UCC. All 15 patients underwent a regular examination with a 1.5-T MRI system. Axial and sagittal T2w 2D turbo spin-echo sequences with voxel size of $0.5 \times 0.5 \times 3$ mm were used. All data sets were manually segmented and staged by an expert radiologist. We used affine registration to align all training axial and sagittal MR images to a common space. Each testing subject is then affinely aligned to the training samples.

Without loss of generality, our goal is to segment multi-organ UCC MR images in both axial and sagittal views. Tumor size, tumor invading in and out of the cervix, and its propagation to distant organs (rectum and bladder wall invasion) are best evaluated in the sagittal plane. High-resolution T2w in the axial oblique plane is essential for assessing the disruption or preservation of the hypointense stromal. The use of the sagittal and axial views is therefore useful to segment multi-organs UCC. This segmentation is learned using the paired axial and sagittal MR images of training subjects, and then applied to a new axial and sagittal image for generating its corresponding segmentation map. Hence, without loss of generalizability to more than two layers, we designed a two-layer SMN to simultaneously segment two image views.

We used leave-one-out cross-validation to evaluate our segmentation and staging approaches. To evaluate our segmentation method, we use the Dice ratio defined as: $Dice = 2(\hat{S} \cap S)/(\hat{S} + S)$, where S denotes the ground-truth label map, manually delineated by an expert radiologist, and $\hat{S}$ the estimated label map.

We also use mean squared error (MSE), which computes the average squared
L2 distance between the ground truth and generated segmentation maps. For a
more comprehensive evaluation, we also use peak signal-to-noise ratio (PSNR)
as its approximates well human perception of reconstruction quality. Thus, a
higher PSNR indicates that the segmented image is of higher quality.

Table 1. Segmentation results. A: axial. S: sagittal.

Method	Bladder			Vagina			Tumor		
	Dice	MSE	PSNR	Dice	MSE	PSNR	Dice	MSE	PSNR
(1a) CycleGAN (S view)	0.8559	0.0121	18.7503	0.5152	0.0075	21.2363	0.8226	0.0057	22.3784
(1b) CycleGAN (A view)	0.8751	0.0109	19.6217	0.6264	0.0103	18.6352	0.7636	0.0158	19.0238
(2a) Cascaded cycleGAN (S view + S segmentation results)	0.9241	0.0042	23.7244	0.5708	0.0090	20.4636	0.8839	0.0188	17.2552
(2b) Cascaded cycleGAN (A view + A segmentation results)	0.8905	0.0099	20.0357	0.6957	0.0076	21.1664	0.7968	0.0101	19.9431
(3a) Cross-view cascaded cycleGAN (S view + A segmentation results)	0.3258	0.0423	15.365	0.2365	0.0236	16.3584	0.5048	0.0718	11.4383
(3b) Cross-view cascaded cycleGAN (A view + S segmentation results)	0.4387	0.0391	14.0807	0.3064	0.0114	18.4374	0.3810	0.0297	14.4726
(4a) Cycle-GAN SMN (S view + A and S segmentation results)	**0.9575**	**0.0024**	**26.1782**	**0.6170**	**0.0012**	**29.2439**	**0.9325**	**0.0116**	**22.3784**
(4b) Cycle-GAN SMN (A view + A and S segmentation results)	**0.9189**	**0.0091**	**20.4196**	**0.7060**	**0.0037**	**24.2909**	**0.8610**	**0.0060**	**19.3681**

Evaluation and Comparison Methods. We compared the proposed method
with several segmentation methods (Table 1): (1) single cycle-GAN (a. sagittal
view, and b. axial view), (2) contextual cycle-GAN cascade with no cross-layer
coupling links (a. sagittal view with sagittal segmentation results, and b. axial
view with axial segmentation results) (Fig. 2B), and (3) cross-view cycle-GAN
cascade with no context coupling links (a. sagittal view with axial segmentation
results, and b. axial view with sagittal segmentation results). We note that cycle-
GAN-Cascade cascade one cycle-GAN. In each layer, we have only two nodes
as the performance improvement becomes negligible when adding a third node.
The detailed experimental results are reported in Table 1. We visually inspect
the results using our framework and comparison methods for 3 representative
patients in views 1 and 2 (sagittal and axial views) displayed in Fig. 4. Our proposed method significantly outperformed all comparison methods ($p < 0.05$ using
two-tailed paired t-test) and produced the best segmentation maps. We also note

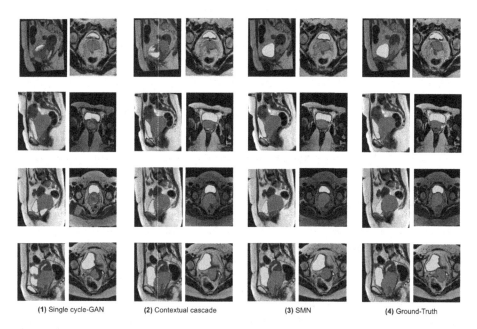

(1) Single cycle-GAN   (2) Contextual cascade   (3) SMN   (4) Ground-Truth

Fig. 4. *Segmentation maps of 3 representative patients in both axial (left) and sagittal (right) views.* (1) independent cycle-GAN. (2) Contextual cascaded cycleGAN (sagittal view with sagittal segmentation results and axial view with axial segmentation results). (3) Cycle-GAN SMN (axial view with axial and sagittal segmentation results). (5) Ground-truth segmentation maps.

a significant increase in the average Dice ratio of the conventional cycle-GAN and the cascaded cycle-GAN when using SMN. Clearly, our proposed synergetic learning architecture achieved the highest average segmentation accuracies for both views. We note that using cross-view information can also be relevant for UCC staging [19]. In our future work, we will extend our SMN architecture to jointly segment and stage UCC.

4   Conclusion

In this paper, we proposed a novel fully automated synergetic multiplex network deep learning-based architecture for joint multi-view and multi-organ segmentation of T2-weighted uterine cervical cancer MR images, leveraging contextual information to enforce consistency between spatial neighborhoods within a view and across views. For the segmentation results, both qualitative and quantitative measures show that our proposed approach produces better multi-organ segmentation compared to other methods. It is shown that the proposed approach has significantly higher accuracy in segmenting bladder, vagina, and tumor. The proposed framework is generic and can be applied to other types of MRIs and organs. In our future work, we will extend the proposed approach to an end-to-end architecture to simultaneously segment and stage UCC and handle the multi-scale anatomical variability across subjects in a coarse-to-fine manner.

References

1. Bray, F., Ferlay, J., Soerjomataram, I., Siegel, R.L., Torre, L.A., Jemal, A.: Global cancer statistics 2018: GLOBOCAN estimates of incidence and mortality worldwide for 36 cancers in 185 countries. CA Cancer J. Clin. **68**, 394–424 (2018)
2. He, K., Cao, X., Shi, Y., Nie, D., Gao, Y., Shen, D.: Pelvic organ segmentation using distinctive curve guided fully convolutional networks. IEEE Trans. Med. Imaging **38**, 585–595 (2018)
3. Kazemifar, S., et al.: Segmentation of the prostate and organs at risk in male pelvic CT images using deep learning. Biomed. Phys. Eng. Express **4**, 055003 (2018)
4. Litjens, G., et al.: A survey on deep learning in medical image analysis. Med. Image Anal. **42**, 60–88 (2017)
5. Trullo, R., Petitjean, C., Dubray, B., Ruan, S.: Multiorgan segmentation using distance-aware adversarial networks. J. Med. Imaging **6**, 014001 (2019)
6. Dong, X., et al.: Automatic multiorgan segmentation in thorax CT images using U-net-GAN. Med. Phys. **46**, 2157–2168 (2019)
7. Lei, Y., et al.: Male pelvic multi-organ segmentation aided by CBCT-based synthetic MRI. Phys. Med. Biol. **65**, 035013 (2020)
8. Lei, Y., et al.: Deep learning in multi-organ segmentation. arXiv preprint arXiv:2001.10619 (2020)
9. Zhu, J.Y., Park, T., Isola, P., Efros, A.A.: Unpaired image-to-image translation using cycle-consistent adversarial networks. In: Proceedings of the IEEE International Conference on Computer Vision, pp. 2223–2232 (2017)
10. Huo, Y., Xu, Z., Bao, S., Assad, A., Abramson, R.G., Landman, B.A.: Adversarial synthesis learning enables segmentation without target modality ground truth. In: IEEE 15th International Symposium on Biomedical Imaging (ISBI 2018), pp. 1217–1220 (2018)
11. Kang, E., Koo, H.J., Yang, D.H., Seo, J.B., Ye, J.C.: Cycle-consistent adversarial denoising network for multiphase coronary CT angiography. Med. Phys. **46**, 550–562 (2019)
12. Chen, C., Dou, Q., Chen, H., Heng, P.-A.: Semantic-aware generative adversarial nets for unsupervised domain adaptation in chest x-ray segmentation. In: Shi, Y., Suk, H.-I., Liu, M. (eds.) MLMI 2018. LNCS, vol. 11046, pp. 143–151. Springer, Cham (2018). https://doi.org/10.1007/978-3-030-00919-9_17
13. Dar, S.U., Yurt, M., Karacan, L., Erdem, A., Erdem, E., Çukur, T.: Image synthesis in multi-contrast MRI with conditional generative adversarial networks. IEEE Trans. Med. Imaging **38**, 2375–2388 (2019)
14. Bnouni, N., Rekik, I., Rhim, M.S., Amara, N.E.B.: Dynamic multi-scale CNN forest learning for automatic cervical cancer segmentation. In: Shi, Y., Suk, H.-I., Liu, M. (eds.) MLMI 2018. LNCS, vol. 11046, pp. 19–27. Springer, Cham (2018). https://doi.org/10.1007/978-3-030-00919-9_3
15. Badrinarayanan, V., Kendall, A., Cipolla, R.: SegNet: a deep convolutional encoder-decoder architecture for image segmentation. IEEE Trans. Pattern Anal. Mach. Intell. **39**, 2481–2495 (2017)

16. Ronneberger, O., Fischer, P., Brox, T.: U-Net: convolutional networks for biomedical image segmentation. In: Navab, N., Hornegger, J., Wells, W.M., Frangi, A.F. (eds.) MICCAI 2015. LNCS, vol. 9351, pp. 234–241. Springer, Cham (2015). https://doi.org/10.1007/978-3-319-24574-4_28
17. Kanawati, R.: Multiplex network mining: a brief survey. IEEE Intell. Inf. Bull. **16**, 24–27 (2015)
18. Lee, K.M., Kim, J.Y., Lee, S., Goh, K.I.: Multiplex Networks. Networks of Networks: The Last Frontier of Complexity, pp. 53–72 (2014)
19. Bnouni, N., Rekik, I., Rhim, M.S., Amara, N.E.B.: Cross-view self-similarity using shared dictionary learning for cervical cancer staging. IEEE Access **7**, 30079–30088 (2019)

Residual Embedding Similarity-Based Network Selection for Predicting Brain Network Evolution Trajectory from a Single Observation

Ahmet Serkan Göktaş[1], Alaa Bessadok[1,2]⬭, and Islem Rekik[1,2(✉)]⬭

[1] BASIRA Lab, Faculty of Computer and Informatics, Istanbul Technical University,
Istanbul, Turkey
irekik@itu.edu.tr
[2] LATIS Lab, ISITCOM, University of Sousse, Sousse, Tunisia
http://basira-lab.com

Abstract. Predicting the evolution trajectories of brain data from *a baseline timepoint* is a challenging task in the fields of neuroscience and neuro-disorders. While existing predictive frameworks are able to handle Euclidean structured data (i.e, brain images), they might fail to generalize to *geometric non-Euclidean* data such as brain networks. Recently, a seminal brain network evolution prediction framework was introduced capitalizing on learning how to select the most similar training network samples at baseline to a given testing baseline network for the target prediction task. However, this rooted the sample selection step in using Euclidean or learned similarity measure between *vectorized* training and testing brain networks. Such sample connectomic representation might include irrelevant and redundant features that could mislead the training sample selection step. Undoubtedly, this fails to exploit and preserve the topology of the brain connectome. To overcome this major drawback, we propose Residual Embedding Similarity-Based Network selection (RESNets) for predicting brain network evolution trajectory from a single timepoint. RESNets first learns a compact geometric embedding of each training and testing sample using adversarial connectome embedding network. This nicely reduces the high-dimensionality of brain networks while preserving their topological properties via graph convolutional networks. Next, to compute the similarity between subjects, we introduce the concept of a connectional brain template (CBT), a fixed network reference, where we further represent each training and testing network as a deviation from the reference CBT in the embedding space. As such, we select the most similar training subjects to the testing subject at baseline by comparing their learned residual embeddings with respect to the pre-defined CBT. Once the best training samples are selected at baseline, we simply average their corresponding brain networks at follow-up timepoints to predict the evolution trajectory of the testing network. Our experiments on both healthy and disordered brain networks demonstrate the success of our proposed method in comparison

© Springer Nature Switzerland AG 2020
I. Rekik et al. (Eds.): PRIME 2020, LNCS 12329, pp. 12–23, 2020.
https://doi.org/10.1007/978-3-030-59354-4_2

to RESNets ablated versions and traditional approaches. Our RESNets code is available at http://github.com/basiralab/RESNets.

Keywords: Brain graph evolution prediction · Connectional brain template · Sample embedding and selection · Dynamic brain connectivity · Residual similarity

1   Introduction

Longitudinal neuroimaging of the brain has spanned several neuroscientific works to examine early disease progression and eventually improve neurological disorder diagnosis [1,2]. Existing studies aiming to predict brain evolution trajectories from a single baseline timepoint are mainly focused on Euclidean neuroimaging data such as magnetic resonance imaging (MRI). For instance, [3] predicted the multishape trajectory of the baby brain using neonatal MRI data. Similarly, [4] and [5] used MR images to predict brain image evolution trajectories for early dementia detection. Although pioneering, such works mainly focused on Euclidean structured data (i.e, images), which is a flat representation of the brain and does not reflect the connectivity patterns existing among brain regions encoded in brain networks (i.e, connectomes). Specifically, a brain network is a graph representation of interactions in the brain between a set of anatomical regions of interests (ROIs) (or nodes). Such interactions are encoded in the edge weights between pairs of ROIs, capturing the function, structure, or morphology of the brain as a complex highly interconnected system.

So far, we have identified a single work on brain network evolution trajectory prediction [6], leveraging multi-kernel manifold learning technique to predict follow-up brain networks from a baseline network. This landmark work predicted the spatiotemporal trajectory of a network by first selecting the closest neighboring training samples (i.e., brain networks) to the testing sample at baseline via learning their pairwise similarities. Second, by averaging the follow-up selected training networks at later timepoints, the evolution trajectory of a testing brain network was generated. However, such approach is limited by the vectorization of baseline brain networks to learn the similarities between pairs of brain networks. Clearly, this fails to preserve and exploit both local and global topologies of the brain connectome [7]. In fact, each brain region has a particular topological property underpinning its function and which can be changed with healthy or atypical aging. The vectorization of brain networks to extract the sample features (i.e., connectivity weights) is widely adopted in connectomic machine learning tasks such as classification [8,9]. However, such connectome feature representations spoil the rich topological properties of the brain as a graph including its percolation threshold, hubness and modularity [10]. A second limitation of [6] lies in comparing pairs of brain networks at baseline without considering their inherently shared connectivity patterns. In other words, one can think of each individual sample as a deviation from a training population center capturing the shared traits across training samples. Hence, estimating a fixed population

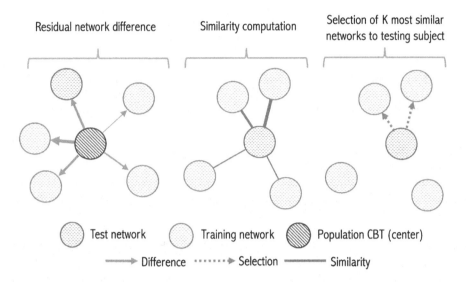

Fig. 1. *Selection principle of similar training subjects to a testing subject at a baseline timepoint* t_0. In this illustration, we sketch the scenario where we first generate the residual networks by computing an element-wise absolute difference between each network and population-driven connectional brain template (CBT). Second, we calculate the similarities between subjects using the resulting residual networks. Finally, we select top K similar subjects in the population to the testing one at baseline for the target prediction task.

network, namely a connectional brain template (CBT) as introduced in [11], presents a powerful tool to integrate complementary information from different brain networks. To capture shared connectivity patterns between training and testing samples, we propose to define a 'normalization' or 'standardization' process of brain networks (Fig. 1). Eventually, we hypothesize that reducing inter-subject variability in the baseline training network population through a normalization process will contribute towards helping better identify the best neighboring samples to the testing sample by modeling them as deviations from the 'standard/normalized' brain network representation (CBT).

This recalls an analogous brain imaging protocol, where one registers an image to an atlas image for group comparison and building classification models [12] following the extraction of 'shared' features in the standard shared space. Following this lead, we will use the estimated CBT to (1) first *normalize* each individual baseline brain connectome to the estimated CBT at baseline timepoint by generating the residual between each connectome and the fixed CBT, (2) then use the normalized individual network (i.e. residual with respect to the population CBT) at baseline to guide the prediction of follow-up brain connectomes acquired at later timepoints. To do so, we leverage netNorm [11] which produces a unified normalized connectional representation of a population of brain networks. Notably, this proposed strategy only solves the second limitation, while the first drawback of existing works remains untackled.

To overcome both limitations in a unified framework, we propose Residual Embedding Similarity-based Network selection (RESNets) for predicting brain connectome evolution trajectory from a single timepoint. To learn a topology-preserving brain network representation in a low-dimensional space for the target sample selection task, we first propose to learn the embedding of each baseline network by leveraging adversarial connectome embedding (ACE) [13]. ACE is rooted in the nascent field of geometric deep learning [14,15] where a brain graph is auto-encoded using an encoder E, defined as a Graph Convolution Network (GCN) [16], and regularized by a discriminator D aiming to align the distribution of the learned connectomic embedding with that of the original connectome. Specifically, we use ACE to embed each training and testing brain network as well as the CBT in a fully independent manner. Next we define the residual embedding of each training and testing sample using the absolute difference between the sample embedding and the CBT embedding. The resulting residual embeddings represent how each brain network deviate from the training population center. To predict the follow-up brain networks of a testing subject, we first compute the cosine similarities between training and testing subjects using their CBT-based residual embeddings, then identify the closest residual embeddings to the testing subject at baseline. Finally, we average their corresponding training networks at consecutive timepoints to ultimately predict the brain network evolution trajectory of a testing subject.

2   Proposed Method

Problem Definition. A brain network can be represented as $\mathbf{N} = \{\mathbf{V}, \mathbf{E}, \mathbf{X}\}$ where $\mathbf{V}$ is a set of nodes (i.e, ROIs) and $\mathbf{E}$ is a set of weighted edges encoding the interaction (connectivity) between each pair of nodes. Let $\mathbf{X} \in \mathbb{R}^{n_r \times n_r}$ denote the connectivity matrix where n_r is the number of nodes (ROIs) in a connectome. Each training sample s in our dataset is represented by a set of *time-depending* brain connectomes $\{\mathbf{X}_{t_g}^s\}_{g=0}^{n_t}$, each measured at a particular timepoint t_g. Given a testing connectome i solely represented by a brain network at first timepoint t_0 denoted as $\mathbf{X}_{t_0}^i$, our objective is to predict its missing brain networks $\{\hat{\mathbf{X}}_{t_h}^i\}$ at later timepoints t_h, $h \in \{1, ..., n_t\}$.

In the following, we present the main steps of our network evolution trajectory prediction framework from a baseline observation. Figure 2 provides an overview of the key three steps of the proposed framework: 1) adversarial connectome embedding of training and testing brain networks and the CBT estimated by netNorm at baseline, 2) construction of residual embeddings, and 3) prediction of brain networks at follow-up timepoints. For easy reference, we summarize the major mathematical notations in Table 1.

A-Adversarial Brain Network Embedding at Baseline t_0. We propose in this step to learn a low-dimensional topology-preserving representation of

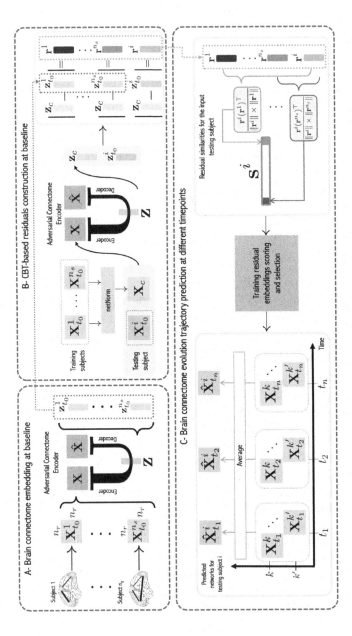

Fig. 2. *Proposed frameworks steps for predicting brain network evolution trajectory from a single observation at baseline timepoint* t_0 *using residual embeddings similarities.* **(A) Adversarial brain network connectome embedding at baseline** t_0. We learn the embeddings of each training brain network in the population at baseline using an adversarial connectome embedding encoder. **(B) CBT-based residuals construction.** We first estimate the CBT of the training networks and learn the embedding of both generated CBT and the testing brain network. Next, we normalize each brain network by computing the residual between the networks and the CBT embeddings. **(C) Brain network prediction at different timepoints.** To predict a follow-up brain network of a testing subject, we (i) compute the cosine similarities between subjects using their CBT-based residual embeddings, (ii) select the top similar subjects to the testing one and (iii) average their corresponding brain networks at a follow-up timepoint t_h where $h \in \{1, \ldots, n_t\}$.

Table 1. *Major mathematical notations used in this paper.*

Mathematical notation	Definition
n_t	Number of timepoints (baseline and follow-up)
n_s	Number of training subjects
n_r	Number of region of interest (ROI) in a brain network
d	Number of features of the embedded graph
K	Number of neighbors of a testing subject
$\mathbf{X}_{t_0}^i$	Brain network of a testing subject i at the baseline timepoint t_0 in $\mathbb{R}^{n_r \times n_r}$
$\mathbf{X}_{t_0}^j$	Brain network of a training subject j at the baseline timepoint t_0 where $j \in \{1, ..., n_s\}$ in $\mathbb{R}^{n_r \times n_r}$
$\hat{\mathbf{X}}_{t_h}^i$	Predicted brain network of a testing subject i at a follow-up timepoint t_h where $h \in \{1, ..., n_t\}$
$\mathbf{X}_{t_h}^l$	Brain network of a training neighbor $l \in \{k, ..., k'\}$ to the testing subject at a follow-up timepoint t_h in $\mathbb{R}^{n_r \times n_r}$
$\mathbf{X}_c$	Connectional brain template (CBT) of the training brain networks in $\mathbb{R}^{n_r \times n_r}$
$\mathbf{s}^i$	Similarity vector between the testing i and training subjects n_s using their CBT-based residuals in $\mathbb{R}^{1 \times n_s}$
$\mathbf{z}_c$	Learned CBT embedding of the training population in $\mathbb{R}^{d \times 1}$
$\mathbf{z}_{t_0}^i$	Learned brain network embedding of a testing subject i at the baseline timepoint t_0 in $\mathbb{R}^{d \times 1}$
$\mathbf{z}_{t_0}^j$	Learned brain network embedding of a training subject j in $\mathbb{R}^{d \times 1}$
$\mathbf{r}^i$	Testing CBT-based residual in $\mathbb{R}^{d \times 1}$
$\mathbf{r}^j$	Training CBT-based residual in $\mathbb{R}^{d \times 1}$
$\mathbf{v}_{ab}^j$	Similarity value for subject j related to ROIs a and b
$\mathbf{H}_{ab}$	High-order graph (graph of a graph) for pair of ROIs a and b $\in \mathbb{R}^{n_s \times n_s}$
$\mathbf{D}_{ab}(j)$	Cumulative distance of node j in $\mathbf{H}_{ab}$
$E(\mathbf{z}_{t_0} \mid \mathbf{F}_{t_0}, \mathbf{X}_{t_0})$	Encoder used for learning the brain network embedding at a baseline timepoint taking as input a feature matrix $\mathbf{F}_{t_0}$ and a brain network $\mathbf{X}_{t_0}$
$D(\hat{\mathbf{X}}_{t_0} \mid \mathbf{z}_{t_0})$	Decoder used to reconstruct the brain network from its embedding $\mathbf{z}_{t_0}$
$\mathcal{D}$	Discriminator used for connectome embedding regularization taking as input the real brain network $\mathbf{X}_{t_0}^s$ and the embedded network $\mathbf{z}_{t_0}^s$ of a subject s

a given brain network at baseline using ACE model [13], which is a subject-based adversarial embedding autoencoder tailored for brain connectomes (Fig. 2-A). ACE architecture is composed of a graph convolution network (GCN) [16] encoder $E(\mathbf{z} \mid \mathbf{F}, \mathbf{X})$ with two layers inputting a feature matrix $\mathbf{F}$ and an adjacency matrix $\mathbf{X}$. Since nodes in a brain connectome have no features, we filled $\mathbf{F}$ matrix with identify values (a set of '1'). At baseline timepoint t_0, we define the layers of our encoder $E(\mathbf{z}_{t_0} \mid \mathbf{F}_{t_0}, \mathbf{X}_{t_0})$ and the graph convolution function used in each mapping layer as follows:

$$\mathbf{z}_{t_0}^{(l)} = f_\phi(\mathbf{F}_{t_0}, \mathbf{X}_{t_0} | \mathbf{W}^{(l)}); \quad f_\phi(\mathbf{F}_{t_0}^{(l)}, \mathbf{X}_{t_0} | \mathbf{W}^{(l)}) = \phi(\widetilde{\mathbf{D}}^{-\frac{1}{2}} \widetilde{\mathbf{X}}_{t_0} \widetilde{\mathbf{D}}^{-\frac{1}{2}} \mathbf{F}_{t_0}^{(l)} \mathbf{W}^{(l)}), \tag{1}$$

$\mathbf{z}_{t_0}^{(l)}$ represents the resulting brain network embedding of the layer l. ϕ is the Rectified Linear Unit (ReLU) and linear activation functions we used in the first and second layers, respectively. $\mathbf{X}_{t_0}$ denotes the input brain network connectivity matrix at baseline timepoint. $\mathbf{W}^{(l)}$ is a learned filter encoding the graph convolutional weights in layer l. $f(.)$ is the graph convolution function where $\widetilde{\mathbf{X}}_{t_0} = \mathbf{X}_{t_0} + \mathbf{I}$ with $\mathbf{I}$ is the identity matrix used for regularization, and $\widetilde{\mathbf{D}}_{aa} = \sum_b \widetilde{\mathbf{X}}_{t_0}(ab)$ is a diagonal matrix storing the topological strength of each node. We note that ACE is trained for each sample independently to learn its embedding. The *individual-based* learning of brain network embedding yields not only to reducing the high-dimensionality of the original brain network but also preserving its topology via a set of layer-wise graph convolutions. To decode the resulting connectomic embedding $\mathbf{z}_{t_0}$, we compute the sigmoid function of the embedding $\mathbf{z}_{t_0}(a)$ and the transposed embedding $\mathbf{z}_{t_0}(b)$ of nodes a and b, respectively. Hence, we define our decoder $D(\hat{\mathbf{X}}_{t_0} | \mathbf{z}_{t_0})$ and the reconstruction error $\mathcal{L}$ as follows:

$$D(\hat{\mathbf{X}}_{t_0} | \mathbf{z}_{t_0}) = \frac{1}{1 + e^{-(\mathbf{z}_{t_0}(a) \cdot \mathbf{z}_{t_0}^\top(b))}}; \quad \mathcal{L} = \mathbf{E}_{E(\mathbf{z}_{t_0} | \mathbf{F}_{t_0}, \mathbf{X}_{t_0})}[\log D(\hat{\mathbf{X}}_{t_0} | \mathbf{z}_{t_0})] \tag{2}$$

Moreover, each brain network embedding is adversarially regularized using a discriminator $\mathcal{D}$ that aligns the distribution of learned embedding $\mathbf{z}_{t_0}^{(l)}$ in the last encoding layer l towards the prior data distribution that is the real baseline brain network $\mathbf{X}_{t_0}$. In particular, $\mathcal{D}$ is a multilayer perceptron aiming to minimize the error in distinguishing between real and fake data distributions. We formulate the adversarial brain network embedding cost function at a first timepoint t_0 as follows:

$$\min_E \max_{\mathcal{D}} \mathbf{E}_{p_{(real)}}[\log \mathcal{D}(\mathbf{X}_{t_0})] + \mathbf{E}_{p_{(fake)}}[\log(1 - \mathcal{D}(\mathbf{z}_{t_0}^{(l)})))] \tag{3}$$

where $\mathbf{E}$ is the cross-entropy cost. E and $\mathcal{D}$ represent our GCN encoder and discriminator, respectively.

B-CBT-Based Residual Construction. To compute the similarity between training and testing brain networks, we propose to consider the inherently shared connectivity patterns which are captured in an 'average' population network called connectional brain template (CBT). To this aim, we leverage netNorm [11] which estimates a normalized connectional map of a population of brain networks (Fig. 2B). Specifically, we learn a CBT for the training baseline brain connectomes in four consecutive stages. Since netNorm was originally designed to handle multi-view brain networks, where each subject is represented by a set of multimodal networks, we adapt it to our aim of integrating a set of *uni-modal* brain networks. Firstly, for each subject, we extract the value of the similarity between ROIs a and b as follows:

$$\mathbf{v}_{ab}^j = \mathbf{X}^j(a, b) \,; \forall \; 1 \le j \le n_s \tag{4}$$

where $\mathbf{X}^j$ represents the brain network of the subject j. Secondly, using these extracted values, we construct the high-order graph, storing for each pair of subjects j and j', the Euclidean distance between their corresponding connectivity weights between ROIs a and b as follows:

$$\mathbf{H}_{ab}(j, j') = \sqrt{(\mathbf{v}_{ab}^j - \mathbf{v}_{ab}^{j'})^2} \; ; \forall \; 1 \leq j, j' \leq n_s \tag{5}$$

This high-order graph will constitute the basis of selecting the connectivity weight between ROIs a and b of the most centered subject (j) with respect to all other subjects (i.e., achieving the lowest distance to all samples). To do so, we use cumulative distance metric for each subject j as:

$$\mathbf{D}_{ab}(j) = \sum_{j'=1}^{n_s} \mathbf{H}_{ab}(j, j') = \sum_{j'=1}^{n_s} \sqrt{(\mathbf{v}_{ab}^j - \mathbf{v}_{ab}^{j'})^2} \; ; \forall \; 1 \leq j, j' \leq n_s \tag{6}$$

Notably, this defines the strength of node j in the high-order graph H_{ab}. In the last step, we define the connectivity weight in the centered final CBT denoted by $\mathbf{X}_c$ as follows:

$$\mathbf{X_c}(a, b) = \mathbf{v}_{ab}^{j'}; \; where \; j' = \min_{1 \leq j \leq n_s} D_{ab}(j) \tag{7}$$

Originally, to fuse these matrices into a single connectome, we need to use a network fusion method [17] which reduces the tensor into a single representative matrix. However, since we design our framework for a single-view brain network evolution prediction, we skip the network fusion step of the multi-view CBT estimation.

Next, we feed the resulting CBT denoted by $\mathbf{X}_c$ to the GCN encoder E to learn its embedding $\mathbf{z}_c$ using Eq. 1. Last, we compute the residual embeddings using the following formula: $\mathbf{r} = |\mathbf{z}_c - \mathbf{z}_{t_0}|$, where $\mathbf{z}_{t_0}$ is the network embedding of a subject in the population (Fig. 2B). By producing these residuals, we are normalizing each baseline brain connectome to a fixed brain network reference (i.e, CBT) of the whole population.

C-Brain Network Prediction at Different Timepoints. To predict the evolution trajectory of a testing brain network, we first search its most similar training networks at baseline timepoint t_0 then average their corresponding brain networks at later timepoints $\{t_h\}_{h=1}^{n_t}$. To this end, we propose to select subjects based on their learned residual embeddings (Fig. 2-C). Specifically, we project the testing subject residual $\mathbf{r}^i$ on each training subject $\mathbf{r}^j$ in population and find the cosine between them using the following formula:

$$\mathbf{s}^i(j) = \frac{\mathbf{r}^i (\mathbf{r}^j)^\top}{\|\mathbf{r}^i\| \times \|\mathbf{r}^j\|} ; \forall \; 1 \leq j \leq n_s \tag{8}$$

The intuition behind this step is that if two embeddings are similar at a particular timepoint, they deviate from the CBT in the same way thus their residuals will also be similar. Notably, if the angle between two residual vectors is smaller then the cosine value will be higher. Next, we select top K subjects with the highest cosine similarities with the testing subject i. Finally, we average the brain networks of the K selected subjects at follow-up timepoints to predict the evolution trajectory of the testing network $\hat{\mathbf{X}}_{t_h}^i$ with $h \in \{1, \ldots, n_t\}$.

3   Results and Discussion

Evaluation Dataset. We evaluated our framework on 67 subjects (35 diagnosed with Alzheimer's disease and 32 diagnosed with late mild cognitive impairment) from ADNI GO public dataset[1] using leave-one-out cross validation. Each subject has two structural T1-w MR images acquired at baseline and 6-months follow-up. We used FreeSurfer to reconstruct both right and left cortical hemispheres for each subject from T1-w MRI. Next, we parcellated each cortical hemisphere into 35 cortical ROIs using Desikan-Killiany Atlas. For each subject, we constructed morphological brain networks (MBN) at each timepoint using the method introduced in [18]. We used the mean cortical thickness measure where the morphological connectivity strength between two regions is defined as the absolute difference between the average cortical thickness in each ROI.

Parameter Setting. Our encoder comprises three hidden layers of 16 neurons. The second hidden layer of the encoder is a Gaussian noise layer with $\sigma = 0.1$. We construct the discriminator with 64- and 16-neuron hidden layers. Both encoder and discriminator learning rates and number of iterations are set to 0.005 and 30, respectively. For the brain network prediction step, we vary the number of selected neighbors K between 2 and 4 and report results in Fig. 3A.

Comparison Methods and Evaluation. We compare the performance of our RESNets framework with two baseline methods: **(1) Similarity-based Network selection (SNets):** is a variant of our framework where the similarities are defined as the dot product between raw feature vectors of brain networks without any embedding. Note that such strategy is adopted in the state-of-the-art work [6] **(2) Embedding Similarity-based Network selection (ESNets):** is an ablated version of RESNets where the similarities are computed as the dot product between learned *embedded* brain networks. Figure 3A.1 and Fig. 3A.2 shows the Mean Absolute Deviance (MAD) and Mean Squared Error (MSE) between the ground truth and predicted testing networks at follow-up timepoint, respectively. Clearly, our RESNets framework consistently achieves the best prediction performance using different K selected neighbors to the testing subject. This demonstrates that our proposed similarity metric using the CBT-based residual embeddings boosts the network evolution prediction accuracy. We display in Fig. 3B.1 and Fig. 3B.2 the residual prediction error computed using Mean Absolute Deviance (MAD) between the ground truth and predicted follow-up brain network for two representative subjects. This clearly shows that our framework leads to a low network residual prediction error in

---

[1] http://adni.loni.usc.edu.

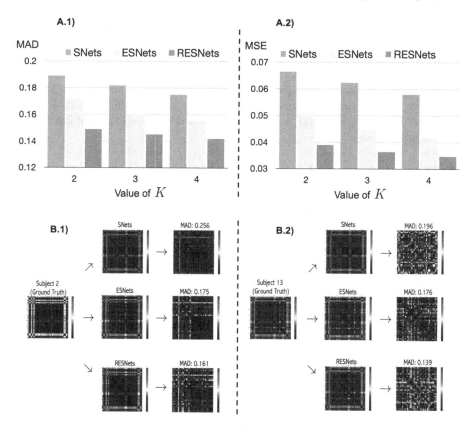

Fig. 3. **A.1–2)** *Comparison of RESNets against baseline methods using Mean Absolute Deviance (MAD) and Mean Squared Error (MSE).* SNets: Similarity-based Network selection method. ESNets: Embedding Similarity-based Network selection method. RESNets: the proposed Residual Embedding Similarity-based Network selection method. **B.1–2)** We display the predicted brain networks at a 6-month follow-up timepoint by RESNets and its ablated versions for two random subjects.

comparison to its variants. There are several exciting research directions to take this work further such as designing a joint end-to-end sample selection and prediction framework within a unified geometric deep learning framework.

4   Conclusion

We proposed a novel brain network evolution trajectory prediction framework from a single timepoint rooted in (i) learning adversarial topology-preserving embeddings of brain networks and (ii) a normalization step with respect to population center, namely connectional brain template, allowing us to compute residual similarities between a testing subject and training subjects for effective sample selection. Our RESNets framework can better identify the most similar training brain networks to a given testing network at baseline. Furthermore, RESNets outperformed baseline methods on autism spectrum disorder connectomic dataset. In our future work, we plan to generalize RESNets to handle multi-view brain network evolution prediction where different follow-up views are simultaneously predicted. Specifically, we aim to learn a joint embedding of all network views using ACE encoder and leverage the generalized netNorm for multi-view CBT estimation [11] to produce a population template that integrates different brain views.

Acknowledgement. I. Rekik is supported by the European Union's Horizon 2020 research and innovation programme under the Marie Sklodowska-Curie Individual Fellowship grant agreement No 101003403 (http://basira-lab.com/normnets/).

References

1. Yang, Q., Thomopoulos, S.I., Ding, L., Surento, W., Thompson, P.M., Jahanshad, N.: Support vector based autoregressive mixed models of longitudinal brain changes and corresponding genetics in Alzheimer's disease. In: Rekik, I., Adeli, E., Park, S.H. (eds.) PRIME 2019. LNCS, vol. 11843, pp. 160–167. Springer, Cham (2019). https://doi.org/10.1007/978-3-030-32281-6_17
2. Zhou, Y., Tagare, H.D.: Bayesian longitudinal modeling of early stage Parkinson's disease using DaTscan images. In: Chung, A.C.S., Gee, J.C., Yushkevich, P.A., Bao, S. (eds.) IPMI 2019. LNCS, vol. 11492, pp. 405–416. Springer, Cham (2019). https://doi.org/10.1007/978-3-030-20351-1_31
3. Rekik, I., Li, G., Lin, W., Shen, D.: Estimation of brain network atlases using diffusive-shrinking graphs: application to developing brains. In: Niethammer, M., et al. (eds.) IPMI 2017. LNCS, vol. 10265, pp. 385–397. Springer, Cham (2017). https://doi.org/10.1007/978-3-319-59050-9_31
4. Gafuroğlu, C., Rekik, I., Alzheimer's Disease Neuroimaging Initiative: Joint prediction and classification of brain image evolution trajectories from baseline brain image with application to early Dementia. In: Frangi, A.F., Schnabel, J.A., Davatzikos, C., Alberola-López, C., Fichtinger, G. (eds.) MICCAI 2018. LNCS, vol. 11072, pp. 437–445. Springer, Cham (2018). https://doi.org/10.1007/978-3-030-00931-1_50
5. Xia, T., Chartsias, A., Tsaftaris, S.A.: Consistent brain ageing synthesis. In: Shen, D., et al. (eds.) MICCAI 2019. LNCS, vol. 11767, pp. 750–758. Springer, Cham (2019). https://doi.org/10.1007/978-3-030-32251-9_82
6. Ezzine, B.E., Rekik, I.: Learning-guided infinite network atlas selection for predicting longitudinal brain network evolution from a single observation. In: Shen, D., et al. (eds.) MICCAI 2019. LNCS, vol. 11765, pp. 796–805. Springer, Cham (2019). https://doi.org/10.1007/978-3-030-32245-8_88
7. Fornito, A., Zalesky, A., Breakspear, M.: The connectomics of brain disorders. Nature Rev. Neurosci. **16**, 159–172 (2015)
8. Wang, J., et al.: Multi-class ASD classification based on functional connectivity and functional correlation tensor via multi-source domain adaptation and multi-view sparse representation. IEEE Trans. Med. Imaging (2020)
9. Richiardi, J., Van De Ville, D., Riesen, K., Bunke, H.: Vector space embedding of undirected graphs with fixed-cardinality vertex sequences for classification. In: 20th International Conference on Pattern Recognition, pp. 902–905 (2010)

10. Bassett, D.S., Sporns, O.: Network neuroscience. Nature Neurosci. **20**, 353 (2017)
11. Dhifallah, S., Rekik, I.: Estimation of connectional brain templates using selective multi-view network normalization. Med. Image Anal. **59**, 101567 (2019)
12. Liu, M., Zhang, D., Shen, D., Initiative, A.D.N.: View-centralized multi-atlas classification for Alzheimer's disease diagnosis. Hum. Brain Map. **36**, 1847–1865 (2015)
13. Banka, A., Rekik, I.: Adversarial connectome embedding for mild cognitive impairment identification using cortical morphological networks. In: Schirmer, M.D., Venkataraman, A., Rekik, I., Kim, M., Chung, A.W. (eds.) CNI 2019. LNCS, vol. 11848, pp. 74–82. Springer, Cham (2019). https://doi.org/10.1007/978-3-030-32391-2_8
14. Bronstein, M.M., Bruna, J., LeCun, Y., Szlam, A., Vandergheynst, P.: Geometric deep learning: going beyond Euclidean data. IEEE Signal Process. Mag. **34**, 18–42 (2017)
15. Hamilton, W.L., Ying, R., Leskovec, J.: Representation learning on graphs: methods and applications. arXiv preprint arXiv:1709.05584 (2017)
16. Kipf, T.N., Welling, M.: Semi-supervised classification with graph convolutional networks. arXiv preprint arXiv:1609.02907 (2016)
17. Wang, B., Mezlini, A., Demir, F., Fiume, M., et al.: Similarity network fusion for aggregating data types on a genomic scale. Nat. Methods **11**, 333–337 (2014)
18. Mahjoub, I., Mahjoub, M.A., Rekik, I.: Brain multiplexes reveal morphological connectional biomarkers fingerprinting late brain dementia states. Sci. Rep. **8**, 1–14 (2018)

Adversarial Brain Multiplex Prediction from a Single Network for High-Order Connectional Gender-Specific Brain Mapping

Ahmed Nebli[1,2] and Islem Rekik[1(✉)]

[1] BASIRA Lab, Faculty of Computer and Informatics, Istanbul Technical University,
Istanbul, Turkey
irekik@itu.edu.tr
[2] National School for Computer Science (ENSI), Mannouba, Tunisia
http://basira-lab.com

Abstract. Brain connectivity networks, derived from magnetic resonance imaging (MRI), non-invasively quantify the relationship in function, structure, and morphology between two brain regions of interest (ROIs) and give insights into gender-related connectional differences. However, to the best of our knowledge, studies on gender differences in brain connectivity were limited to investigating *pairwise* (i.e., *low-order*) relationship ROIs, overlooking the complex *high-order* interconnectedness of the brain as a network. A few recent works on neurological disorder diagnosis addressed this limitation by introducing *the brain multiplex*, which in its shallow form, is composed of a source network intra-layer, a target intra-layer, and a convolutional inter-layer capturing the *high-level* relationship between both intra-layers. However, brain multiplexes are built from at least two different brain networks, inhibiting its application to connectomic datasets with single brain networks such as functional networks. To fill this gap, we propose the first work on *predicting brain multiplexes from a source network* to investigate gender differences. Recently, generative adversarial networks (GANs) submerged the field of medical data synthesis. However, although conventional GANs work well on *images*, they cannot handle brain networks due to their non-Euclidean topological structure. Differently, in this paper, we tap into the nascent field of *geometric-GANs* (G-GAN) to design *a deep multiplex prediction architecture* comprising (i) a geometric source to target network translator mimicking a U-Net architecture with skip connections and (ii) a conditional discriminator which classifies predicted target intra-layers by conditioning on the multiplex source intra-layers. Such architecture simultaneously learns the latent source network representation and the deep non-linear mapping from the source to target multiplex intra-layers. Our experiments on a large dataset demonstrated that predicted multiplexes significantly boost gender classification accuracy compared with source networks and identifies both low and high-order gender-specific multiplex connections.

GitHub: http://github.com/basiralab.

© Springer Nature Switzerland AG 2020
I. Rekik et al. (Eds.): PRIME 2020, LNCS 12329, pp. 24–34, 2020.
https://doi.org/10.1007/978-3-030-59354-4_3

Keywords: Geometric-generative adversarial networks · Brain multiplex prediction · Graph convolutional neural network · Graph translation · Gender differences

1 Introduction

The brain is a complex interconnected network encoding the connectional fingerprint of each individual and representing a notable biomarker of its gender [1]. In fact, several studies suggest that gender is a result of a natural distinction caused by human genetics and translated into dimorphic cortical connectivities. For instance, [2] showed that males excel in memory and motor tasks while females have better linguistic and emotional processing yet more prone to anxiety and depression [3]. Therefore, an accurate gender classification of brain networks might help better spot gender-biased brain disorders and contribute to more reliable and personalized treatments. Despite the breadth of research on gender differences in brain functional and structural connectivity [1] as well as morphological connectivity [4], existing works are limited to investigating *pairwise* (i.e., *low-order*) relationship between ROIs, overlooking not only the complex *high-order* interconnectedness of the brain as a network but also the topological configuration of brain ROIs connectivities.

To address the limitation of conventional low-order brain network representation, recent pioneering works [5,6] introduced the concept of a *brain multiplex*, which in its shallow form, is composed of a source network intra-layer, a target intra-layer, and a convolutional inter-layer capturing the *high-order* relationship between both intra-layers. Basically, a brain multiplex can be viewed as a tensor stacking two brain networks (also called intra-layers) and one inter-layer that encodes the similarity between these two intra-layers. While the intra-layers capture the *low-order* pairwise relationship between ROIs, the inter-layer models the *high-order* relationship between both intra-layer networks. In particular, the inter-layer is estimated by convolving one intra-layer with the other. The multiplex representation of brain connectivities boosted the classification accuracy in patients with early mild cognitive impairment [5] and patients with late mild cognitive impairment compared to the low-order brain network as well as their simple concatenation [6]. Although compelling, building a brain multiplex depends on the availability of different intra-layer brain networks [5,6], limiting its applicability to only multi-view (or multi-modal) brain connectomic datasets. One way to circumvent the issue of connectomic data with missing observations is to discard those samples, however this might not be convenient for devising learning-based classification frameworks. Ideally, one would learn how to predict a multiplex from a single intra-layer network (i.e., a source network) to (i) boost classification results, and (ii) discover low-order and high-order connectional biomarkers for the target classification task.

In recent years, the in-vogue generative adversarial networks (GANs) submerged the field of medical data synthesis [7] with unprecedented results in learning how to generate a target brain imaging modality from a different modality (e.g., computed tomography (CT) from MRI or T1-w from T2-w imaging) [7]. Despite the high efficiency of GANs in solving generative-related problems, all these methods focused on generating *only images*. However, brain connectivities as well as manifolds and graphs are essentially non-Euclidean spaces. To fill this gap in graph deep learning, *geometric* deep leaning has been recently proposed to handle such data [8,9] and propose new graph convolution and deconvolution operations. Given the absence of works on predicting brain multiplex as well as investigating the discriminative potential of these high-order brain connectional representations for gender classification, we design in this paper a deep brain multiplex prediction (DBMP) architecture comprising (i) a geometric source to target network translator mimicking a U-Net architecture with skip connections and (ii) a conditional discriminator which classifies predicted target intra-layers by conditioning on the multiplex source intra-layers. Such architecture *simultaneously* learns the latent source network representation and the deep non-linear mapping from the source to target multiplex intra-layers. Taking into account its insensitivity to overtraining and its notable performance in paired classification, we train a support vector machine (SVM) classifier in combination with a feature selection step on the predicted brain multiplexes for gender classification and connectional gender marker discovery. The main innovative contributions of our work on both methodological and clinical levels are listed below.

Methodological Advance. We propose the first geometric deep learning on *brain multiplex prediction* based on G-GAN. This allows to *learn* the multiplex instead of predefining it for each individual in the population and circumvents the scarcity of multi-view connectomic brain data compared to the breadth of computer vision datasets. Furthermore, to the best of our knowledge, this is the first work adapting geometric deep learning for brain connectome synthesis and classification in general.

Clinical/Scientific Advances. This is the first attempt to explore gender differences using brain multiplexes and reveal new connectional gender markers on both low and high-order levels. This contribution will enable early and personalized treatments for gender-biased brain disorders.

2   Proposed Deep Brain Multiplex Prediction Using G-GAN for Gender Fingerprinting

In this section, we introduce the different steps of deep multiplex prediction framework from a source network for connectional gender fingerprinting. The proposed DBMP framework draws inspiration from [9], which has pioneered the concept of graph or network translator. In typical GAN models, network generation is designed only for learning the distribution of network representations whereas network translation learns not only the latent network representation but also the generic translation mapping from source network to the target network simultaneously [9]. Figure 1 illustrates the proposed pipeline for DBMP

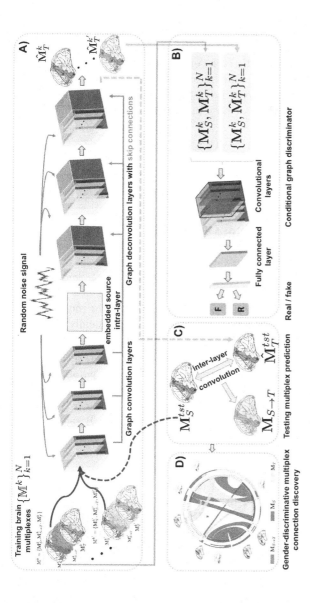

Fig. 1. *Proposed deep brain multiplex prediction (DBMP) framework from a source network for gender classification and fingerprinting.* **(A)** Given a set of morphological brain multiplexes, we train a brain network translator to learn how to translate a source multiplex intra-layer M_S to the target intra-layer M_T. The translator architecture mimics that of U-Net comprising encoding and decoding layers with additional skip connections to pass over sample-specific representations to the encoding layers. **(B)** The conditional network discriminator aims to provide the translator with useful information about the multiplex generation quality. To do so, for each of the k training subjects, the conditional network discriminator inputs two sets of pairs of multiplex layers: $\{M_S^k, M_T^k\}_{k=1}$ and $\{M_S^k, \hat{M}_T^k\}_{k=1}^N$ and outputs one value between 0 and 1 representing the *realness* of the translator's predicted multiplex $\hat{M}_T^k$. **(C)** We produce the final multiplex $\mathbb{M}^k = \{M_S^k, \hat{M}_{S\rightarrow T}^k, \hat{M}_T^k\}$ by stacking the source intra-layer, the predicted intra-layer, and inter-layer which is the result of a convolving both intra-layers. **(D)** We use an infinite feature selection strategy that selects the most gender discriminative brain multiplex connections to train a support vector machine classifier to assign each subject's brain multiplex gender. We display the most discriminative brain multiplex connections which belong to both intra-layers (source derived from mean average curvature and target from mean cortical thickness) as well as the high-order inter-layer.

with application to gender fingerprinting comprising the following steps: 1) network translator training, 2) conditional network discriminator learning, 3) linear SVM classifier training with feature selection, and 4) connectional gender discriminative brain multiplex connections discovery.

Conventional Shallow Brain Multiplex Construction. Given N training subjects, let $\{\mathbf{M}_S^k\}_{k=1}^N$ denote the set of N source intra-layers and $\{\mathbf{M}_T^k\}_{k=1}^N$ the set of N target intra-layers. A conventional shallow brain multiplex $\mathbb{M}^k$ for subject k is defined as a tensor stacking three layers: a source intra-layer $\mathbf{M}_S^k$, a target intra-layer $\mathbf{M}_T^k$, and a convolutional inter-layer $\mathbf{M}_{S \to T}^k$ encoding the similarity between the source and the target intra-layers [5]. The inter-layer is typically generated by convolving both multiplex intra-layers as follows [5,6]:

$$\mathbf{M}_{S \to T}^k(a,b) = \sum_p \sum_q \mathbf{M}_S^k(p,q) \mathbf{M}_T^k(a-p+1, b-q+1) \tag{1}$$

Where a and b respectively denote the row and the column of a specific element in the inter-layer while p and q respectively denote the row and column of a specific element in the intra-layers.

Deep Brain Multiplex Prediction Using G-GAN. For the target prediction task, we assume that each sample is represented by a ground-truth source network intra-layer. Our goal is to learn the target intra-layer from the source, then convolve both to ultimately synthesize a shallow brain multiplex. To do so, inspired by the graph translator model introduced in [9] proposing new graph convolution and deconvolution operations on graphs, we formulate our multiplex prediction task in the spirit of generative adversarial learning. Specifically, given an input ground-truth source intra-layer $\mathbf{M}_S^k$ and a random noise, we predict the target intra-layer $\hat{\mathbf{M}}_T^k$ by learning a local and global source to target $\mathbf{M}_T^k$ mapping where ground-truth and predicted target intra-layers are enforced to share sparse patterns. This is achieved via an adversarial training of a *network translator* learning to generate fake target data from input source data by which it tries to *fool* the conditional discriminator aiming to learn to tell real and fake samples apart. The main advantage of such architecture is its adversarial training resulting in one network training the other in a bi-directional way.

Given a brain multiplex $\mathbb{M}^k$ of subject k, let $\mathbf{M}_S^k = (V, E, \mathbf{W})$ denote a source intra-layer, represented as a fully-connected (directed or undirected) graph. V is a set of n nodes, $E \subseteq V \times V$ is the set of edges and the set of weights for their corresponding edges are encoded in matrix $\mathbf{W} \in R^{n \times n}$, namely a weighted adjacency matrix. Let $e(i,j) \in E$ denote the edge from the node $v_i \in V$ to the node $v_j \in V$ and $\mathbf{W}_{i,j} \in \mathbf{W}$ denotes the corresponding weight of the edge $e(i,j)$. Analogously, $\mathbf{M}_T^k = (V', E', \mathbf{W}')$ denote the target intra-layer in $\mathbb{M}^k$. The translation T_r from source to target intra-layer mapping is defined as $T_r : U, S \to T$, where U refers to the random noise and S and T respectively denote the domains of both source and the target intra-layers. The proposed G-GAN based DBMP framework aims to synthesize a fake target intra-layer $\hat{\mathbf{M}}_T^k = T(\mathbf{M}_S^k, U)$ that mimics the real target intra-layer $\mathbf{M}_T^k$ in its topological and structural properties by minimizing the following adversarial loss function over all k samples:

$$\mathcal{L}(T_r, D) = \mathbb{E}_{\mathbf{M}_S^k, \mathbf{M}_T^k}[log D(\mathbf{M}_T^k|\mathbf{M}_S^k)] + \mathbb{E}_{\mathbf{M}_S^k, U}[log(1 - D(T_r(\mathbf{M}_S^k, U)|\mathbf{M}_S^k))], \quad (2)$$

where both T_r and D are trying to minimize the output of this loss function in an adversarial way. Since we translate the source into the target intra-layer which might lie on different manifolds, we enforce sparsely shared patterns across translated source intra-layer and ground-truth target intra-layer via L_1 regularization which can boost the optimization process. The updated loss function is defined as follows to estimate the mapping translator T_r:

$$T_r^* = argmin_{T_r} max_D \mathcal{L}(T_r, D) + \mathcal{L}_{L_1}(T_r), \quad (3)$$

Where $\mathcal{L}_{L_1}(T_r) = \mathbb{E}_{\mathbf{M}_S^k, \mathbf{M}_T^k, U}[||\mathbf{M}_T^k - T_r(\mathbf{M}_S^k, U)||_1]$. This is solved using ADAM optimizer for learning the translator and discriminator mappings alternatingly.

Source to Target Intra-layer Translator. As displayed in Fig. 1A, the geometric translator acts as a U-Net with skip connections based on graph convolution in the three encoding layers and deconvolution in the three decoding layers. Specifically, the encoder network comprises two edge-to-edge convolutional layers and one edge-to-node convolutional layer, while the decoder network is composed of a node-to-edge deconvolutional layer and two edge-to-edge deconvolutional layers.

Conditional Network Discriminator (Fig. 1C). The conditional discriminator is trained by minimizing the sum of two losses: the loss between the target intra-layers $\{\mathbf{M}_T^k\}_{k=1}^N$ and the source $\{\mathbf{M}_S^k\}_{k=1}^N$ and the loss between the predicted target multiplex intra-layers $\{\hat{\mathbf{M}}_T^k\}_{k=1}^N$ and ground-truth target intra-layers $\{\mathbf{M}_T^k\}_{k=1}^N$. In order to compute these losses separately, the conditional network discriminator inputs for training sets of pairs of multiplex layers: $\{\mathbf{M}_S^k, \mathbf{M}_T^k\}_{k=1}^N$ and $\{\mathbf{M}_T^k, \hat{\mathbf{M}}_T^k\}_{k=1}^N$ to distinguish the pair including the ground truth $\mathbf{M}_T^k$ from the predicted one $\hat{\mathbf{M}}_T^k$ by the translator for each training subject k. The discriminator architecture comprises four stacked layers organized in the following order: two edge-to-edge convolutional layers, one edge-to-node convolutional layer, and fully connected layer followed by a softmax layer to output real or fake label for each input target intra-layer.

Brain Multiplex Prediction from Source Network and Classification. Given the predicted target intra-layer for a testing subject tst, we synthesize its brain multiplex $\hat{\mathbb{M}}^{tst} = \{\mathbf{M}_S^{tst}, \mathbf{M}_{S \rightarrow T}^{tst}, \hat{\mathbf{M}}_T^{tst}\}$. Using 2-fold cross-validation, we train and test the proposed G-GAN DBMP model along a linear SVM classifier to label the multiplex $\hat{\mathbb{M}}$ into male or female. The training of the SVM classifier is proceeded by a feature selection step using the training samples. We particularly use infinite feature selection (IFS) [10] to select the most reproducible features distinguishing between male and female brain multiplexes.

Gender-Related Brain Multiplex Connectivity Discovery. Following feature selection, we identify the top n_f gender-discriminative features. We design a feature scoring algorithm by quantifying feature reproducibility across validation folds depending on the occurrence of each selected feature and its weight given by the IFS algorithm. Indeed, the more frequently a feature appears in the top n_f set, the higher its score is.

3   Results and Discussion

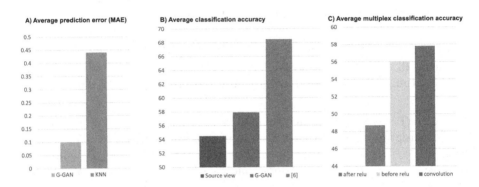

Fig. 2. *Average classification accuracy using linear SVM classifier and multiplex prediction error.* (**A**) We report the mean absolute error (MAE) between the predicted and ground truth target intra-layers by (i) the proposed G-GAN method and (ii) KNN algorithm. (**B**) Average classification accuracy using: (i) a single source intra-layer network, (ii) the predicted multiplex, and (iii) the ground-truth multiplex [5]. (**C**) Predicted multiplex classification accuracy while defining the multiplex inter-layer as: (i) the learned G-GAN inter-layer preceding relu, (ii) the learned G-GAN inter-layer following relu, and (iii) the convolutional layer between both intra-layers as in [5].

Evaluation Dataset and Method Parameters. We evaluated our proposed framework on a dataset of 400 healthy subjects (226 females with mean age $= (21.6 \pm 0.8)$ and 174 males with mean age $= (21.6 \pm 0.9)$ from the Brain Genomics Superstruct Project [11]. T1-weighted images were acquired using a 1.2 mm isotropic resolution. Test-retest reliability was established with a correlations range from 0.75 for the estimated cortical thickness of the right medial prefrontal cortex to 0.99 for the estimated intracranial volume. We used FreeSurfer processing pipeline to reconstruct the left and right cortical hemispheres. Then we parcellated each hemisphere into 35 regions using Desikan-Killiany atlas. For each subject, we created 4 morphological brain networks (MBN) of size 35×35 as introduced in [6,12], derived from the following cortical attributes respectively: cortical thickness, sulcal depth, mean average curvature, and maximum principal curvature.

Method Evaluation and Comparison Methods. Due to the absence of state-of-the-art methods focusing on learning how to predict brain multiplexes using G-GAN as well as investigating how gender differences manifest in brain

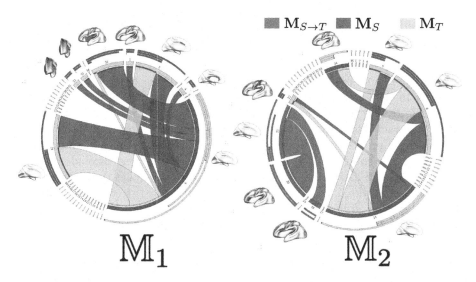

Fig. 3. *Discovery of the top gender discriminative multiplex connectivities.* We display the top 10 most discriminative multiplex connections for $\mathbb{M}_1$ (S = maximum principal curvature MBN and T = mean cortical thickness MBN) and $\mathbb{M}_2$ (S = mean average curvature and T = mean cortical thickness).

multiplexes, we resorted to comparing our framework against widely used methods such as KNN. This is a valid approach adopted by high-impact publication venues such as [13], where innovative proposed frameworks are benchmarked against the most commonly used techniques. KNN is a widely used algorithm due to its robustness to noisy data. Basically, for each testing subject with a source network, we first identify its top K most similar training source brain networks. Next, we retrieve their corresponding target networks, which we average to predict the target testing intra-layer. To evaluate the potential of the predicted multiplex in boosting gender classification, we benchmarked our predicted multiplexes by G-GAN against classification using: (i) solely source intra-layer (i.e., from a single network), and (ii) ground truth shallow multiplexes where multiplexes were generated using two MBNs and one convolutional layer between them as in [5,14].

Figure 2A shows the mean absolute error (MAE) between the predicted target intra-layers and the ground truth ones. For KNN, we report the average performance when varying the number of top K selected neigbnors from 2 to 10. Notably, G-GAN predicted multiplexes significantly outperforms the baseline KNN method. Figure 2B displays classification results averaged across multiplexes and number of selected features $n_f \in \{310, \ldots, 350\}$ using three methods: source MBN, predicted multiplex by G-GAN, and ground-truth multiplexes. The predicted multiplexes significantly boosted the classification results in comparison to solely using the ground-truth source MBN. We also notice that it is quite close to the ground-truth multiplex. This classification experiments present an indirect method for evaluating the quality and reliability of the predicted multiplexes.

Insights into Learning the Multiplex Inter-layer. Instead of computing the inter-layer by convolving both intra-layers, we extracted the *learned* final inter-layer in the encoding part of the translator: before and after the rectified linear unit (ReLU) activation function. Figure 2C displays the average classification accuracy using the learned embedding of the source intra-layer as its gets translated into the target intra-layer (i.e., a hybrid inter-layer bridging the gap between the source and target intra-layers) and the conventional convolutional inter-layer [5]. Although, this experiment is considered as the first attempt to learn the multiplex inter-layer in the state-of-the-art, the convolutional predefined inter-layer still achieved the best classification result. This might be explained that the learned inter-layer is learned without any supervision by the sample class labels.

Gender Multiplex Fingerprint Discovery. As a proof of concept, Fig. 3 displays results from two multiplexes $\mathbb{M}_1$ and $\mathbb{M}_2$, where we report the top 10 most discriminative multiplex connectional biomarkers for distinguishing between male and female morphological brain networks. These connectional fingerprints were captured on both low and high-order levels. For instance, in $\mathbb{M}_1$ (S = maximum principal curvature MBN and T = mean cortical thickness MBN), we found that the most gender-discriminative connectivity links (entorhinal cortex ↔ pericalcarine cortex) in both intra-layers. In fact, the entorhinal cortex is known to be correlated with spatial memory processing, where [15] showed that male participants outperform female participants. Besides, the pericalcarine cortex controlling visual processing and spatial navigation was identified as a gender discriminative region in [16]. While in the multiplex $\mathbb{M}_2$ (S = mean average curvature and T = mean cortical thickness), we found that the most discriminative connectivity included the (pars triangularis ↔ pericalcarine cortex). For instance, the pars triangularis is known to be related to language and speech processing, which is in line with the observation that females are better at language processing than males as reported in [17]. This hallmark connectivity was found in the convolutional inter-layer. We also notice other relevant brain multiplex connectivities distributed across intra-layers. In our future work, we will investigate the reproducibility of the discovered multiplex biomarkers fingerprinting gender using different perturbation strategies of the training set while tracking the reproducibility of the top ranked features [18].

4 Conclusion

In this paper, we presented the first framework for brain multiplex synthesis from a source brain network with application to gender classification. Specifically, we rooted our method in geometric generative adversarial network (G-GAN) nicely preserving local and global brain connectional patterns, where a network translator and discriminator are adversarially trained. The predicted multiplexes significantly boosted the classification results compared to using single source networks. More importantly, we identified for the first time both low-order and high-order morphological brain connectivities encoding gender differences using large GSP dataset. There are many possible future directions yet to explore, such as learning *discriminative* multiplex inter-layers by integrating a second conditional discriminator by class labels.

Acknowledgement. This project has been funded by the 2232 International Fellowship for Outstanding Researchers Program of TUBITAK (Project No: 118C288, http://basira-lab.com/reprime/) supporting I. Rekik. However, all scientific contributions made in this project are owned and approved solely by the authors.

References

1. Gong, G., He, Y., Evans, A.C.: Brain connectivity: gender makes a difference. Neuroscientist **17**, 575–591 (2011)
2. Shirao, N., Okamoto, Y., Okada, G., Ueda, K., Yamawaki, S.: Gender differences in brain activity toward unpleasant linguistic stimuli concerning interpersonal relationships: an fMRI study. Eur. Arch. Psychiatry Clin. Neurosci. **255**, 327–333 (2005). https://doi.org/10.1007/s00406-005-0566-x
3. Saunders, P.A., et al.: The prevalence of dementia, depression and neurosis in later life: the Liverpool MRC-ALPHA study. Int. J. Epidemiol. **22**, 838–847 (1993)
4. Nebli, Ahmed, Rekik, Islem: Gender differences in cortical morphological networks. Brain Imaging Behav. 1–9 (2019). https://doi.org/10.1007/s11682-019-00123-6
5. Raeper, R., Lisowska, A., Rekik, I., The Alzheimer's Disease Neuroimaging Initiative: Joint correlational and discriminative ensemble classifier learning for dementia stratification using shallow brain multiplexes. In: Frangi, A.F., Schnabel, J.A., Davatzikos, C., Alberola-López, C., Fichtinger, G. (eds.) MICCAI 2018. LNCS, vol. 11070, pp. 599–607. Springer, Cham (2018). https://doi.org/10.1007/978-3-030-00928-1_68
6. Mahjoub, I., Mahjoub, M.A., Rekik, I.: Brain multiplexes reveal morphological connectional biomarkers fingerprinting late brain dementia states. Sci. Rep. **8**, 4103 (2018)
7. Yi, X., Walia, E., Babyn, P.: Generative adversarial network in medical imaging: a review. arXiv preprint arXiv:1809.07294 (2018)
8. Bronstein, M.M., Bruna, J., LeCun, Y., Szlam, A., Vandergheynst, P.: Geometric deep learning: going beyond Euclidean data. IEEE Signal Process. Mag. **34**, 18–42 (2017)
9. Guo, X., Wu, L., Zhao, L.: Deep graph translation. arXiv preprint arXiv:1805.09980 (2018)
10. Roffo, G., Melzi, S., Cristani, M.: Infinite feature selection. In: Proceedings of the IEEE International Conference on Computer Vision, pp. 4202–4210 (2015)
11. Buckner, R., et al.: The brain genomics superstruct project. Harvard Dataverse Network (2012)
12. Soussia, M., Rekik, I.: High-order connectomic manifold learning for autistic brain state identification. In: Wu, G., Laurienti, P., Bonilha, L., Munsell, B.C. (eds.) CNI 2017. LNCS, vol. 10511, pp. 51–59. Springer, Cham (2017). https://doi.org/10.1007/978-3-319-67159-8_7

13. Samusik, N., Good, Z., Spitzer, M.H., Davis, K.L., Nolan, G.P.: Automated mapping of phenotype space with single-cell data. Nature Methods **13**, 493 (2016)
14. Lisowska, A., Rekik, I.: Pairing-based ensemble classifier learning using convolutional brain multiplexes and multi-view brain networks for early dementia diagnosis. In: Wu, G., Laurienti, P., Bonilha, L., Munsell, B.C. (eds.) CNI 2017. LNCS, vol. 10511, pp. 42–50. Springer, Cham (2017). https://doi.org/10.1007/978-3-319-67159-8_6
15. Cherney, I.D., Brabec, C.M., Runco, D.V.: Mapping out spatial ability: sex differences in way-finding navigation. Percept. Motor Skills **107**, 747–760 (2008)
16. Ingalhalikar, M., et al.: Sex differences in the structural connectome of the human brain. Proc. Nat. Acad. Sci. **111**, 823–828 (2014)
17. Bourne, V.J.: Lateralised processing of positive facial emotion: sex differences in strength of hemispheric dominance. Neuropsychologia **43**, 953–956 (2005)
18. Georges, N., Mhiri, I., Rekik, I.: Alzheimer's disease neuroimaging initiative and others: identifying the best data-driven feature selection method for boosting reproducibility in classification tasks. Pattern Recognit. **101**, 107183 (2020)

Learned Deep Radiomics for Survival Analysis with Attention

Ludivine Morvan[1,2(✉)], Cristina Nanni[3], Anne-Victoire Michaud[4],
Bastien Jamet[4], Clément Bailly[2,4], Caroline Bodet-Milin[2,4],
Stephane Chauvie[5], Cyrille Touzeau[2,6], Philippe Moreau[2,6], Elena Zamagni[7],
Francoise Kraeber-Bodéré[2,4,8], Thomas Carlier[2,4], and Diana Mateus[1]

[1] Ecole Centrale de Nantes, Laboratoire des Sciences Numériques de Nantes (LS2N),
CNRS UMR 6004, Nantes, France
ludivine.morvan@ls2n.com
[2] CRCINA, INSERM, CNRS, University of Angers, University of Nantes,
Nantes, France
[3] Nuclear Medicine, AOU Policlinico S. Orsola-Malpighi, Bologna, Italy
[4] Nuclear Medicine Department, University Hospital of Nantes, Nantes, France
[5] Medical Physics Division, Santa Croce e Carle Hospital, Cuneo, Italy
[6] Haematology Department, University Hospital of Nantes, Nantes, France
[7] School of Medicine, Seragnoli Institute of Hematology, Bologna University,
Bologna, Italy
[8] Nuclear Medicine, ICO Cancer Center, Saint-Herblain, France

Abstract. In the context of multiple myeloma, patient diagnosis and treatment planning involve the medical analysis of full-body Positron Emission Tomography (PET) images. There has been a growing interest in linking quantitative measurements extracted from PET images (radiomics) with statistical methods for survival analysis. Following very recent advances, we propose an end-to-end deep learning model that learns relevant features and predicts survival given the image of a lesion. We show the importance of dealing with the variable scale of the lesions, and propose to this end an attention strategy deployed both on the spatial and channels dimensions, which improves the model performance and interpretability. We show results for the progression-free survival prediction of multiple myeloma (MM) patients on a clinical dataset coming from two prospective studies. We also discuss the difficulties of adapting deep learning for survival analysis given the complexity of the task, the small lesion sizes, and PET low SNR (signal to noise ratio).

Keywords: Survival analysis · Multiple myeloma · PET imaging · Convolutional NN · Attention models · Spatial pyramidal pooling

This work has been partially funded by the SIRIC ILIAD (INCa-DGOS-Inserm_12558), the LabEx IRON (ANR-11-LABX-0018-01) and by the European Regional Development Fund, the Pays de la Loire region on the Connect Talent scheme (MILCOM Project) and Nantes Métropole (Convention 2017-10470).

1   Introduction

Survival analysis aims to quantitatively link patient data to disease progression over time. It enables identifying bio-markers useful for splitting patient population into risk (e.g. low and high) subgroups. It is also used for training models that, given the data of a new patient, are able to predict the time to the next event (e.g. relapse, progression, death, etc.). Traditional survival methods rely on Cox proportional hazards regression and Kaplan Meier curves [12].

The goal of this paper is to adapt deep learning methods to survival analysis for prognosis in multiple myeloma (MM) patients using PET images. The use of quantitative image analysis for survival analysis based on PET images is a relatively recent field, commonly addressed with handcrafted (radiomics) features [4]. There are several challenges in adapting CNNs to instead learn discriminative features for survival. Firstly, PET images have low resolution, especially when considering the size of MM lesions. Secondly, prospective datasets that control patient treatment and follow-up are needed but often limited to a low number of patients. Finally, survival data often suffers from censorship (missing data) related to patients presenting no event during the study.

In this paper, we revisit recent deep learning methods for survival analysis, and propose a method that handles the challenges described previously. We manage the small-sized lesions and their scale variability of lesions with SPP [7,14] or with an attention model [19]. At the same time, the low number of data samples imposes architectural and learning choices such as the reduction of the number of neurons in the fully connected layers, leaky ReLU, instance normalization, learning rate decay, and kernel regularisation to avoid overfitting. Finally, a specific survival loss function (negative partial log-likelihood) enables us to deal with missing data in the form of censorship. At the same time, the low number of data samples imposes architectural and learning choices such as the reduction of the number of neurons in the fully connected layers, leaky ReLU, instance normalization, learning rate decay, and kernel regularisation to avoid overfitting. Finally, a specific survival loss function (negative partial log-likelihood) enables us to deal with missing data in the form of censorship.

This work investigates for the first time the use of learned deep radiomics for survival prognosis in the context of MM using PET images. To the best of our knowledge, we are the first to combine channel and spatial attention in the context of survival analysis using images as input. Our work improves prediction results over state-of-the-art methods for image-based multiple myeloma survival prediction.

2   Related Work

Early adaptions of Deep Learning (DL) to survival tasks extract deep features with a pre-trained Neural Network and feed them to prediction models such as Lasso Cox [13] or Random Survival Forest (RSF) [17]. The survival problem has also been simplified to the *classification* of different risk groups (e.g., low, middle, high risk) [2], or to the *regression* of the time-to-event [17]. However, such formulations do not natively handle *censored data*.

Risk-predicting methods adapt the learning loss to take into account the censorship. Faraggi and Simon [5] adapted the linear Cox Proportional Hazards (CPH) model with a more flexible feedforward network. Katzman et al. revisits (in the so called DeepSurv approach) the Faraggi-Simon's loss in the context of deeper networks [11]. Some other variants stick to the CPH linear model, $w^\top x$, but use the network either for non-linear dimensionality reduction of the input x [3], or for predicting the weights w [16]. Recent alternatives include combining a regression and a ranking loss [3] or using discrete survival model [6].

Regarding the data type, Xinliang *et al.* [20] were the first to adapt DeepSurv to Convolutional Layers (DeepConvSurv) and dealt with images data as input. Zhu *et al.*, extend in [1] and subsequent papers the DeepConvSurv to handle very large whole slide histopathological images. We are instead interested in the problems raised by the low-resolution and SNR of PET images. Both [2] and [14] propose 3D CNN models for survival analysis from PET images. Amyar *et al.* [2] target radio-chemotherapy response in esophageal cancer by simplifying the survival problem to a classification without censorship and using an input layer of relative large size ($100 \times 100 \times 100$) compared to our MM lesions. To predict treatment response in colorectal cancer, Li et al. [14] modify the DeepConvSurv model with an additional spatial pyramid pooling (SPP) layer [7] in order to deal with small lesions of multiple scales. Both PET and CT data are considered as inputs, showing that multi-modality improves the performance. Although our study is performed on PET images only, we borrow from the idea of using SPPs to handle multiple-scales of even smaller lesions for the MM survival analysis. In addition, we propose a novel strategy to handle the variability of small lesions, by means of attention models. Attention has been successfully used in a large variety of medical applications including reconstruction [9], segmentation, detection [18] or classification [8]. Kaji et al. [10] use LSTM to predict daily sepsis from clinical data while Liu et al. [15] focus on spatial attention. Instead, our work integrates a CBAM model, which also includes channel attention to determine the most predictive "learned radiomics" filters.

Moreover, our work is the first to adapt CNNs for MM survival from PET lesion images only.

3   Method

The input to our model is a data-set of N samples, $\{x_i, t_i, \delta_i\}_{i=1}^N$, each consisting of an image x_i associated to a target time-to-event t_i and a binary censorship δ_i. $\delta_i = 0$ means that the event of interest did not happen during the studied period, while $\delta_i = 1$ means that the event did occur. In the particular case of study, our images come from manually identified lesions in full-body PET images and time is given in days. We consider both 2D and 3D images. The proposed method adapts a CNN to predict progression free survival (PFS), i.e. the time to (or risk of) the next disease progression, from images and in presence of censored data. The output of the method is the scalar risk value. An overview of the method is presented in Fig. 1. In the following, we describe the loss function for survival (Sect. 3.1) and the deep learning model including the SPP and attention strategies (Sect. 3.2).

3.1   From Cox Survival Model to Loss Function

A common approach to survival analysis with CNNs has been to derive a loss function from the Cox proportional hazard model. Cox assumes that each variable independently affects a baseline hazard $h_0(t)$ (a measure of risk at time t), multiplied by a constant factor independent of time. The risk for patient i is then modelled as $h(\boldsymbol{x}_i, t) = h_0(t)e^{h_\beta(\boldsymbol{x}_i)} = h_0(t)e^{\beta^\top \boldsymbol{x}_i}$ where $\boldsymbol{x}_i \in \boldsymbol{R}^m$ and $\beta \in \boldsymbol{R}^m$ are respectively, the vector of input variables and their associated coefficients. The partial likelihood for one coefficient is the product of probabilities over time, where for each event-time t_i the probability is computed as the ratio between the risk of patient i and the cumulative risk of all individuals still at risk at time t_i:

$$L_{\text{cox}}(\beta) = \prod_{\{i|\delta_i=1\}} \frac{e^{h_\beta(\boldsymbol{x}_i)}}{\sum_{\{j|t_j \geq t_i\}} e^{h_\beta(\boldsymbol{x}_j)}}, \tag{1}$$

where the product is done over the defined (uncensored) time events.

DeepSurv. Following [5,11], the linear model $h_\beta(\boldsymbol{x})$ is replaced by the output of a neural network $h_\theta(\boldsymbol{x})$ parameterised by weights θ while the same partial likelihood is kept. Computing the negative log likelihood from Eq. 1 leads to the following loss to optimise the parameters θ:

$$l_{\text{cox}}(\theta) = - \sum_{\{i|\delta_i=1\}} [h_\theta(\boldsymbol{x}_i) - \log \sum_{\{j|t_j \geq t_i\}} e^{h_\theta(\boldsymbol{x}_j)}] \tag{2}$$

This loss function pushes the network to predict risks that explain the order of events in the dataset. Note that the risk of the current patient depends on all patients at risk at the event time. We use the loss in Eq. 2 to optimize the parameters of the CNN architecture described next.

3.2   CNN Model for Survival Analysis

The core of the risk prediction model $h(\boldsymbol{x}_i, \theta)$ is a CNN learning radiomics features and whose architecture was inspired from [14]. We consider both a 2D and 3D version of the model and two additional (optional) blocks: i) a Spatial Pyramidal block to deal with small lesions of multiple-sizes [7] ii) a spatial and channel attention block [19] to localise respectively the lesion and the filters, and enhance model interpretability.

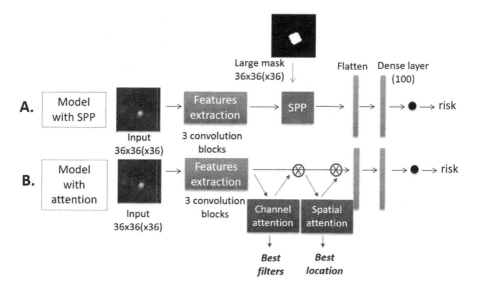

Fig. 1. Models with SPP (A) or Attention part (B)

Radiomics Feature Learning Block. This block is a standard CNN transforming the 3-D image of a lesion x_i into C feature maps each of size $H \times W \times L$. It is composed of three convolutional blocks. Each block has one convolution with leaky RELU activations (+ Maxpooling when SPP is not used).

In practice, the input layer is set to $36 \times 36 (\times 36)$, according to the distribution of MM lesions' scale in our database, where the bounding polygons surrounding the lesions were shown to be between $3 \times 3(\times 3)$ and $32 \times 40(\times 53)$ pixels size.

The kernel size of the convolutions are $3 \times 3(\times 3)$, $5 \times 5(\times 5)$ and $3 \times 3(\times 3)$ with padding and a stride at 1. The difference with model [14] is in the added layers as Leaky RELU, dropout or Instance normalisation.

Spatial Pyramidal Pooling. (SPP) was designed to handle multi-scale images efficiently. Multiple max pooling layers at different scales are applied to the features from the last convolutional layer to later flattened and concatenated (see Fig. 2). Different to classical pooling, the size of the resultant feature maps is fixed, and thus the output feature vector dimension remains constant irrespective of the input image size.

The SPP method was used in [14] to handle PET/CT rectal-cancer lesions of different sizes. A bounding box delimiting the tumour was given as an auxiliary input to the SPP. Moreover, each feature map was pooled to three 2-D matrices of size $8 \times 8 \times 8$, $4 \times 4 \times 4$ and $2 \times 2 \times 2$ (in the case of 3D) and 8×8, 4×4 and 2×2 (in the case of 2D). In this work, we also use the tumour mask. However, for our MM application, many of the lesions are small (the smallest is less than $3 \times 3(\times 3)$), and thus a choice has to be made (on our 2D model) between either

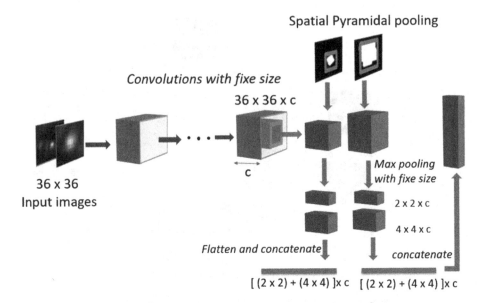

Fig. 2. SPP block for a 2D model.

keeping the 8×8 as in [14] dominated by background information, or retaining the limited amount of information from the smaller 4×4 and 2×2 maps. An alternative is to use a spatial attention model.

CBAM Attention Model. An attention mechanism learns to assign weights to the extracted features according to their relevance for a given task, with the side effect of improving the task performance. The mechanism is flexible in the sense the weights adapt to the input image. After the feature-extraction, we add a Convolutional Block Attention Module (CBAM) to sequentially infer attention maps for both the feature channels and spatial axes [19]. Channel attention is computed squeezing spatial information from the convolutional layers with max and average pooling operations. The pooled values are passed through a shared MultiLayer Perceptron network to predict the attention weights. The MLP is trained along with the survival prediction layers following a parallel branch from the output back to the convolutional layers (See Fig. 3).

Spatial attention weights are calculated at each location of the image. They are computed applying max pooling and average pooling to squeeze the channels. They are then applied to the feature maps by an element-wise multiplication. In this way, CBAM focuses spatial attention within the lesion and not around. For this reason, it is an interesting alternative to the SPP. Spatial attention maps can also, in some cases, show the most important part within the lesion. Channel attention provides information about the most informative filters and thus, give interpretability to the model.

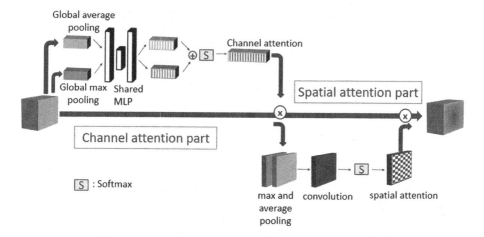

Fig. 3. Attention block for a 2D model [19].

Survival Prediction Output. The prediction layer consists of 3 fully connected layers, and an output layer with a single neuron predicting the risk $h(\boldsymbol{x}_i, \theta)$.

Optimisation Details. An ADAM optimizer was used. Hyperparameter optimisation was done on the batch size (10, 32, 64), the learning rate (1e−03, 1e−04, 1e−05, 1e−06), the learning rate decay (1e−06, 1e−07, 1e−08, 1e−09) and the number of epochs (until 150). Dropout was added after the first fully connected layer and also on the input but was not retained. Batch and instance normalisation were enforced. The Leaky RELU activation is set to 0.1. Leaky RELU, instance normalisation, kernel regularisation and dropout are used to avoid overfitting.

4   Experimental Validation

Experimental Set-Up. We evaluate our survival model on a dataset composed of two prospective multi-centric MM studies with respectively 87 and 65 patients. The 3D baseline PET-images and survival time (until 7 years) are available for each patient. The most intense lesion for each patient was selected and a global polygon (no segmentation step involved) around the lesion was drawn by a nuclear physician. According to the version, 2D or 3D information was used for both the PET image and its corresponding mask. For the 2D case, we extract the 2D transverse, coronal, and sagittal sections from the middle of the bounding polygon, and use them individually. For 3D we use a single cube encompassing the bounding box. Finally, we use data augmentation (rotation, translation, zoom, flip) to obtain 30 different images per input image. This leads to a total of 13850 images in 2D and 4560 in 3D, split patient-wise into 4 sets for cross-validation.

Table 1. Comparison vs baseline models. Average c-index over 4-fold cross validation.

Model	C-index
Lasso-Cox	0.494 ($\pm$0.0025)
RSF	0.529 ($\pm$0.036)
VIMP+RSF	0.583 ($\pm$0.017)
CNN 2D	0.6100 ($\pm$0.041)
Our model (3D+Attention)	0.6414 ($\pm$0.023)

Regarding the input layer size, the median lesion size is $116 \times 116 \times 12$, and only 4 of the 155 patients have a box bigger than $36 \times 36 \times 36$. Therefore, we define the input size to $36 \times 36 \times 36$. This choice avoids deteriorating the smallest lesions with the interpolation step or having too much background information (in the case of spatial attention). For the SPP and attention methods, we extract a $36 \times 36(\times 36)$ cube around the center of polygon. For the baseline CNNs for comparison (without SPP or attention), we take the parallelepiped englobing the bounding box of the lesion, and we resize it with cubic interpolation to a size of $36 \times 36(\times 36)$.

Evaluation Metrics. To evaluate the model's performance, we rely on the C-index measuring if the predicted risk respects the events order.

$$\text{Cindex} = \frac{\sum_{ij} \mathbf{1}_{t_j < t_i} \cdot \mathbf{1}_{h(x_j,\theta) > h(x_i,\theta)} \cdot \delta_j}{\sum_{ij} \mathbf{1}_{t_j < t_i} \cdot \delta_j} \tag{3}$$

4.1 Experiment 1. CNNs vs Classical Methods for Survival Analysis

Herein, we compare a CNN-based model against three baselines: Lasso-Cox, and Random Survival Forest (RSF) with and without Variable importance selection (VIMP). Input to the baseline models were 19 handcrafted radiomics. VIMP feature selection was done on 100 runs of the initial RSF model trained on all the variables. Both models were optimized to their best performance. The results of a 4-fold cross-validation are shown in Table 1. We report the average and standard deviation across the 4 folds. Our simplest CNN model, adapted from DeepConvSurv [1] and trained on 2D input data, shows improvements over the baselines.

4.2 Experiment 2. Evaluation of Deep Learning Methods

Here, we perform a comparative study based on the 4-fold cross-validation results of different configurations of the method. We consider 2D and 3D versions to explore the performance variability for two extremes of the model capacity: with the 2D models we search for a compact model capable of predicting meaningful risks; with the 3D models we look for a high complexity model we can still train with the available data. The results are reported in Table 2. The reported values in the table are taken at the best validation performance.

Among the 2D models, the SPP seems to most effectively learn discriminative features for survival probably due to the concentration of the information in the compact pooling layers, it also corresponds to the most compact model. Attention adds relatively few additional parameters, but does not improve the results any further. Actually, when looking at the learning curves we notice instead an acceleration of the overfitting. Conversely, the 3D model with attention can take full advantage of the extra model parameters, effectively guiding the convergence and significantly improving the results over the baseline. The difference might come from the spatial constraints enforced by the 3D data. Despite performing similar to 2D+SPP, the cost of a larger complexity is worthwhile when interpretability of the model is sought.

Table 2. Comparison of different deep models. The result is for each model the average C-index over 4-cross validation.

Model	Validation c-index	Train c-index	Number of parameters
2D simple	0.6100 (±0.041)	0.7814 (±0.066)	554,003
2D+SPP	**0.6396** (±0.061)	**0.7671** (±0.045)	163,603
2D+Attention	0.5059 (±0.017)	0.7526 (±0.201)	555,197
2D+SPP+Attention	0.4869 (±0.017)	0.7398 (±0.101)	163,783
3D simple	0.5712 (±0.028)	0.5525 (±0.048)	4,800,557
3D+Attention	**0.6414** (±0.023)	**0.6384** (±0.044)	4,802,339

5   Discussion and Conclusions

In this paper, we address survival analysis of MM patients from PET image lesions. We present a deep learning approach that adapts CNNs to learn relevant radiomics features from the data in an end-to-end fashion. We develop two strategies to deal with the small and variable size of the input lesions, SPP and Attention, and explore their effect on model capacity and performance. When looking for compact models, SPP seems to be more appropriate. If more complexity is affordable, then the 3D + CBAM attention model is preferred: for a similar performance, it removes the need for segmentation masks, it can be used to verify if the model has correctly focused on a lesion, and provides additional hints to the importance of the learned features. Such double attention mechanism is new in the context of deep survival analysis with images.

In future work, we will further analyse the clinical relevance of our method, study the attention matrix and the incidence of considering a multi-modal PET/CT approach.

References

1. Zhu, X., Yao, J., Zhu, F., Huang, J.: WSISA: making survival prediction from whole slide histopathological images. In: CVPR, pp. 970–975 (2017)
2. Amyar, A., Ruan, S., Gardin, I., Chatelain, C., Decazes, P., Modzelewski, R.: 3-D RPET-NET: development of a 3-D pet imaging convolutional neural network for radiomics analysis and outcome prediction. IEEE Trans. Radiat. Plasma Med. Sci. **3**(2), 225–231 (2019)
3. Ching, T., Zhu, X., Garmire, L.X.: Cox-nnet: an artificial neural network method for prognosis prediction of high-throughput omics data. PLoS Comput. Biol. **14**(4), 1–18 (2018). https://doi.org/10.1371/journal.pcbi.1006076
4. Cook, G.J.R., Siddique, M., Taylor, B.P., Yip, C., Chicklore, S., Goh, V.: Radiomics in PET: principles and applications. Clin. Transl. Imaging **2**(3), 269–276 (2014). https://doi.org/10.1007/s40336-014-0064-0
5. Faraggi, D., Simon, R.: A neural network model for survival data. Stat. Med. **14**(1), 73–82 (1995). https://doi.org/10.1002/sim.4780140108
6. Gensheimer, M.F., Narasimhan, B.: A scalable discrete-time survival model for neural networks. PeerJ **2019**(1), 1–17 (2019). https://doi.org/10.7717/peerj.6257
7. He, K., Zhang, X., Ren, S., Sun, J.: Spatial pyramid pooling in deep convolutional networks for visual recognition. In: Fleet, D., Pajdla, T., Schiele, B., Tuytelaars, T. (eds.) ECCV 2014. LNCS, vol. 8691, pp. 346–361. Springer, Cham (2014). https://doi.org/10.1007/978-3-319-10578-9_23
8. Herent, P., et al.: Detection and characterization of MRI breast lesions using deep learning. Diagn. Interv. Imaging **100**(4), 219–225 (2019). https://doi.org/10.1016/j.diii.2019.02.008
9. Huang, Q., Yang, D., Wu, P., Qu, H., Yi, J., Metaxas, D.: MRI reconstruction via cascaded channel-wise attention network. In: 2019 IEEE 16th International Symposium on Biomedical Imaging (ISBI 2019), pp. 1622–1626 (2019). https://doi.org/10.1109/ISBI.2019.8759423
10. Kaji, D.A., Zech, J.R., Kim, J.S., et al.: An attention based deep learning model of clinical events in the intensive care unit. PLoS ONE **14**(2), e0211057 (2019). https://doi.org/10.1371/journal.pone.0211057
11. Katzman, J.L., Shaham, U., Cloninger, A., Bates, J., Jiang, T., Kluger, Y.: Deep-Surv: personalized treatment recommender system using a cox proportional hazards deep neural network. BMC Med. Res. Methodol. **18**, 24 (2018). https://doi.org/10.1186/s12874-018-0482-1
12. Kleinbaum, D.G., Klein, M. (eds.): Survival Analysis: A Self-Learning Text. Springer, New York (2012). https://doi.org/10.1007/978-1-4419-6646-9
13. Lao, J., et al.: A deep learning-based radiomics model for prediction of survival in glioblastoma multiforme. Sci. Rep. **7**(1) (2017). https://doi.org/10.1038/s41598-017-10649-8
14. Li, H., et al.: Deep convolutional neural networks for imaging data based survival analysis of rectal cancer. In: ISBI, April, vol. 2019, pp. 846–849 (2019). https://doi.org/10.1109/ISBI.2019.8759301
15. Liu, Z., Sun, Q., Bai, H., Liang, C., Chen, Y., Li, Z.: 3D deep attention network for survival prediction from magnetic resonance images in glioblastoma. In: 2019 IEEE International Conference on Image Processing (ICIP), pp. 1381–1384 (2019)
16. Mobadersany, P., et al.: Predicting cancer outcomes from histology and genomics using convolutional networks. Proc. Natl. Acad. Sci. **115**(13), E2970–E2979 (2018). https://doi.org/10.1073/pnas.1717139115.   https://www.pnas.org/content/115/13/E2970

17. Shboul, Z.A., Alam, M., Vidyaratne, L., Pei, L., Elbakary, M.I., Iftekharuddin, K.M.: Feature-guided deep radiomics for glioblastoma patient survival prediction. Front. Neurosci. **13**, 966 (2019). https://doi.org/10.3389/fnins.2019.00966. https://www.frontiersin.org/article/10.3389/fnins.2019.00966
18. Tong, Q., et al.: RIANet: recurrent interleaved attention network for cardiac MRI segmentation. Comput. Biol. Med. **109**, 290–302 (2019). https://doi.org/10.1016/j.compbiomed.2019.04.042
19. Woo, S., Park, J., Lee, J.-Y., Kweon, I.S.: CBAM: convolutional block attention module. In: Ferrari, V., Hebert, M., Sminchisescu, C., Weiss, Y. (eds.) ECCV 2018. LNCS, vol. 11211, pp. 3–19. Springer, Cham (2018). https://doi.org/10.1007/978-3-030-01234-2_1
20. Zhu, X., Yao, J., Huang, J.: Deep convolutional neural network for survival analysis with pathological images. In: 2016 IEEE International Conference on Bioinformatics and Biomedicine (BIBM), vol. 1, pp. 544–547. IEEE (2016). https://doi.org/10.1109/BIBM.2016.7822579

Robustification of Segmentation Models Against Adversarial Perturbations in Medical Imaging

Hanwool Park[1][(✉)], Amirhossein Bayat[1,2], Mohammad Sabokrou[3],
Jan S. Kirschke[2], and Bjoern H. Menze[1]

[1] Department of Informatics, Technical University of Munich, Munich, Germany
zerg468@gmail.com
[2] Department of Neuroradiology, Klinikum rechts der Isar, Munich, Germany
[3] School of Computer Science, IPM Institute for Research in Fundamental Sciences,
Tehran, Iran

Abstract. This paper presents a novel yet efficient defense framework for segmentation models against adversarial attacks in medical imaging. In contrary to the defense methods against adversarial attacks for classification models which widely are investigated, such defense methods for segmentation models has been less explored. Our proposed method can be used for any deep learning models without revising the target deep learning models, as well as can be independent of adversarial attacks. Our framework consists of a frequency domain converter, a detector, and a reformer. The frequency domain converter helps the detector detects adversarial examples by using a frame domain of an image. The reformer helps target models to predict more precisely. We have experiments to empirically show that our proposed method has a better performance compared to the existing defense method.

Keywords: Deep learning · Adversarial attacks · Image segmentation · Medical imaging

1 Introduction

Recently, Deep learning plays an important role on medical industry since the deep learning system makes it possible to help medical imaging segmentation to identify the pixels of different lesions or organs in medical imaging such as MRI images. However, many researchers discovered that the deep learning neural networks are vulnerable to adversarial examples [3,11]. To defend against the adversarial attacks, numerous defense algorithms and methods have been introduced and can be grouped under different approaches: (1) training the target deep learning neural networks with the adversarial examples to be more robust; namely adversarial training [3,11] (2) changing training procedures of the target deep learning models for the attackers hard to attack by reducing the magnitude of gradient, e.g., defensive distillation [12] and (3) building a defense

© Springer Nature Switzerland AG 2020
I. Rekik et al. (Eds.): PRIME 2020, LNCS 12329, pp. 46–57, 2020.
https://doi.org/10.1007/978-3-030-59354-4_5

framework, which is independent of the adversarial attacks, to defend the target deep learning models against any adversarial attacks [5,17]. However, All of these approaches have limitations. (1) needs the specific adversarial examples to train the models, so it is only resistant against the limited adversarial attacks. For (2), this approach does not show a good defensive performance against some of the adversarial attacks. (3) shows good generalization and robustness against any adversarial attacks, but some of the defense frameworks only prove their capacities against the small size of images and it is still a challenging task to appropriately train and tune for some of the defense frameworks.

The related works for our proposed defense method are defense approach (3). This approach does not need to modify the target models, as well as it does not need to know any knowledge of the process for crafting adversarial examples. MagNet [5] and Defense-GAN [17] are known for this approach. MagNet is created to defend the neural network classifiers against the adversarial examples in 2017. MagNet consists of a detector and a reformer. The detector discerns between normal images and adversarial images by measuring how far the input images differ from the manifold of the normal images. The reformer pushes the adversarial images close to the manifold of the legitimate images to help target models to correctly predict. MagNet is the attack-independent defense framework but it works only with the small size of images and classifier models. Dense-GAN was introduced by Samangoeui et al. in 2018. This defense framework leverages Generative Adversarial Networks (GANs) [10] to defend the deep learning models against any adversarial attacks. Defense-GAN utilizes GANs for the main architecture as well as Gradient Descent (GD) minimization to find latent codes for GANs instead of using the detector network and the reformer network. The authors believed if GAN is trained properly and has enough capacity to represent the data, its reconstructions and the original images should not defer much. However, it is very challenging to train GANs and if GANs are neither trained nor tuned appropriately, the performance of Defense-GAN decreases.

In this paper, we introduce a new defense mechanism to defend the deep learning segmentation models against the adversarial examples in medical imaging. Our approach does not require the target networks to modify the model architectures or training procedures. Moreover, it does not need to know the information about the adversarial examples. Additionally, we use frequency domain of an image instead of spatial domain because we can analyze the geometric characteristic of an image and show more clearly differences between a normal image and an adversarial image in the frequency domain of image because of the difference between low and high frequency domain information. Our contributions are as followed. Firstly, we show that our method can be robust and generalized well against the adversarial examples for semantic segmentation tasks in medical imaging. Secondly, we utilize a frequency domain of an image to differentiate the legitimate examples and the adversarial examples. Thirdly, our defense mechanism can be used for any deep learning neural network models.

2   Methodology

The purpose of our defense strategy is to design the defense mechanism to be robust and generalized well across any adversarial attacks. Our defense strategy is similar to MagNet. The main differences between MagNet and our approach are: (1) we exploit the deep semantic segmentation models (e.g. UNet [14], DenseNet [16]) instead of auto-encoders, (2) we utilize a frequency domain of an image to detect the adversarial examples rather than a spatial domain of an image. The main components in our defense strategy are the frequency domain converter, the detector network, and the reformer network. Figure 1 demonstrates the workflow of our approach in the test phase.

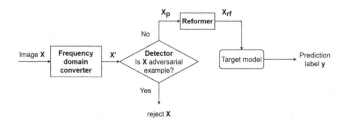

Fig. 1. The workflow of our defense strategy in the test phase

At the test time, the input image X is given to the frequency domain converter at first. The role of the frequency domain converter is to convert the spatial domain of an image into the frequency domain of an image. The detector gets frequency domain of X' which is the output of the frequency domain converter and then differentiates whether X' is the normal image or the adversarial image by measuring the reconstruction error between X' and the manifold of the normal examples, which are also in the frequency domain. If X' is far from the majority boundary (i.e. the reconstruction error is large), the detector network rejects X'. The output of the detector is the information of indices of X' which is not rejected by the detector network. We extract the passed input image X_p by using the output of the detector. Then, the reformer pushes X_p close to the manifold of an original image. The important point is that the reformer does not use the frequency domain of an image for its function, but uses the spatial domain of an image. At the final step, the output of the reformer network X_{rf} is given as the input of the target deep segmentation models. Our defense framework only needs these three components. Therefore, we do not need the target networks to change training procedures as well as the model architecture. Moreover, we do not require the information about the adversarial examples.

Frequency Domain Converter. The frequency domain converter is a function to return the frequency domain of an image from the spatial domain of an image. The purpose of this function is to help the detector to distinguish between the normal examples and the adversarial examples more precisely. The frequency domain is a space that represents the sine and cosine components of images by using the Fourier Transform [15]. In the frequency domain, each point in domain shows a particular frequency in the spatial domain of an image. To be more specific, high-frequency components correspond to edges or boundaries in an image, and low-frequency components represent smooth regions in an image. Hence, we can analyze the geometric characteristics of an image by the frequency domain of the image. The different images have their own frequency domains. Each frequency domain has their dominating directions, which are represented the regular patterns in the background of the images. But, all of the frequency domains have one thing in common. Their magnitudes get smaller for higher frequencies. Therefore, more image information is at low frequencies than at high frequencies. Since the frequency domain represents the rate at which the pixel values are changing in an image, we assume that the frequency domain shows more clearly differences between the normal examples and the adversarial examples than the spatial domain does.

The difference between the spatial domain and the frequency domain of the normal image and its corresponding adversarial example is as shown in Fig. 2. Figure 2(b) represents the frequency domain of the clean image, whereas Fig. 2(d) represents frequency domain of the adversarial image crafted by DAG [4]. There are a couple of differences between (b) and (d). Firstly, the dominating directions which are shown in (b) are blurred in (d). Also, (d) has more magnitude for high frequencies than (b). We assume that adding small perturbations to the clean image increases edges and breaks the regular patterns of the clean image. Therefore, we believe that this characteristic of the frequency domain makes the detector to differentiate the adversarial examples more precise compared to the detector using the spatial domain.

To convert image from spatial domain to frequency domain, we use Discrete Fourier Transform (DFT) [9] because images are discrete signal. The DFT is defined as:

$$F(u, v) = \frac{1}{WH} \sum_{x=0}^{W-1} \sum_{y=0}^{H-1} f(x, y) e^{-j2\pi(ux/W + vy/H)}$$

where F(u, v) is the coefficient of the periodic function component with frequency u in the x-axis and v in the y-axis and f(x, y) is the coefficient of the image with the size W x H. The ranges of each component are $x = 0, 1, ..., W-1$, $y = 0, 1, ..., H-1$, $u = 0, 1, ..., W-1$, and $v = 0, 1, ..., H-1$.

However, the zero-frequency component(0, 0) of the frequency domain of an image by DFT is not at the center of the image as shown in Fig. 3. It is hard to understand the shape of the frequency domain with (b) since the magnitude becomes bigger close to edges. If we want better to understand the frequency domain of an image, it is better to shift the zero-frequency component to the center of the image. Because F(u, v) is the periodic function that is symmetric with the origin, we can use the shift function to shift the zero-frequency component. We evaluate the performance between the frequency domain detector without using the shift function and with using the shift function in experiments.

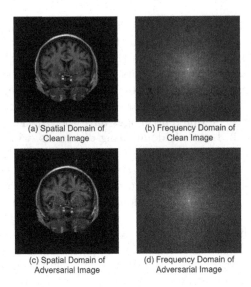

Fig. 2. The spatial domain and the frequency domain of one clean image and its corresponding adversarial image

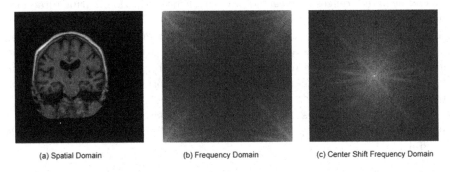

Fig. 3. A whole-brain MRI image in the spatial domain, the frequency domain and the frequency domain using the shift function

Detector. The detector is a function that classifies whether the input image is the adversarial image or the legitimate image. We utilize the distance metrics to access the distance between the input examples and the manifold of the normal examples. We train the detector networks with mean squared error (MSE):

$$MSE(X) = \frac{1}{|X|} \sum_{x \in X} \|x - D(x)\|_2$$

We use a reconstruction error for our distance metrics. D is referred as the detector. The reconstruction error RE(x) on test data x is defined:

$$RE(x) = \|x - D(x)\|_p$$

If the input sample is drawn from the same data generation process as the training samples which are used for training the detector, the reconstruction error is small. Otherwise, the reconstruction error is big. Hence, we can utilize the reconstruction error for our distance metrics to tell how far a test image is from the majority of the normal images. Also, it is very essential to choose suitable norms when we calculate the reconstruction errors because the norm has a big impacts on the sharpness of detection results. Smaller p in p-norm averages its depth to each pixel. On the other hand, a larger p is more responsive to the maximum difference among all pixels. Empirically, we found out that 2-norm is sufficient. Hence, we use 2-norm to calculate the reconstruction error for the detector network.

Moreover, we must set a threshold t_{re} to decide the decision boundary to detect the adversarial examples since the reconstruction error is a continuous value. Hence, the threshold is a hyperparameter which is an instance of the detector network. The one thing to note is that we should care to select the correct threshold. To detect little perturbed adversarial examples, the threshold should be as low as possible. If the threshold is too low, the detector classifies the normal examples as the adversarial examples. To choose t_{re}, we exploit the validation dataset including the normal examples. We calculate all of the thresholds on the validation dataset and then we discover the highest t_{re} below the threshold t_{fp}, which is the false positive rate of the detector on the validation dataset. t_{fp} should be chosen by the requirement of the system. We give one example of t_{fp} and t_{re} to explain the relationship between them. If the t_{fp} is set to 0.1 by the system, the detector rejects no more than 10% examples on the validation dataset. So, the threshold t_{re} is the highest value in the threshold set which are already computed by using the validation dataset.

In MagNet, they implemented the autoencoder architecture for the detector network. However, we assume that the autoencoder appropriately works only with the small size images because the autoencoder architecture is simple network. Hence, we utilize more complicated architectures than autoencoder architectures to have better the detector network. For this, we implement the deep image segmentation models such as UNet and DenseNet.

Reformer. The reformer is a function to try to reconstruct the input image to push close to the majority of the normal examples. The output of the reformer is then given as the input to the target deep learning neural network model. The one thing is to note that the reformer is used only at the inference time. We train the reformer network to minimize the reconstruction error on the training dataset including the legitimate images. Since the reformer is trained with the normal examples, the output of the reformer should be very similar when the input image is reconstructed in the same process as the training normal examples. However, when the adversarial example comes to the reformer, the reformer moves the adversarial example closer to the majority of the normal examples. Therefore, the reformer can help the target deep neural network model to improve the accuracy of the prediction of the adversarial examples while keeping the accuracy of the prediction of the normal examples.

3   Experiments

The following sections describe experiments and results to evaluate the performance of our defense strategy outlined in Sect. 2. We introduce our setup for the experiment. Then, we evaluate the performance of the detector networks, as well as we compare our defense approach and MagNet under the adversarial attacks.

Setup. Since we are motivated by the paper where Paschali M. et al., evaluated the performance of SegNet [18], UNet and DenseNet in unseen clean and adversarial examples [13], we also select the same segmentation models(SegNet, UNet and DenseNet) for our target models to evaluate the performance of our defense method against the adversarial examples. SegNet does not have skip connection, UNet has long-range skip connections and DenseNet has long-range and short-range skip connections. In the paper [13], DenseNet shows the best robustness results against adversarial attacks and noisy attacks because of long-range and short-range skip connections followed by UNet and SegNet.

The semantic segmentation models are trained with the special loss function [1] combined with weighted multi-class logistic loss and Dice loss [7]. The loss function is

$$L = -\sum_x w(x)g_l(x)log(p_l(x))) - \frac{2\sum_x p_l(x)g_l(x)}{\sum_x p_l^2(x) + \sum_x g_l^2(x)}$$

where the estimated probability of pixel x belonging to class l represents $p_l(x)$ and the its actual class is $g_l(x)$. The first term is the weighted multi-class logistic loss and the second term is the Dice loss. The details are described in the paper written by Roy A.G. et al. [1]. Model optimization is performed with ADAM optimizer with an initial learning rate of 0.001.

For our experiments, we use special MRI data from the publicly-available whole-brain segmentation benchmark which is a subset of Open Access Series of Imaging Studies (OASIS) [6]. OASIS dataset has 35 different volumes. The OASIS dataset consists of three-dimensional images, but we split the dataset into two-dimensional images. The adversarial examples are crafted for all of the trained segmentation models by using DAG. To measure the performance of the semantic segmentation models, we use Dice score [8].

To compare our defense framework and MagNet, we implement two segmentation models (UNet, DenseNet) for our detector and reformer. For the detector, we use the training dataset that is trained for the semantic segmentation models. But, we transform the training dataset from the spatial domain to the frequency domain. For the reformer, we train the training examples in the spatial domain. The optimizer is ADAM which is set to the initial learning rate of 0.001 and we use L^2 regularization.

Evaluation for Detection. We evaluate the performance of the different detector architectures. The purpose of this experiment is not only to compare the auto-encoder architectures and the segmentation architectures that we implement for our detector network, but also to compare the detector based on the frequency domain and the detector based on the spatial domain. For this, we utilize the Receiver Operating Characteristics (ROC) - Area Under The Curve (AUC) curve [2].

For this experiment, we design the new OASIS dataset including the normal examples and all types of the adversarial examples crafted by DAG that sets for the three trained segmentation models. The ratio of each examples is the normal examples (50%), DAG adversarial examples (50%).

Table 1. The ROC-AUC score of each detector network

	ROC_AUC score %			
	UNet	SegNet	DenseNet	Average
Autoencoder I	54.27	57.87	57.18	56.44
Autoencoder II	53.17	56.09	56.10	55.12
UNet_spatial	84.58	97.36	92.49	91.48
DenseNet_spatial	80.29	95.21	87.56	87.69
UNet_frequency	52.74	53.81	52.90	53.15
DenseNet_frequency	52.39	55.35	55.49	54.41
UNet_shiftFrequency	**96.12**	**98.82**	**99.34**	**98.09**
DenseNet_shiftFrequency	90.62	98.09	97.42	95.38

Table 1 shows the ROC-AUC score of the different detectors. Autoencoder I and autoencoder II for MagNet show that they are not capable of discerning the adversarial examples. Our methods with the segmentation models in the spatial domain demonstrate the good performance of classification. Now, we observe the detectors based on the frequency domain. The UNet and DenseNet frequency domain detectors without using the shift function show bad capacity to distinguish between the adversarial examples and the legitimate examples. However, the frequency domain detectors using the shift function show very good measurement of separability.

As a result, this experiment provides empirical pieces of evidence to our assumptions. Firstly, deep segmentation models achieve better performance than auto-encoders because auto-encoders cannot differentiate the big size of adversarial images and normal images. Lastly, the detector can differentiate the normal examples and the adversarial examples better when the detector uses the frequency domain instead of the spatial domain.

Overall Performance Against Adversarial Attacks. We evaluate different defense architectures including MagNet and our defense method against the DAG adversarial attacks. Firstly, we introduce the different defense architectures for the detectors and the reformers. Then, we evaluate the different defense architectures for the trained segmentation models using the DAG adversarial attacks.

Table 2. The combination of detector and reformer networks

	Detector	Reformer		Detector	Reformer
1	Autoencoder I	Autoencoder I	9	UNet_frequency	UNet
2	Autoencoder I	Autoencoder II	10	UNet_frequency	DenseNet
3	Autoencoder II	Autoencoder I	11	DenseNet_frequency	UNet
4	Autoencoder II	Autoencoder II	12	DenseNet_frequency	DenseNet
5	Autoencoder I	UNet	13	UNet_shiftFrequency	UNet
6	Autoencoder I	DenseNet	14	UNet_shiftFrequency	DenseNet
7	Autoencoder II	UNet	15	DenseNet_shiftFrequency	UNet
8	Autoencoder II	DenseNet	16	DenseNet_shiftFrequency	DenseNet

Table 2 depicts all the combinations of the detector and the reformer networks for experiments. Diversified defense architectures boost the defense performance. The total number of defense architectures is 16. The combinations of the defense architectures are between the number 1 and the number 4 for MagNet. To compare the performance of the reformers between the auto-encoders and the segmentation models, we design the defense architectures which include the auto-encoders for the detector and the segmentation models for reformer in the number 5 to the number 8. The number 9 to the number 16, we design the frequency domain detectors using UNet and DenseNet. The difference between "frequency" and "shiftFrequency" is that the "shiftFrequency" detectors use the shift function. In this experiment, we do not use the detectors using the segmentation models for the spatial domain because our main idea of the defense framework uses the detector for the frequency domain rather than the spatial domain, as well as we already empirically proved that the frequency domain detector has better power to detect adversarial examples than the spatial domain detector.

Since we have the 16 different defense architectures, we can evaluate the performances of the reformer networks between the auto-encoders and the segmentation models as well as the performances of the detectors between the spatial domain and the frequency domain. Lastly, we can ultimately measure the performance of the defense strategies between our defense method and MagNet. For convenience, we refer to the combination of the defense architectures between the number 1 and the number 16 as between (1) and (16).

Figure 4 demonstrates the overall performances of the diversified defense architectures for the semantic segmentation models (SegNet, UNet, DenseNet) with the average score against all of the DAG adversarial attacks. We choose the false positive rate of the detector on the validation set t_{fp} to 0.05 to set the threshold of reconstruction error t_{re}.

In Fig. 4, we can compare the performance of each semantic segmentation model without defense. DenseNet shows the best dice score against DAG adversarial attacks followed by UNet and SegNet. Therefore, we can say that the skip connections help to be robust against adversarial attacks.

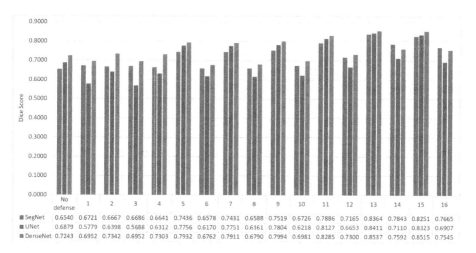

Fig. 4. Bar charts for the average Dice scores of SegNet, UNet and DenseNet using the different defense strategies against all of the attacks

Firstly, we look at the bar charts of SegNet with the different defense strategies. MagNet((1)–(4)) slightly improves the performance rather than no defense SegNet. Compared with the reformer networks between the auto-encoders((1)–(4)) and the segmentation models, the DenseNet reformers((6), (7)) show the same or less performances than the auto-encoders, but the performance of the UNet reformers((5), (7)) improves around 10% better than the auto-encoders. Compared with the frequency domain detectors((9)–(16)), the UNet shift frequency domain detectors((13), (14)) achieve the better performances than the UNet no shift frequency domain detectors((9), (10)). The DenseNet shift frequency domain detectors((15), (16)) also shows the better achievements than the DenseNet no shift frequency domain detectors((11), (12)). Furthermore, we can compare the detectors between the auto-encoders((5)–(8)) and the segmentation models using the shift function in the frequency domain((13)–(16)). We observe that the shift frequency domain detectors have better achievements than the auto-encoders detectors. In conclusion, the shift frequency domain detector using UNet and the UNet reformer network (13) shows the best Dice score accuracy compared with the other defense strategies followed by (15). Furthermore, our defense mechanism(13) achieves better than MagNet in SegNet.

Secondly, we observe the bar charts of UNet. MagNet((1)–(4)) shows the worse average Dice score than no defense UNet. The combinations with detectors using the auto-encoders and the DenseNet reformers((6), (8)) also display that they are not able to defend against the adversarial examples. The defense strategies with the shift frequency domain detectors and the DenseNet reformers((10), (12)) show the bad performances too. We only observe that the defense strategies using the UNet reformers((5), (7), (9), (11), (13), (15)) are capable of defending against the adversarial attacks. The reformers using UNet architecture ((5), (7)) show better achievements 17% than the reformers using the auto-encoders((1)–(4)). The shift frequency domains((13)–(16)) achieve more than 7% than the auto-encoders detectors((5)–(8)). The best performance of the defense strategy is the shift frequency domain detector using UNet and the UNet reformer(13). This strategy shows around 23% better performance than MagNet(2).

Next, we observe the overall performances of DenseNet using the different defense combinations. DenseNet also shows that MagNet ((1)–(4)) is not very useful to defend against the adversarial attacks. The defense strategies using the UNet reformer((5), (7), (9), (11), (13), (15)) achieve better Dice scores than the defense strategies using the DenseNet reformer((6), (8), (10), (12), (14), (16)). The shift frequency domain detectors((13)–(16)) show better achievements than the auto-encoder detectors((5)–(8)). The reformer using segmentation models((5)–(8)) are more powerful to defend facing the adversarial attacks compared with the reformer using the auto-encoders((1)–(4)). The defense strategy(13) shows the best performance among the other defense strategies and the other semantic segmentation models.

In conclusion, these experiments result provide empirical shreds of evidence of our assumptions. Firstly, the reformer using the UNet has better capability to move closer to the majority of the original examples than auto-encoders. Secondly, the shift frequency domain which has zero frequency component is located at the center of an image helps the detector networks to differentiate the adversarial examples and the normal examples more accurately than the spatial domain as well as the frequency domain without using the shift function. Finally, the experiment results prove that our new defense strategy is powerful and generalized well to the various adversarial attacks.

4   Conclusion

We proposed the new defense methodology for defending the medical image semantic segmentation models against adversarial attacks. Our defense framework improves the prediction accuracy and decreases the power of the adversarial attacks. Furthermore, our defense framework is attack-independent. Besides, our method is independent of the target deep learning neural network models. These characteristics of our defense method lead to better generalization across the adversarial attacks.

References

1. Roy, A.G., Conjeti, S., Sheet, D., Katouzian, A., Navab, N., Wachinger, C.: Error corrective boosting for learning fully convolutional networks with limited data. In: Descoteaux, M., Maier-Hein, L., Franz, A., Jannin, P., Collins, D.L., Duchesne, S. (eds.) MICCAI 2017. LNCS, vol. 10435, pp. 231–239. Springer, Cham (2017). https://doi.org/10.1007/978-3-319-66179-7_27
2. Bradley, A.P.: The use of the area under the ROC curve in the evaluation of machine learning algorithms. Pattern Recogn. **30**, 1145–1159 (1997)

3. Szegedy, C., et al.: Intriguing properties of neural networks. Preprint at https://arxiv.org/abs/1312.6199 (2013)
4. Xie, C., Wang, J., Zhang, Z., Zhou, Y., Xie, L., Yuille, A.: Adversarial examples for semantic segmentation and object detection. In: 2017 IEEE International Conference on Computer Vision (ICCV) (2017)
5. Meng, D., Chen, H.: MagNet. In: Proceedings of the 2017 ACM SIGSAC Conference on Computer and Communications Security (2017)
6. Marcus, D.S., Wang, T.H., Parker, J., Csernansky, J.G., Morris, J.C., Buckner, R.L.: Open access series of imaging studies (OASIS): cross-sectional MRI data in young, middle aged, nondemented, and demented older adults. J. Cogn. Neurosci. **19**(9), 1498–1507 (2007)
7. Milletari, F., Navab, N., Ahmadi, S.-A.: V-Net: fully convolutional neural networks for volumetric medical image segmentation. In: 2016 Fourth International Conference on 3D Vision (3DV) (2016)
8. Zou, K.H., et al.: Statistical validation of image segmentation quality based on a spatial overlap index1. Acad. Radiol. **11**, 178–189 (2004)
9. Cooley, J.W., Tukey, J.W.: An algorithm for the machine calculation of complex Fourier series. Math. Comput. **19**, 297 (1965)
10. Goodfellow, J., et al.: Generative adversarial nets. Preprint at https://arxiv.org/abs/1406.2661 (2014)
11. Goodfellow, J., Jonathon, S., Christian, S.: Explaining and harnessing adversarial examples. Preprint at https://arxiv.org/abs/1412.6572 (2014)
12. Papernot, N., Mcdaniel, P., Wu, X., Jha, S., Swami, A.: Distillation as a defense to adversarial perturbations against deep neural networks. In: 2016 IEEE Symposium on Security and Privacy (SP) (2016)
13. Paschali, M., Conjeti, S., Navarro, F., Navab, N.: Generalizability *vs.* robustness: investigating medical imaging networks using adversarial examples. In: Frangi, A.F., Schnabel, J.A., Davatzikos, C., Alberola-López, C., Fichtinger, G. (eds.) MICCAI 2018. LNCS, vol. 11070, pp. 493–501. Springer, Cham (2018). https://doi.org/10.1007/978-3-030-00928-1_56
14. Ronneberger, O., Fischer, P., Brox, T.: U-Net: convolutional networks for biomedical image segmentation. In: Navab, N., Hornegger, J., Wells, W.M., Frangi, A.F. (eds.) MICCAI 2015. LNCS, vol. 9351, pp. 234–241. Springer, Cham (2015). https://doi.org/10.1007/978-3-319-24574-4_28
15. Bracewell, R.N.: The Fourier Transform and Its Applications. McGraw-Hill, New York (1986)
16. Jegou, S., Drozdzal, M., Vazquez, D., Romero, A., Bengio, Y.: The one hundred layers tiramisu: fully convolutional DenseNets for semantic segmentation. In: 2017 IEEE Conference on Computer Vision and Pattern Recognition Workshops (CVPRW) (2017)
17. Pouya, S., Maya, K., Rama, C.: Defense-GAN: protecting classifiers against adversarial attacks using generative models. Preprint at https://arxiv.org/abs/1805.06605 (2018)
18. Badrinarayanan, V., Kendall, A., Cipolla, R.: SegNet: a deep convolutional encoder-decoder architecture for image segmentation. IEEE Trans. Pattern Anal. Mach. Intell. **39**, 2481–2495 (2017)

Joint Clinical Data and CT Image Based Prognosis: A Case Study on Postoperative Pulmonary Venous Obstruction Prediction

Xinrong Hu[1]($\boxtimes$), Zeyang Yao[2], Furong Liu[2], Wen Xie[2], Hailong Qiu[2], Haoyu Dong[2], Qianjun Jia[2], Meiping Huang[2], Jian Zhuang[2], Xiaowei Xu[1], and Yiyu Shi[1]

[1] University of Notre Dame, Notre Dame, IN 46556, USA
{xhu7,xxu8,yshi4}@nd.edu
[2] Guangdong Provincial People's Hospital, Guangdong 510000, China

Abstract. Very often doctors diagnose diseases and prescribe treatments through cross-referencing patients' clinical data as well as radiology reports. On the other hand, while a few existing machine learning frameworks for diagnosis, treatment planning, and prognosis have used both clinical data and medical images, they all have prior knowledge about what information should be extracted from medical images. However, this is not the case for many diseases. For example, cardiac anatomical structure and tissue shapes are essential for pulmonary venous obstruction (PVO) prediction after correction of total anomalous pulmonary venous connection (TAPVC), but the exact graphical features in the computed tomography (CT) images that should be measured remain unclear. In this paper, we propose to use convolutional neural network to automatically obtain features from CT images and combine them with clinical data in an end-to-end trainable manner. We further collect a dataset consisting of 132 TAPVC patients for evaluation, and find that jointly using clinical data and CT images to predict postoperative PVO outperforms the method based on either clinical data or CT images alone. Our dataset is released to the community to promote further research.

Keywords: Cardiac CT images · Pulmonary venous obstruction · Total anomalous pulmonary venous connection · Convolutional neural network

1 Introduction

Over the past decades, machine learning has demonstrated great power in the medical domain and been applied for different tasks, including diagnosis, treatment planning, and disease prognosis. In an analogy to the common practice of human doctors where both the clinical data (e.g. demographic information

© Springer Nature Switzerland AG 2020
I. Rekik et al. (Eds.): PRIME 2020, LNCS 12329, pp. 58–67, 2020.
https://doi.org/10.1007/978-3-030-59354-4_6

and lab results) and radiology reports (e.g., X-ray, CT, and MRI) are cross-referenced, there is a growing trend involving both clinical data and medical images in machine learning based frameworks to handle various diseases (e.g., [2,8,9,12]). In [8], all metrics in coronary computed tomographic angiography (CCTA) are measured visually by experienced cardiologists or radiologists, which combined with hospital records are used to predict 5-year all-cause mortality. [9] benefits from considering both the auxiliary information with the imaging data and non-imaging information in a graphical neural network for brain analysis in populations. Recently, [2] combines clinical information and myocardial perfusion imaging (MPI) data to predict major adverse cardiac events. They take advantage of professional software to preprocess MPI and to automatically quantify variables in images.

However, all these works require predefined features of medical images, either measured by software or manually, to be combined with clinical data. Prior knowledge about what information should be extracted from medical images is needed. Unfortunately, such knowledge is not always available for many diseases. In this paper, we use postoperative pulmonary venous obstruction (PVO) prediction problem as a vehicle to explore the practicability of combining clinical data and CT images under such a scenario. The relationship between graphical features on CT images and PVO recurrence remains unknown as of today.

Total anomalous pulmonary venous connection (TAPVC) contributes to about 3% of all congenital heart diseases [5] and yet has notoriously high mortality achieving nearly 80% if without intervention [3]. It is characterized by failure of the pulmonary venous confluence (PVC) to be absorbed into the dorsal portion of the left atrium (LA) in combination with a persistent splanchnic connection to the systemic venous systems. Even with surgical repair, the death rate is still reported as 5% to 7%. PVO is one of the most frequent causes of death after operations. Accurate prediction model can identify patients with high PVO recurrence risk, and then their chance of survival will be improved by early preventive treatment.

Previous works only focus on finding features in the clinical data that have a close association with recurrent PVO, like [6]. An automatic model for PVO prediction is still missing. In addition, it remains unknown if CT images would be helpful in such prediction, and if so, the graphical features that may be of relevance. To answer these questions, in this paper we build a prediction model that explicitly indicates whether a patient will suffer from PVO after surgery. Specifically, we put forward three machine learning based methods: i) applying logistic regression with features selected from the clinical data; ii) using a convolutional neural network (CNN) to extract features from patients' 3D cardiac CT images for prediction; and iii) building an architecture where clinical data features are combined with graphical features through an end-to-end trainable CNN.

The limited number of TAPVC patients and biased distribution of postoperative PVO and non-PVO cases introduce additional challenges. To address these issues, we adopt a series of practical techniques regarding data preprocessing and learning strategies: i) image augmentation is utilized to increase the size of CT dataset; ii) for training epochs, positive cases are over-sampled in an attempt to balance the biased distribution; iii) we modify the loss function, adding L2 normalization of weights in the last fully connected layer of the CNN for generalization performance, and adjusting the weights of the PVO and non-PVO samples.

The main contributions of this paper are concluded as follows:

- For the first time in the literature, we present an automatic prognosis model for PVO after TAPVC surgery and demonstrate its promising accuracy on test dataset.
- We propose clinical data based, CT image based, and joint data and image based methods for the prognosis model. By comparison, we find that jointly considering both clinical data and medical images in an end-to-end trainable manner can indeed provide better prediction.
- Several empirical techniques of data preprocessing and training are discussed in order to deal with small and biased dataset pertinent to TAPVC.
- The method can possibly be extended to various diagnosis, treatment planning and prognosis problems where both clinical data and medical images are important yet the related graphical feature is unknown.
- Our dataset composed of both clinical data and CT images of 132 patients is released [1] to promote further research on this topic.

2   Methods

2.1   Clinical Data Based Method

Prognosis about the onset of PVO after TPAVC correction can be treated as a binary classification problem. With only clinical data taken into consideration, each patient A_k is defined by several features $\{x_{k1}, x_{k2}, x_{k3}, ...\}$, and a target label y_k indicating whether PVO occurs after surgery (either 1 or 0). The problem is then to generate predictions $\widetilde{y}_1, \widetilde{y}_2, \widetilde{y}_3, ...$ and to optimize a defined loss function $\sum_k L(y_k, \widetilde{y}_k)$. The most prevalent methods for such a binary classification problem include logistic regression, support vector machine, and random forest, etc. Among these machine learning models, we find that logistic regression is the most effective method for PVO prognosis in practice.

To decide which features to feed into the prediction model, we initially select a set of candidate features which cardiologists believe to have direct or indirect effects on the recurrence of PVO. For example, sutureless operation is believed to have a potential impact on the geometric distortion of pulmonary venous suture line and thus on the postoperative PVO, according to the previous study [16]. Then, we recursively prune features from the candidate set in the ascending order of the features' importance score until the optimal prediction accuracy is achieved. Such an iterative pruning can help to remove redundant information and reduce potential overfitting.

2.2   CT Image Based Method

Cardiac CT images have never been used in traditional prognosis of TAPVC repair. Yet CT images provide spatial information like anatomical structure and tissue development, which clinical data fails to provide. However, those graphical features are not specified by any measurable parameters. Hence, we apply a convolutional neural network to extract information from patients' CT and then to make a prediction on postoperative PVO. The input of the network is 3D images, and thus it resembles a 3D classification network. Because of the memory bottleneck induced by 3D medical images, very deep CNNs like VGG [13] and ResNet [4] is not suitable. Figure 1(a) illustrates our 3D CNN's architecture. The original 3D cardiac CT images are first cropped to the region of interest and resized to a uniform shape, after which a batch of images are passed to the model. The model consists of 3 resolution stages, and for each resolution stage, there are two convolutional layers followed by max pooling with stride two to half the resolution as well as double the number of channels. The size of feature maps maintains the same for every convolutional operation. We replace the max pooling with global pooling to flatten the feature maps in the last stage, which will be followed by a fully connected layer for predicting postoperative PVO. For the global pooling layer, inspired by [15], we use a combination of global max pooling and global average pooling. These two types of pooling act like two filters with different frequency responses, so that our model takes advantage of both high-frequency and low-frequency information. All the convolutionnal and pooling operations mentioned above are 3D counterparts. Besides, the number of resolution stages and initial filters are both adjustable. After comparison of different combinations, we decide on this architecture that strikes a balance between computational efficiency and generalization performance.

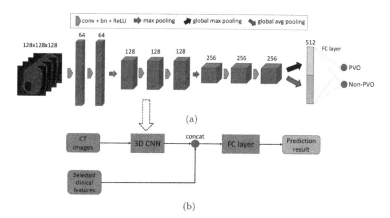

(a)

(b)

Fig. 1. (a) Architecture of CT image based 3D CNN. The blue cuboid represents 3D feature maps, and the number of channels is marked above it. (b) Framework of joint clinical data and image based postoperative PVO prediction method. (Color figure online)

2.3   Joint Data and Image Based Method

Actually, CT images and clinical data give the prediction based on factors from two distinct domains. Thus, it is a natural thought to combine the knowledge from those two "experts" skilled in different fields, in other words, using CT images and clinical data jointly for the prediction task. We concatenate the selected features from clinical data (based on the method described in Sect. 2.1) with the flattened activations right before the fully connected layer in our 3D CNN, as shown in Fig. 1(b). In this way, we build an end-to-end deep learning model making use of both CT images and clinical data, which we find demonstrates better performance than the methods using either one of the data sources solely.

3   Dataset

Our study enrolls 306 patients who were diagnosed with TAPVC and received surgical treatment from January 2009 to September 2019 with complete clinical data and CT images. There are four types of TAPVC, including supracardiac, infracardiac, cardiac, and mixed. In terms of image-based methods, these four types have heterogeneous anatomical structure, so it is hard for a single neural network to learn all distinct spatial information. Thus, we only consider the most common type, the supracardiac, that accounts for 30%–50% of total TAPVC. Among the 306 patients, there are 132 (43.1%) cases of supracardiac TAPVC which are used to create the dataset.

For clinical data, suggested by expert cardiologists, we focus on 14 features, which are patient weight at the time of operation (operation weight), length of hospital stay (hospital stay), Alanine Transaminase value (ALT), Aspartate Aminotransferase value (AST), Total Bilirubin value (TBIL), Direct Bilirubin value (DBIL), INR (International Normalized Ratio), Prothrombin activity time (PT), aortic cross-clamp time (cross-clamp), CPB time (Cardiopulmonary Bypass time), Deep hypothermic circulatory arrest time (DHCA), and binary features including gender, the use of sutureless operation (sutureless), and ligation. All lab results are collected before the operation. These features along with their ranges are summarized in Table 1. As for medical images, all 3D CT were captured by a Siemens Biography 64 CT scanner, and the typical voxel size is $0.25\,\text{mm} \times 0.25\,\text{mm} \times 0.5\,\text{mm}$.

Based on the patients' follow-up record after surgery (which is not part of this dataset and is not used in model training), when at least one of the following three conditions is met, there is postoperative PVO recurrence: i) blood flow in the vertical vein or common trunk of pulmonary vein greater than $1.8\,\text{m/s}$; ii) atrial septal defect smaller than 3 mm; iii) color ultrasonic diagnosis suggesting obstruction. Finally, 10% of the patients in the dataset are labeled with postoperative PVO. This ratio agrees with epidemiology studies, suggesting that our dataset is relatively unbiased.

Table 1. The 14 candidate features in the clinical data that may be relevant to post-operative PVO recurrence, their respective ranges, and the importance score (IS) from logistic regression (clinical data based method).

Feature	Range	IS	Feature	Range	IS
Operation weight	2.63–53.0 kg	**21.8**	Hospital stay	0–77 d	**0.819**
ALT	5–948 IU/L	0.771	AST	20–2420 IU/L	0.237
TBIL	6.8–211.6 μ mol/L	0.324	DBIL	1.9–104.9 μ mol/L	0.498
INR	0.83–2.55	**44.8**	PT	31–140 s	0.040
Cross-clamp	0–153 min	0.409	CPB	40–290 min	**1.38**
DHCA	0–40 min	**4.35**	Gender	{0, 1}	**19.0**
Sutureless	{0, 1}	**55.4**	Ligation	{0, 1}	**59.1**

4   Preprocessing and Learning Techniques

4.1   Image Augmentation

To make full use of all cardiac CT images in the limited dataset, we deploy classic augmentation methods to enlarge the dataset. Traditional image augmentation methods include translation, rotation, scaling, and flipping [10,11]. In order to preserve the spatial structure and relative position of atrial and vessels, we only adopt rotation to increase both the training set and test set. Firstly, we crop the CT images so that the region of interest is centered. Then, we rotate the images clockwise by ($10°$, $-10°$, $90°$, $180°$, $270°$). As a result, we can expand the dataset by six times. Note that we first divide all the data into four folds with PVO patients evenly distributed. Only then do we augment the images in each fold and do four-fold cross-validation. This trick only works for the two methods described in Sects. 2.2 and 2.3, as it cannot expand clinical data.

4.2   Resampling

The distribution of our dataset is highly biased, which genuinely reflects the recurrence rate of PVO. To deal with the imbalance problem, resampling the dataset is a simple and effective method. There are two main methods called over-sampling and under-sampling. Over-sampling is to add copies of samples from the under-presented class, and under-sampling is to remove instances belonging to the over-presented class. In practice, we find over-sampling fits our dataset better than under-sampling because the dataset is already small, and reducing training samples would compromise models' generalization performance.

4.3 Loss Function Modification

The loss function L we choose for the 3D CNN is cross entropy. However, during training, we find the training loss is smaller than validation loss, indicating potential overfitting of our model on the training dataset. L2 normalization is a common way to alleviate overfitting by restraining weights from growing too large. The modified loss function for every batch is defined as:

$$L_{batch} = -\sum_{k \in B} weight[class] * \ln s_k[class] + \beta |w|^2, \qquad (1)$$

in which B is the batch set, $s_k[class]$ is the softmax value of a class (PVO or non-PVO) at the output layer, w is the weight vector of the last fully connected layer, and β is an adjustable parameter which we set to be 2. Additionally, we assign different $weight[class]$ to the two classes, since positive samples appear at a lower frequency in a batch. A larger weight for the PVO class forces the model to be more sensitive to wrongly predicting PVO patients as non-PVO, i.e., false negative, which is more critical than the other way around. On the other hand, if it is too large, it would lead to high false positive rate. Our experiments suggest that the optimal of weights for PVO and non-PVO classes is $(30, 1)$.

Table 2. Impact of the techniques described in Sect. 4 on the three prediction methods. "8" or "14" stands for the number of features used (pruned features v.s. all candidate features). For the CT image based method and the joint method, over-sampling is always applied.

	Clinical data based (8, w/o over-sample)	Clinical data based (8, w/over-sample)	CT image based (-, w/L2 norm)
AUC	0.824 ± 0.060	0.856 ± 0.061	0.618 ± 0.061
	Joint method (14, w/L2 norm)	Joint method (8, w/o L2 norm)	Joint method (8, w/L2 norm)
AUC	0.818 ± 0.081	0.933 ± 0.041	**0.941 ± 0.027**

5 Experiments

The metric we use to evaluate and compare different methods is AUC, which represents the area under the ROC (Receiver Operating Characteristics) curve, and is an important measurement for a classification model's performance as used in [7,14]. In our setting, it shows the ability of a method to predict the postoperative PVO recurrence of a patient. For the four-fold cross-validation, the AUC scores of four test sets are recorded and the resulting average is reported.

For clinical data based method, logistic regression is applied to make the prediction as well as to calculate the importance score of each feature. The importance score is obtained from the absolute value of features' coefficients in the logistic regression model, as listed in Table 1. We gradually remove some features from the 14 candidates following the ascending order of importance score. We observe that, when the number of predictors is eight, logistic regression model achieves the best performance. The eight features that are finally selected as postoperative PVO predictors by the clinical data based method are operation weight, hospital stay, INR, CPB, DHCA, gender, sutureless, and ligation.

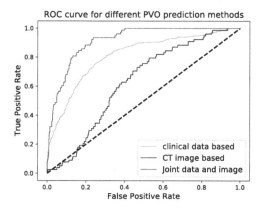

Fig. 2. ROC curves of the three different prediction methods. All the techniques in Sect. 4 are applied as appropriate on the three methods. The joint data and image based method is consistently better than the other two.

Table 2 displays the impact of the techniques discussed in Sect. 4 on AUC when applied on the three prediction methods. For the sake of clarity, we choose not to enumerate all the possible combinations in this ablation study; rather we illustrate six cases which are sufficient to observe the effectiveness of the techniques. From the table, several interesting points can be observed. First, comparing the clinical data based method with and without data over-sampling, the technique can increase the AUC by 0.032. Second, comparing the joint method with and without L2 norm, when both methods use eight features, the technique can increase the AUC by 0.008. Third, comparing the joint method with eight features and 14 features, when both methods use L2 norm, the technique can increase the AUC by 0.123. This suggests that feature pruning is not only effective for clinical data based method, but also the joint one. Finally, comparing all the methods, the joint method achieves the highest AUC score of 0.941. The corresponding ROC curves of the three methods are shown in Fig. 2, where the joint method is consistently better than the other two. This result supports the speculation that the 3D CNN is capable of extracting useful information from CT images for PVO prediction, complementing that from the clinical data.

6 Conclusion

In this paper, we explore how to combine clinical data and CT images for prognosis when the relationship between graphical features on CT images and the outcome is unknown. We use postoperative PVO prediction as a case study. A novel neural network architecture that jointly learns from clinical data and CT images in an end-to-end trainable manner is built. We also introduce a group of implementation tips involving data preprocessing and learning to manipulate the limited and biased dataset pertinent to the disease. Experimental results clearly demonstrate the advantage of the proposed method of joint learning.

References

1. link omitted for blind review
2. Betancur, J., et al.: Prognostic value of combined clinical and myocardial perfusion imaging data using machine learning. JACC: Cardiovascular Imaging **11**(7), 1000–1009 (2018)
3. Burroughs, J.T., Edwards, J.E.: Total anomalous pulmonary venous connection. Am. Heart J. **59**(6), 913–931 (1960)
4. He, K., Zhang, X., Ren, S., Sun, J.: Deep residual learning for image recognition. In: Proceedings of the IEEE Conference on Computer Vision and Pattern Recognition, pp. 770–778 (2016)
5. Herlong, J.R., Jaggers, J.J., Ungerleider, R.M.: Congenital heart surgery nomenclature and database project: pulmonary venous anomalies. Annal. Thorac. Surg. **69**(3), 56–69 (2000)
6. Husain, S.A., et al.: Total anomalous pulmonary venous connection: factors associated with mortality and recurrent pulmonary venous obstruction. Annal. Thorac. Surg. **94**(3), 825–832 (2012)
7. Kourou, K., Exarchos, T.P., Exarchos, K.P., Karamouzis, M.V., Fotiadis, D.I.: Machine learning applications in cancer prognosis and prediction. Comput. Struct. Biotechnol. J. **13**, 8–17 (2015)
8. Motwani, M., et al.: Machine learning for prediction of all-cause mortality in patients with suspected coronary artery disease: a 5-year multicentre prospective registry analysis. Eur. Heart J. **38**(7), 500–507 (2017)
9. Parisot, S., et al.: Spectral graph convolutions for population-based disease prediction. In: Descoteaux, M., Maier-Hein, L., Franz, A., Jannin, P., Collins, D.L., Duchesne, S. (eds.) MICCAI 2017. LNCS, vol. 10435, pp. 177–185. Springer, Cham (2017). https://doi.org/10.1007/978-3-319-66179-7_21
10. Roth, H.R., et al.: Improving computer-aided detection using convolutional neural networks and random view aggregation. IEEE Trans. Med. Imaging **35**(5), 1170–1181 (2015)
11. Setio, A.A.A., et al.: Pulmonary nodule detection in ct images: false positive reduction using multi-view convolutional networks. IEEE Trans. Med. Imaging **35**(5), 1160–1169 (2016)

12. Shah, S.J., et al.: Phenomapping for novel classification of heart failure with preserved ejection fraction. Circulation **131**(3), 269–279 (2015)
13. Simonyan, K., Zisserman, A.: Very deep convolutional networks for large-scale image recognition. arXiv preprint arXiv:1409.1556 (2014)
14. Weng, S.F., Reps, J., Kai, J., Garibaldi, J.M., Qureshi, N.: Canmachine-learning improve cardiovascular risk prediction using routineclinical data? PloS one **12**(4) (2017)
15. Yuan, B., Xing, W.: Diagnosing cardiac abnormalities from 12-lead electrocardiograms using enhanced deep convolutional neural networks. In: Liao, H., Balocco, S., Wang, G., Zhang, F., Liu, Y., Ding, Z., Duong, L., Phellan, R., Zahnd, G., Breininger, K., Albarqouni, S., Moriconi, S., Lee, S.-L., Demirci, S. (eds.) MLMECH/CVII-STENT -2019. LNCS, vol. 11794, pp. 36–44. Springer, Cham (2019). https://doi.org/10.1007/978-3-030-33327-0_5
16. Yun, T.J., et al.: Conventional and sutureless techniques for management of the pulmonary veins: evolution of indications from postrepair pulmonary vein stenosis to primary pulmonary vein anomalies. J. Thorac. Cardiovasc. Surg. **129**(1), 167–174 (2005)

Low-Dose CT Denoising Using Octave Convolution with High and Low Frequency Bands

Dong Kyu Won[1], Sion An[1], Sang Hyun Park[1(✉)], and Dong Hye Ye[2(✉)]

[1] Department of Robotics Engineering, DGIST, Daegu, South Korea
{won548,sion_an,shpark13135}@dgist.ac.kr
[2] Department of Electrical and Computer Engineering, Marquette University, Milwaukee, WI, USA
donghye.ye@marquette.edu

Abstract. Low-dose CT denoising has been studied to reduce radiation exposure to patients. Recently, deep learning-based techniques have improved the CT denoising performance, but it is difficult to reflect the characteristics of signals concerning different frequencies properly. Even though high-frequency components play an essential role in denoising, the deep network with a large number of parameters doesn't concern it and tends to generate the image still having noise and losing the structure. To address this problem, we propose a novel CT denoising method that decomposes high- and low-frequency features and learns more parameters on important features during training. We introduce a network consisting of Octave convolution layers that take feature maps with two frequencies and extract information directly from both maps with inter- and intra-convolutions. The proposed method effectively reduces the noise while maintaining edge sharpness by reducing the spatial redundancy in the network. For evaluation, the 2016 AAPM Low-Dose CT challenge data set was used. The proposed method achieved better performance than the existing CT denoising methods in quantitative and qualitative evaluations.

Keywords: Computational Tomography · Low-dose CT denoising · High and low frequency · Octave convolution

1 Introduction

Computed Tomography (CT) is one of the most widely used non-invasive imaging techniques for diagnosis, stage classification, and disease detection. However, even with high availability, radiation from CT scans can potentially harm patients [1,2]. Low-dose CT (LDCT) scanners are being developed to reduce the potential radiation damage to patients, but the LDCT often contains unexpected artifacts causing inaccurate diagnosis. Accordingly, several methods using filtering [3–7], dictionary learning [8,9] and deep learning [10–16] have been proposed to make high quality images by denoising the LDCT.

© Springer Nature Switzerland AG 2020
I. Rekik et al. (Eds.): PRIME 2020, LNCS 12329, pp. 68–78, 2020.
https://doi.org/10.1007/978-3-030-59354-4_7

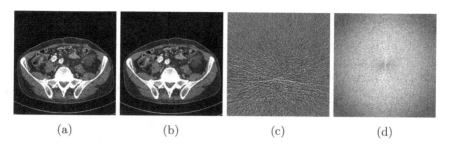

(a)   (b)   (c)   (d)

Fig. 1. An example of (a) LDCT, (b) NDCT (c) difference map if LDCT and NDCT, and (d) Discrete Fourier Transform of (c). (d) indicates that most of the noise is laid on high-frequency band.

Though the deep learning methods have significantly improved the denoising performance by learning dense model parameters to minimize the difference between LDCT and normal-dose CT (NDCT), spatial redundancy between feature maps is not alleviated during training. Thus, many parameters are used for processing low-frequency signals with high redundancy, making it difficult to properly handle the high-frequency signals that are important for CT denoising. Figure 1 shows evidence of the importance of high-frequency components for CT denoising as most of the residuals between LDCT and NDCT are located in the high-frequency band. Thus, in general, the traditional deep learning methods for image quality improvement often generate over-smoothed images, making it difficult to distinguish detailed structures.

To address this problem, we propose a novel CT denoising method that divides feature maps into low- and high-frequency components and learns the parameters focusing on important frequency information. We introduce a novel CT denoising network consisting of a residual path with Octave convolution, which takes feature maps with two frequencies and extracts information directly from both maps without decoding the low-frequency components to high-frequency explicitly. We extend the Octave convolution proposed in image classification and integrate this convolution on the residual network for CT denoising.

The main contributions of this work are as follows: (1) We adopt multi-scale representation learning to the CT denoising problem. Spatial redundancy in low-frequency components is implicitly alleviated in our network. (2) We extend the Octave convolution proposed in image classification to the CT denoising. Since there are lots of spatial redundancy in CT images, the Octave convolution is suitable for addressing the CT denoising. (3) Lastly, we show better performance for CT denoising in quantitative, qualitative, and efficiency of our network. The proposed method can be applied to not only CT denoising but also various medical image quality enhancement problems.

1.1   Related Work

CT Denoising. For LDCT denoising, several techniques such as non-local means [3–5], dictionary learning [8,9], and block matching [6,7] have been proposed. These methods perform the denoising using relevant dictionary patches searched from a target image or from training images. Model-based iterative reconstruction (MBIR) methods [17] also have been studied to further impose additional requirements such as smoothness or sparsity. Though these methods generated reasonable denoising results, the performance was often limited due to the non-uniform distribution of LDCT artifacts.

Recently, deep learning based methods have been proposed. For example, Chen et al. [10] proposed a convolutional neural network (CNN) consisting of 3 convolutional layers to minimize the mean square error (MSE) between a prediction and NDCT. Yang et al. [11] proposed a deeper network with the perceptual loss to preserve structural details. Chen et al. [16] proposed an encoder-decoder network with residual paths, while Yang et al. [13] proposed a ResNet. M. Gholizadeh-Ansari et al. [14] proposed a dilated residual network to capture contextual information of a large receptive field and used a non-trainable edge detector to utilize the edge of LDCT for learning. However, above-mentioned approaches cannot capture high- and low-frequency feature representations separately in the feature embedding space, which leads to failure to maintain the detailed structures related to the high frequency components.

Recently, Kang et al. [15] addressed this limitation and proposed a method that performs a wavelet transform to divide an image into multiple frequency components and then learn a CNN to minimize the difference between those components. However, this method does not provide a way to reduce the spatial redundancy; *i.e.*, it performs the wavelet transform explicitly and then learns the network using all coefficients with concatenation. Our proposed method performs the decomposition within the network and effectively reduces the spatial redundancy.

Multi-scale Representation Learning. Several studies have been conducted to decompose a signal or an image into multiple scales. Szegedy et al. [18] outperformed in image classification problems with multiple scales of the image and various sizes of convolution kernels. Lin et al. [19] and Zhao et al. [20] used pyramid structure to enlarge the receptive fields that are helpful to extract the feature for object detection and scene parsing. [21] proposed the MG-Conv operator to represent a multi-grid pyramid feature representation for image classification. Moreover, Ghaisi et al. [22] discovered the architecture of feature pyramid network for object detection Neural Architecture Search (NAS).

In other domains, Chen et al. [23] transformed the input data into different scales and performed object and speech recognition using the features obtained from multiple scales. Dai et al. [24] decomposed EEG signals into multiple bands with different frequencies, extracted features using CNN, and then performed classification using the concatenated features. Li et al. [25] applied multi-instance multi-scale CNN which expands feature maps obtained by pretrained CNN to various sizes of feature maps and aggregated them for retinal OCT image classification.

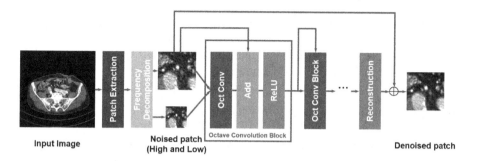

Fig. 2. Proposed CT Denoising Network using Octave convolution. Our network consists of a frequency decomposition layer, denoising layers using Octave convolution, and a reconstruction layer. Residual path is connected between input and output to focus on residual learning.

Recently, Chen et al. [12] proposed Octave convolution to simply separate high- and low-frequency features borrowing the concept in scale-space theory and effectively reduce the spatial redundancy of low-frequency components. Inspired by this concept applied to the classification tasks, our proposed method performs multi-scale learning for CT denoising. To do so, we integrate a modified Octave convolution to the proposed denoising network that learns residuals between LDCT and NDCT.

2 Method

The proposed framework is shown in Fig. 2. The framework consists of three parts: a frequency decomposition layer, denoising blocks, and a reconstruction layer. The frequency decomposition layer decomposes the input image into low and high-frequency bands with a convolutional layer. Given the output of the frequency decomposition layer, the denoising blocks extract and remove noise interacting between high and low-frequency bands. Finally, the reconstruction layer generates a denoised image with a convolutional layer. During training, the proposed network is trained end-to-end using LDCT as input and NDCT as ground truth.

Frequency Decomposition Layer. The frequency decomposition layer takes an image and decomposes into high- and low-frequency bands increasing 1 channel to C channels. The output of the frequency decomposition layer is X with the size of $C \times H \times W$ where H and W are height and width, respectively, and we factorize it along the channel dimension to define low and high-frequency bands.

$X^{(1-\alpha)C \times H \times W}$ is defined as the high-frequency band X^h, which captures detail structures and $X^{\alpha C \times H \times W}$ is defined as low-frequency band X^l which captures overall structures. X^l is downsampled to half size of X^h along the height and width dimensions for denoising block. The number of channels for denoising is determined by α. α is a hyper-parameter ranging $[0, 1]$ which controls how many low-frequency channels will be used among the base channels C. The number of low-frequency feature channels C_l is defined as αC while the number of high-frequency feature channels C_h is defined as $(1 - \alpha)C$.

Denoising Blocks. To process for each frequency band and interact with each other, we use Octave convolution [12] O repeating N times. Octave convolution is shown in Fig. 3. n^{th} denoising block takes low-frequency features f_l^n and high frequency features f_h^n as input and has multi-branch structure consisting of four convolutional layers: intra-convolution $(Low - Low, High - High)$ and inter-convolution $(Low - High, High - Low)$. Each layers predict feature maps while maintaining the number of channels, but $High - Low$ convolutional layer uses downsampled high-frequency inputs to get feature maps of same size as output of $Low - Low$ convolutional layer (i.e. $f_{l2l}(f_l^n)$, $f_{l2h}(f_l^n)$, $f_{h2h}(f_h^n)$ and $f_{h2l}(down(f_h^n))$). Finally, to combine information of frequency bands, we sum the outputs of intra- and inter-convolution element-wise. Here $f_{l2h}(f_l^n)$ is upsampled to the same size as high frequency band. Then output of Octave convolution are as follows:

$$f_l^{n+1} = f_{l2l}(f_l^n) + f_{h2l}(down(f_h^n)), \qquad (1)$$

$$f_h^{n+1} = f_{h2h}(f_h^n) + up(f_{l2h}(f_l^n)), \qquad (2)$$

$$O_n(f_l^n, f_h^n | \theta^n) = (f_l^{n+1}, f_h^{n+1}). \qquad (3)$$

The outputs of denoising block are used as the input of $n + 1$ denoising block or reconstruction layer. Ultimately, the denoising blocks balance the sharpness and smoothness of the original image.

Reconstruction Layer. The reconstruction layer generates a residual image based on feature maps from denoising blocks O_N. The noise image estimated through the reconstruction layer and LDCT is added to generate the NDCT. To remove noise in the original image, we put a residual connection between the original image and output of denoising blocks. Here the α of the last denoising block is set to 0. Then perform convolution reducing the number of the channel to 1.

Implementation Details. The proposed network trains a 64×64 size patch. When testing the network, it is possible to test the images of any size larger than 64×64 size patch used for training. Field of view (FOV) sampling and Data augmentation were performed to improve the model's training efficiency and robustness. FOV sampling is a method of extracting a training patch based on the FOV of a CT image so that the training patches can include various

$0.5H \times 0.5W \times C_l$ $H \times W \times C_h$

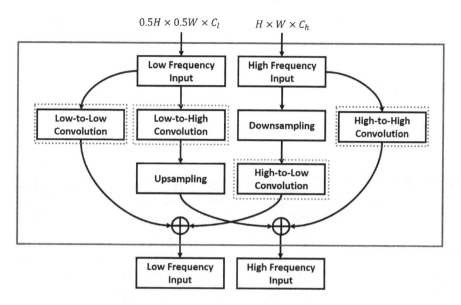

Fig. 3. Diagram of Proposed Octave Convolution. Red boxes indicate intra-convolution and Green boxes indicate inter-convolution. (Color figure online)

organs and boundaries and exclude the air part. For data augmentation, random rotation $[-45, 45]$, random rescale $[0.5, 2]$, random flip [Horizontal, Vertical] were used. For the loss function, we used L1 loss to optimize our network. We used PyTorch framework, Adam for the optimizer and set 100 epochs for training. We decreased the learning rate by 10% from 0.0001 whenever if the performance does not have any improvement within 10 epochs in the validation stage. This training was performed on a desktop with Intel i7-8700K, 64 GB RAM, NVIDIA GTX 1080Ti. The number of the base channels was set to 64 channels for convolution.

3 Experimental Results

3.1 Dataset and Experimental Settings

For evaluation, we used the 2016 AAPM Low Dose CT Grand Challenge dataset. The dataset consists of abdominal LDCT and NDCT image data taken from 10 patients. Image size is 512×512, voxel space is $0.5\,\mathrm{mm} \times 0.5\,\mathrm{mm}$, and slice thickness is 3 mm. To verify the denoising performance of our proposed network, we compared the performance of our proposed network to several networks: CNN10 [10], WavResNet [15], and RED-CNN [16]. CNN10 follows the conventional CNN structure with standard convolution layers. WavResNet is based on ResNet structure, which learns Wavelet coefficient of LDCT and NDCT image instead of the CT image itself. RED-CNN follows Encoder-Decoder structure with some residual connections, which encodes the features of LDCT image and

Table 1. Quantitative results on 2016 AAPM dataset for LDCT denoising.

	PSNR	SSIM	RMSE
LDCT	41.4231 ± 1.7833	0.9375 ± 0.0208	0.0320 ± 0.0050
CNN10	45.6908 ± 1.5377	0.9766 ± 0.0071	0.0054 ± 0.0010
WavResNet	45.7048 ± 1.7152	0.9792 ± 0.0069	0.0054 ± 0.0010
RED-CNN	45.8616 ± 1.5508	0.9774 ± 0.0070	0.0053 ± 0.0010
Ours	**46.1487 ± 1.5829**	**0.9785 ± 0.0068**	**0.0051 ± 0.0009**

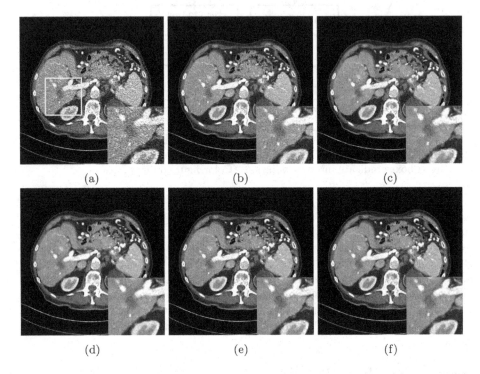

Fig. 4. Comparison of the abdominal image in the liver with patch. (a) LDCT, (b) NDCT, (c) CNN10, (d) WavResNet, (e) REDCNN [16] and (f) Ours. Other results show still noisy and over smoothed parts. The result of our method provides a much cleaner image than other methods.

decodes to NDCT image. For fair comparison, the number of parameters or layers has been set to be similar. We measured the denoising performance by Peak Signal-to-Noise Ratio (PSNR), Structural Similarity (SSIM), and Root-Mean-Square Error (RMSE), which are widely used in image enhancement problems. For all experiments, 10-fold cross-validation was performed on 10 patients' data.

Table 2. Network parameters and computation for denoising networks

	#Params	FLOPs(G)	×FLOPs
CNN10	**0.2966**	19.44	×2.434
WavResNet	0.4617	46.23	×5.934
RED-CNN	0.3000	16.01	×2.008
Ours	0.3711	**7.97**	×1.000

3.2 Quantitative Results

Table 1 shows the average PSNR, SSIM, and RMSE results obtained by cross-validating 10 patients' data with other denoising networks. Since CNN10 using the conventional convolution layers uses filters that may not focus on high- and low-frequency bands, it cannot effectively remove artifacts. WavResNet learns various aspects of noise patterns with Wavelet coefficients, but it did not show significant improvement in quantitative measures compared to CNN10. The Encoder-Decoder structure in REDCNN improved denoising performance, but this method cannot focus on the important information concerning frequencies while contracting and expanding their features. On the other hand, our proposed network has shown better results than other networks by effectively reducing and considering the spatial redundancy while focusing on important information using Octave convolution.

In Table 2, we analyzed the number of parameters and computation cost of CT Denoising networks. #Params means the number of parameters that has been used in training. FLOPs (Floating Point Operations) denotes the amount of calculation processing in the network. We marked how much computations other networks require compared to our network, with ×FLOPs. CNN10 and RED-CNN used simple standard convolution or transposed convolution layers which require large parameters or high computation cost. WaveResNet used batch normalization layer and concatenated the features from their denoising blocks to increase receptive field, but a large number of parameters and high computation are needed. These approaches might work fine in broad tasks, but for image enhancement tasks such as CT Denoising, Super-Resolution, etc., they are not effective in extracting the features properly. Using Octave convolution, we could decrease the computation cost with reasonable parameters. Even though the number of parameters is similar to other methods, our method's computation cost was at least 2 to 5 times less than other methods. This shows that our methods with Octave convolution is much efficient than other methods using standard convolution layers.

3.3 Qualitative Results

For qualitative evaluation, it is very important to provide images for visualizing shapes of organs, removing noise, and keeping their sharpness at the same time.

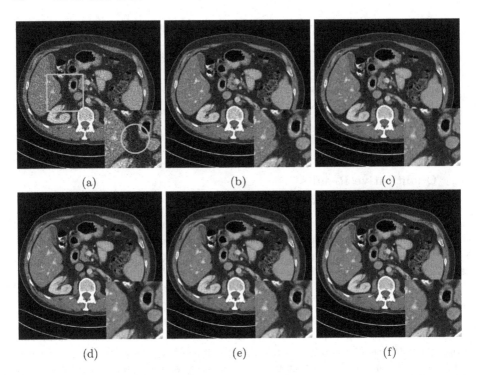

(a)   (b)   (c)

(d)   (e)   (f)

Fig. 5. Comparison of the abdominal image in difficult part to preserve. (a) LDCT, (b) NDCT, (c) CNN10, (d) WavResNet, (e) REDCNN [16] and (f) Ours. Other result makes the small part blurry or disappeared. Our method preserves a small part showing more sharper and clearer than other methods.

If the CT image is not denoised well or is too smooth, there may be difficulty in actual reading. To verify that our proposed network can provide high quality denoised CT images, we have evaluated qualitative results by comparing existing CT denoising network and our proposed network. Figure 4 and Fig. 5 shows the visualization of patient data from the dataset.

In Fig. 4, CNN10 seems over-smoothed, and WavResNet tries to keep the structure of the image but still shows the noisy image. RED-CNN seems to remove much noise, but their image looks blurry and over-smoothed so that it is challenging to represent the structure of the organ in detail. In Fig. 5, most of the previous methods show still noisy and blurry images, even though there is a small structure that could be used for actual reading. On the other hand, our proposed method does not only remove much noise but also show a clear and balanced sharpness of structure by focusing on the high- and low-frequency bands separately. Through this, we confirmed that the denoising performance of our proposed network shows better than existing networks.

4   Conclusions

In this paper, we focused on high- and low-frequency bands for Low-dose CT denoising problem and proposed a CT denoising network using Octave convolution. We confirmed that our proposed network could effectively remove the noise of LDCT and clarify the shape and boundary of organs in CT images. We believe that this CT denoising technique can reduce the radiation damage in patients and help radiologists analyze CT images and be applied to various medical image enhancement problems.

Acknowledgement. This research was supported by the MSIT (Ministry of Science, ICT), Korea, under the High-Potential Individuals Global Training Program (2019-0-01557) supervised by the IITP (Institute for Information & Communications Technology Planning & Evaluation).

References

1. Brenner, D.J., Hall, E.J.: Computed tomography—an increasing source of radiation exposure. N. Engl. J. Med. **357**(22), 2277–2284 (2007)
2. de Gonzalez, A.B., Darby, S.: Risk of cancer from diagnostic X-rays: estimates for the UK and 14 other countries. Lancet **363**(9406), 345–351 (2004)
3. Chen, Y., et al.: Thoracic low-dose CT image processing using an artifact suppressed large-scale nonlocal means. Phys. Med. Biol. **57**(9), 2667 (2012)
4. Ma, J., et al.: Low-dose computed tomography image restoration using previous normal-dose scan. Med. Phys. **38**(10), 5713–5731 (2011)
5. Li, Z., et al.: Adaptive nonlocal means filtering based on local noise level for CT denoising. Med. Phys. **41**(1), 011908 (2014)
6. Fumene Feruglio, P., Vinegoni, C., Gros, J., Sbarbati, A., Weissleder, R.: Block matching 3D random noise filtering for absorption optical projection tomography. Phys. Med. Biol. **55**(18), 5401 (2010)
7. Kang, D., et al.: Image denoising of low-radiation dose coronary CT angiography by an adaptive block-matching 3D algorithm. In: Medical Imaging 2013: Image Processing, vol. 8669, p. 86692G. International Society for Optics and Photonics (2013)
8. Chen, Y., et al.: Improving abdomen tumor low-dose CT images using a fast dictionary learning based processing. Phys. Med. Biol. **58**(16), 5803 (2013)
9. Zhang, H., Zhang, L., Sun, Y., Zhang, J.: Projection domain denoising method based on dictionary learning for low-dose CT image reconstruction. J. X-ray Sci. Technol. **23**(5), 567–578 (2015)
10. Chen, H., et al.: Low-dose CT via convolutional neural network. Biomed. Opt. Express **8**, 679–694 (2017)
11. Yang, Q., Yan, P., Kalra, M.K., Wang, G.: CT image denoising with perceptive deep neural networks. ArXiv, abs/1702.07019 (2017)
12. Chen, Y., et al.: Drop an octave: reducing spatial redundancy in convolutional neural networks with octave convolution. ArXiv, abs/1904.05049 (2019)
13. Yang, W., et al.: Improving low-dose CT image using residual convolutional network. IEEE Access **5**, 24698–24705 (2017)

14. Gholizadeh-Ansari, M., Alirezaie, J., Babyn, P.: Low-dose CT denoising using edge detection layer and perceptual loss. In: 2019 41st Annual International Conference of the IEEE Engineering in Medicine and Biology Society (EMBC), pp. 6247–6250, July 2019
15. Kang, E., Chang, W., Yoo, J., Ye, J.C.: Deep convolutional framelet denosing for low-dose CT via wavelet residual network. IEEE Trans. Med. Imaging **37**(6), 1358–1369 (2018)
16. Chen, H., et al.: Low-dose CT with a residual encoder-decoder convolutional neural network. IEEE Trans. Med. Imaging **36**(12), 2524–2535 (2017)
17. Ziabari, A., et al.: 2.5 D deep learning for CT image reconstruction using a multi-GPU implementation. In: 2018 52nd Asilomar Conference on Signals, Systems, and Computers, pp. 2044–2049. IEEE (2018)
18. Szegedy, C., et al.: Going deeper with convolutions. CoRR, abs/1409.4842 (2014)
19. Lin, T.-Y., Dollár, P., Girshick, R.B., He, K., Hariharan, B., Belongie, S.J.: Feature pyramid networks for object detection. CoRR, abs/1612.03144 (2016)
20. Zhao, H., Shi, J., Qi, X., Wang, X., Jia, J.: Pyramid scene parsing network. CoRR, abs/1612.01105 (2016)
21. Ke, T.-W., Maire, M., Yu, S.X.: Multigrid neural architectures. In: Proceedings of the IEEE Conference on Computer Vision and Pattern Recognition, pp. 6665–6673 (2017)
22. Ghiasi, G., Lin, T.-Y., Pang, R., Le, Q.V.: NAS-FPN: learning scalable feature pyramid architecture for object detection. CoRR, abs/1904.07392 (2019)
23. Chen, C.-F., Fan, Q., Mallinar, N., Sercu, T., Feris, R.: Big-little net: an efficient multi-scale feature representation for visual and speech recognition. arXiv preprint arXiv:1807.03848 (2018)
24. Dai, G., Zhou, J., Huang, J., Wang, N.: HS-CNN: a CNN with hybrid convolution scale for EEG motor imagery classification. J. Neural Eng. **17**(1), 016025 (2020)
25. Li, S., et al.: Multi-instance multi-scale CNN for medical image classification. CoRR, abs/1907.02413 (2019)

Conditional Generative Adversarial Network for Predicting 3D Medical Images Affected by Alzheimer's Diseases

Euijin Jung, Miguel Luna, and Sang Hyun Park[(✉)]

Department of Robotics Engineering, DGIST, Daegu, South Korea
{euijin,shpark13135}@dgist.ac.kr

Abstract. Predicting the evolution of Alzheimer's disease (AD) is important for accurate diagnosis and the development of personalized treatments. However, learning a predictive model is challenging since it is difficult to obtain a large amount of data that includes changes over a long period of time. Conditional Generative Adversarial Networks (cGAN) may be an effective way to generate images that match specific conditions, but they are impractical to generate 3D images due to memory resource limitations. To address this issue, we propose a novel cGAN that is capable of synthesizing MR images at different stages of AD (i.e., normal, mild cognitive impairment, and AD). The proposed method consists of a 2D generator that synthesizes an image according to a condition with the help of 2D and 3D discriminators that evaluate how realistic the synthetic image is. We optimize both the 2D GAN loss and the 3D GAN loss to determine whether multiple consecutive 2D images generated in a mini-batch have real or fake appearance in 3D space. The proposed method can generate smooth and natural 3D images at different conditions by using a single network without large memory requirements. Experimental results show that the proposed method can generate better quality 3D MR images than 2D or 3D cGAN and can also boost the classification performance when the synthesized images are used to train a classification model.

Keywords: Deep learning · Conditional GAN · Alzheimer's disease · 3D discriminator · 3D MRI generation

1 Introduction

Alzheimer's disease (AD) progresses from normal to mild cognitive impairment (MCI), and finally to AD. To learn an accurate prediction model, a large number of data is required, but the data including longitudinal Magnetic Resonance images (MRI) are usually limited. Recently, many studies have been proposed to address the data limitation problem through generation of synthetic data based on supervised learning and generative adversarial networks (GAN) [4]. Supervised learning based methods generate target image based on reducing pixelwise loss of paired data. For example, supervised learning is used to generate

© Springer Nature Switzerland AG 2020
I. Rekik et al. (Eds.): PRIME 2020, LNCS 12329, pp. 79–90, 2020.
https://doi.org/10.1007/978-3-030-59354-4_8

enhanced Perivascular space MRI [8]. GAN models have been applied to generate a computational tomography (CT) image from a MRI [10,15,22], a positron emission tomography (PET) image from a MRI [14] and a PET image from a CT image [1]. However, these methods perform domain translation between 2 predefined domains, and thus it is difficult to generate an image with respect to a specific condition such as normal, MCI or AD.

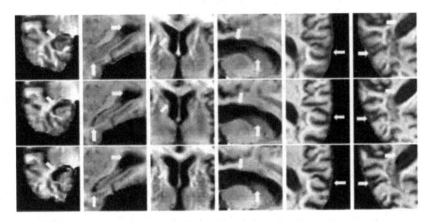

Fig. 1. Synthesized images with respect to normal (top row), MCI (middle row), and AD (bottom row) conditions using the proposed method on hippocampus, ventricle, and gray matter regions. Yellow arrows indicates significant differences. (Color figure online)

The limitation of traditional GANs has been addressed by conditional generative adversarial networks (cGAN) [11] which can transform a latent space into a target domain by applying a specific target condition. The cGAN is used to generate high quality synthesized images with auxiliary classifier based on input imaeg and target condition [13]. Star-GAN [3], Ganimation [16], and SMIT [17] are examples of methods that are able to convert source into target images according to a target condition. In terms of brain images, several methods have been proposed to generate images depending on age [2,20,23] or contrast [12,18,21]. However, the generation of temporal evolution of AD at multiple stages was not considered and most models for 3D image generation were based on 2D GAN [3,11,16] since 3D GAN models are hard to optimize with modern computers. Thus, the final synthesized 3D image is usually reconstructed by the concatenation of independently generated 2D images, which causes a discontinuity problem across the other two axes that are not used in training by the 2D GAN models.

In this work, we propose a novel cGAN to generate MR images at 3 different stages of AD (normal, MCI, and AD) from a MR image and a target condition (see Fig. 1). We introduce a model that includes a 2D generator to synthesize 2D brain MR slices, a 2D discriminator to ensure to synthesize 2D brain MR slices that meet the target condition and a 3D discriminator to account for 3D structural information with smaller memory requirement than 3D GAN. The 3D discriminator works with concatenated neighboring 2D slices generated by the 2D generator in a mini-batch. Thus, the 2D generator learns to generate smooth transformation of consecutive 2D images.

The main contribution points of this work are as follows: (1) we propose a cGAN model that can predict changes in the brain from the current state to other stages of AD condition. Thus, the proposed method can play an important role in learning an accurate predictive model with a small dataset. (2) By simply adding the 3D discriminator to a 2D cGAN structure, our 2D generator can synthesize a smooth and natural 3D images by considering consecutiveness of 2D images. (3) Our method provides a general and efficient 3D image generator that benefits from less memory utilization of 2D images. It is also a consistent data augmentation method that improves the classification accuracy to identify AD in MR brain images. (4) Lastly, the effectiveness of the proposed method is demonstrated by using various measurements that are commonly used to evaluate the performance of GAN for 2D image generation when the ground truth is absent.

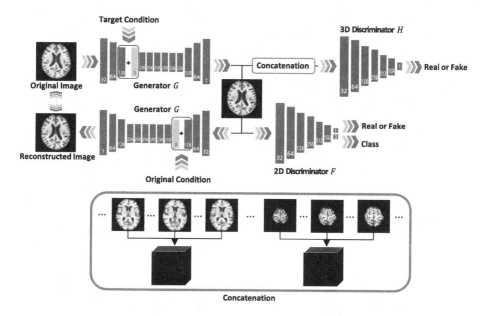

Fig. 2. The proposed conditional generative adversarial network.

2 Method

The structure of our conditional GAN is described in Fig. 2. The network consists of a 2D generator, a 2D discriminator, and a 3D discriminator. The 2D generator

G generates a 2D synthetic image s_{2D} from a 2D MR image x_{2D} with respect to a condition c (i.e., normal, MCI, or AD). The generator is trained by adversarial learning to modify the brain areas affected by the illness, while maintaining the identity of a patient by reversing the transformation through cycle learning. The 2D discriminator F classifies if the condition of its input matches the label c and also if it corresponds to a real 2D slice x_{2D} or a fake one s_{2D}.

In addition to the 2D conditional GAN structure, we add the 3D discriminator H that helps to generate a smooth 3D image. In G, we sequentially put k neighboring images in the axial direction to consider the smoothness of the synthesized images in 3D space. In a mini-batch, $s_{2D}^1, s_{2D}^2, ..., s_{2D}^k$ are generated for each image. H focuses on the image quality in 3D space by identifying whether it corresponds to a real 3D slice x_{3D} or a fake one s_{3D} where x_{3D} and s_{3D} are concatenations of $x_{2D}^1, x_{2D}^2, ..., x_{2D}^k$ and $s_{2D}^1, s_{2D}^2, ..., s_{2D}^k$, respectively.

2.1 Details of Proposed Network

G consists of an encoder, a transition layer, and a decoder. The encoder reduces the feature maps to $\frac{1}{4}$ of the original size of x_{2D} through three convolutional layers. After encoding, encoded feature maps are concatenated with c. c is consist of $\frac{1}{4}$ of the original size height and width and 3 channels. Channels of c follow one-hot encoding depend on disease class of input images. Then, the transition layer processes the feature maps through six residual blocks. In the final stage of G, the decoder defined by three transpose convolution layers transforms the latent representation into an image s_{2D} with the same size of x_{2D}.

F is defined as a convolutional neural network (CNN) with five 2D convolutional layers and two fully connected layers that perform the reality classification of an image F_a (real or fake) and the condition classification F_b (normal, MCI or AD). Note that the input of F is either a real 2D axial image x_{2D} or a synthesized image s_{2D}. H is also defined as a CNN, but with five 3D convolutional layers and a single fully connected layer that discriminates whether its input corresponds to a section of real neighboring 2D slices x_{3D} or a synthesized one s_{3D}. H ensures that our model generates 3D images with good quality in all 3 axes. Figure 2 visualizes how s_{3D} is reconstructed by concatenating k consecutive 2D slices s_{2D}.

2.2 Objective Function

We train the network with the Wasserstein loss functions with gradient penalty [5] as adversarial losses for both on 2D and 3D spaces. The first two terms in L_{2D-adv}, L_{3D-adv} measure the Wasserstein distance and last term is the gradient penalty which use average sample defined z_{2D}, z_{3D} as:

$$L_{2D-adv} = \mathbb{E}_{x_{2D},c}[F_a(s_{2D})] - \mathbb{E}_{x_{2D}}[F_a(x_{2D})] + \lambda_{GP}(||\nabla_{z_{2D}}F_a(z_{2D})||_2 - 1)^2, \quad (1)$$

$$L_{3D-adv} = \mathbb{E}_{x_{3D},c}[H(s_{3D})] - \mathbb{E}_{x_{3D}}[H(x_{3D})] + \lambda_{GP}(||\nabla_{z_{3D}}H(z_{3D})||_2 - 1)^2. \quad (2)$$

$$z_{2D} = \epsilon x_{2D} + (1 - \epsilon)s_{2D}, \epsilon \sim U[0, 1]. \tag{3}$$

$$z_{3D} = \epsilon x_{3D} + (1 - \epsilon)s_{3D}, \epsilon \sim U[0, 1]. \tag{4}$$

s_{2D} should be similar to x_{2D} and also meet the target condition c. To address this, F_b classifies the condition of a 2D input slice. However, the predicted condition of s_{2D} is used to optimize G, while the predicted condition of x_{2D} is used to optimize F. Therefore, the classification loss L_{cls}^r for real images and the loss L_{cls}^s for synthesized images are defined as:

$$L_{cls}^r = \mathbb{E}_{x_{2D}}[-log F_b(c|x_{2D})], \tag{5}$$

$$L_{cls}^s = \mathbb{E}_{x_{2D},c}[-log F_b(c|s_{2D})]. \tag{6}$$

Since the synthesized image should maintain the identity of input image, we added the cycle consistency loss [24] with the adversarial losses. The cycle consistency loss takes s_{2D} and the original condition c' of x_{2D} to revert the transformation by using the same generator G as:

$$L_{cyc} = \mathbb{E}_{x_{2D},c'}[||x_{2D} - G(s_{2D}, c')||_1]. \tag{7}$$

Finally, G, F, and H are trained simultaneously by optimizing their respective loss functions L_G, L_F and L_H

$$L_G = L_{2D-adv} + L_{3D-adv} + \lambda_{cls}L_{cls}^s + \lambda_{cyc}L_{cyc}, \tag{8}$$

$$L_F = L_{2D-adv} + \lambda_{cls}L_{cls}^r, \tag{9}$$

$$L_H = L_{3D-adv}, \tag{10}$$

where $\lambda_{cls} = 1, \lambda_{cyc} = 0.1, \lambda_{GP} = 10$ are hyperparameters to balance the effect of each loss.

3 Experimental Results

Dataset: For evaluation, we used the Alzheimer's Disease Neuroimaging Initiative (ADNI) dataset [7]. We collected 200 MR images of AD patients, 400 images of MCI patients, and 200 images of normal control (NC) subjects. We aligned the images by using an affine transformation and performed resizing so that all images have the size of $192 \times 192 \times 160$.

Implementation Details: We divided the data into two even subsets (set A and set B). We generated synthesized images (set A') using our model with the axial view of the MR images of size 192×192 in set A. For each image, we generated two images with respect to two conditions except the original condition c' (e.g., NC, MCI images were generated from a AD image while MCI, AD images were generated from a NC image). We sampled k consecutive 2D slices from MR images to construct the training mini-batch to train G, F and H simultaneously. In our experiment, k was evaluated with the values 3, 6 and 8 which is maximum fitting size for graphic memory. The model was trained for 150,000 iterations with Adam optimizer [9] and learning rate of 0.0001 with constant decay. The code was developed on top of the PyTorch deep learning framework and run on a GTX TITAN X NVIDIA GPU.

Evaluation Setting: To quantitatively measure the quality of a generated 3D image, the Fréchet Inception Distance (FID) [6] was measured between set A' and set B. FID evaluates the difference between real and generated images by transforming them into an embedded representation and measuring their mean and covariance differences. The embedded representation was computed by encoding the images to the penultimate layer of a pre-trained Inception network on the ImageNet dataset. To apply a pre-trained 2D Inception network to a 3D image, 2D slices were extracted from 3 axes and then the FID scores were respectively measured by axis.

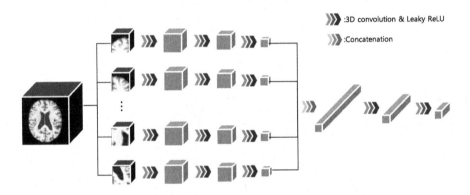

Fig. 3. Network architecture for classification

Furthermore, we also measured GAN-train and GAN-test scores. As pointed in Schmelkov et al. [19], the FID score assumes that real and generated images have Gaussian distributions similar to the images in the ImageNet dataset, which is not a good representation for biomedical images. On the other hand, the distribution similarity between real and generated biomedical images can still be measured by the GAN-train and GAN-test scores. To compute the GAN-train score, a classification model was trained with the generated data and then tested on the real data. For GAN-test, the model was trained with real data and then tested on the generated data. A GAN model is considered to be effective if both scores, GAN-train and GAN-test, have close performance to the case when the classifier is trained and tested on real data. We measured these scores on 3 classes (NC vs MCI vs AD) classification and also NC vs AD binary classification that is a relatively easy task.

For the classification model, we follow the work of Pan et al. [14]. Specifically, we extracted 27 patches of size $48 \times 48 \times 48$ from multiple positions of a whole 3D volume. The patches were encoded into an embedded representation and then all embedded vectors were concatenated to finally estimate a single classification result for the 3D image. The classification model details are shown in Fig. 3. Note that any classification model can be used and the accuracy can vary with respect to that model.

We compared our method to 2D cGAN and 3D cGAN methods. The 2D cGAN has similar structure of the proposed method, but does not use the 3D discriminator. The 3D cGAN also has similar structure, but it uses a 3D generator and a 3D discriminator. Due to memory limitation, the 3D cGAN was implemented to generate 20 adjacent 2D images at a time instead of the whole 3D image. For fair comparison, the same experiments were performed using 2D cGAN and 3D cGAN with the same hyper-parameters used in the proposed method. Furthermore, the FID and GAN-train scores were also measured between the set A and set B to show the upperbound.

Quantitative Results: Table 1 shows the image quality scores for the generated images by our proposed model and the related cGANs. The 2D cGAN achieved a good FID score in axial view, while the FID in coronal and sagittal views was relatively high. In addition, the GAN-train and GAN-test scores are low or inconsistent. The 3D cGAN achieved the worst results. As the 3D model was trained with a limited mini batch size by using a small amount of data, the model for image generation was not well trained. On the other hand, our model with $k = 8$ outperforms other setting in terms of FID in 3 axes and GAN-train and GAN-test scores in both the multiclass and the binary classification setting. This metric shows how our proposed method achieves a significant improvement over conventional 2D and 3D cGAN methods to model the underlying distributions of the real data with scores slightly below or above the real data reference.

Table 1. Results of proposed methods with different k and the related methods for image quality measurements. FID scores are computed in axial(A), coronal(C), and sagittal(S) views, respectively, and GAN-Train and GAN-Test scores are computed for 3 class classification and binary classification.

Models	FID (A)	FID (C)	FID (S)	NC vs MCI vs AD		NC vs AD	
				GAN-Train	GAN-Test	GAN-Train	GAN-Test
Real image	0.86	1.04	0.84	49.00	–	74.68	–
2D cGAN	34.30	40.36	46.36	43.67	42.27	56.32	75.95
3D cGAN	60.74	144.26	134.72	37.16	29.43	50.00	47.26
Our (k = 3)	42.66	49.44	52.33	43.00	45.88	71.52	**82.09**
Our (k = 6)	44.79	37.18	30.52	45.33	52.74	72.79	79.76
Our (k = 8)	**30.70**	**26.82**	**27.25**	**50.00**	**52.74**	**73.42**	80.32

Qualitative Results: Qualitative results are shown in Fig. 1, Fig. 4 and Fig. 5. We confirmed that our proposed model accurately predicts how hippocampus and gray matter become noticeably smaller in AD patients than in NC subjects. Figure 1 and Fig. 4 show the disease stages when the disease progresses from

Table 2. Binary classification performances using the classification model learned with real data and that with real and synthesized images.

	AD vs NC	MCI vs AD	NC vs MCI
Real data	78.48	62.90	64.25
Real + Synthesized data	81.25	63.35	66.06

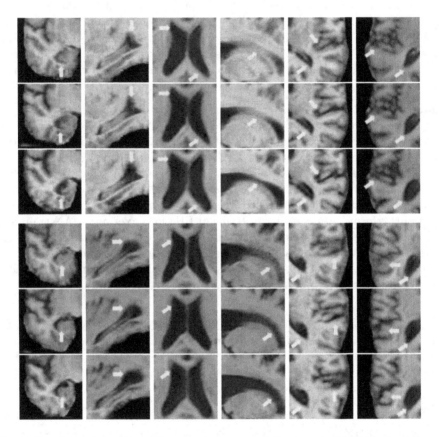

Fig. 4. Synthesized images with respect to normal (1, 4 row), MCI (2, 5 row), and AD (3, 6 row) conditions using the proposed method on hippocampus, ventricle, and gray matter regions. Yellow arrows indicates significant differences. The results of first column are coronal view of hippocampus, and second column is sagittal view of hippocampus. Third and forth column are ventricle of aixal and sagittal view. Fifth and sixth column are gray matter of axial view. (Color figure online)

normal to AD. As AD progresses from normal to AD, hippocampus and gray matter are shrinking, and the space around hippocampus is wider. Also, ventricle region is wider.

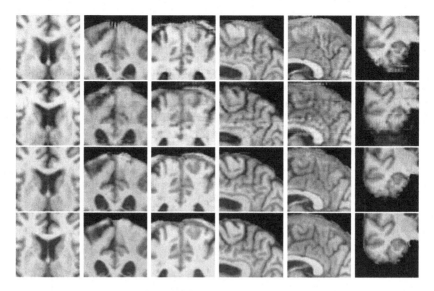

Fig. 5. Comparisons of qualitative results of 2D cGAN (top row), 3D cGAN (2nd row), the proposed method (3rd row), and original images (bottom row). The first column shows axial results of 2D cGAN, 3D cGAN, proposed method, and original images. Second and third columns show coronal results of each method. Forth and fifth columns show sagittal results of each method. Sixth column shows coronal results of each method.

In addition, the images generated by our method have less artifacts than images from 2D and 3D cGAN models. In Fig. 5, the results viewed in axial perspective were mostly satisfactory in all methods, but the differences arise when viewed in coronal or sagittal perspective. For most cases, our method generates better 3D images showing clearer boundaries than the 2D and 3D cGAN models.

Effect on Data Augmentation: To study the effect of our generated images for data augmentation, we also implemented binary classification models to separate NC from MCI and AD, and MCI and AD. We trained 6 classification models, 3 with only real data (set A) and 3 with real and augmented data (set A + set A') and then tested on set B. The results are shown in Table 2. The model trained with the augmented data achieved consistent improvement of about 2% across all combinations of the binary classification setting. Since the difference between NC and AD images is relatively clear, higher classification accuracy was obtained. On the other hand, Classification of MCI patients from NC or AD was relatively low due to the ambiguity.

4   Conclusion

In this work, we have presented a conditional generative adversarial network that is capable of synthesizing MR images at normal condition and 2 different stages of the Alzheimer's disease from a MR image and a target condition. Our model might help medical professionals to better understand how the patient's condition may evolve and focus their efforts on the brain areas that can potentially suffer major damage as the illness progresses. The model is also able to efficiently generate good quality 3D images that are consistent across all directions in 3D space. Finally, we prove that the synthetic images generated by our model resemble the similar features to the real ones by comparing the GAN-train and GAN-test scores. For most cases, the performance of classification task is improved when the synthesized data generated by our model is used to train the classifier. In the future, we will extend our method to generate images by considering both disease and age in a single framework.

Acknowledgement. This research was supported by the National Research Foundation of Korea (NRF) grant funded by the Korean Government (MSIT) (No. 2019R1C1C1008727) and the MSIT (Ministry of Science, ICT), Korea, under the High-Potential Individuals Global Training Program (2019-0-01557) supervised by the IITP (Institute for Information & Communications Technology Planning & Evaluation).

References

1. Ben-Cohen, A., Klang, E., Raskin, S.P., Amitai, M.M., Greenspan, H.: Virtual PET images from CT data using deep convolutional networks: initial results. In: Tsaftaris, S.A., Gooya, A., Frangi, A.F., Prince, J.L. (eds.) SASHIMI 2017. LNCS, vol. 10557, pp. 49–57. Springer, Cham (2017). https://doi.org/10.1007/978-3-319-68127-6_6
2. Choi, H., Kang, H., Lee, D.S., The Alzheimer's Disease Neuroimaging Initiative: Predicting aging of brain metabolic topography using variational autoencoder. Front. Aging Neurosci. **10**, 212 (2018). https://doi.org/10.3389/fnagi.2018.00212
3. Choi, Y., Choi, M.J., Kim, M., Ha, J.W., Kim, S., Choo, J.: StarGAN: unified generative adversarial networks for multi-domain image-to-image translation. CoRR abs/1711.09020 (2017). http://dblp.uni-trier.de/db/journals/corr/corr1711.html
4. Goodfellow, I., et al.: Generative adversarial nets. Adv. Neural Inf. Process. Syst. **27**, 2672–2680 (2014)
5. Gulrajani, I., Ahmed, F., Arjovsky, M., Dumoulin, V., Courville, A.C.: Improved training of Wasserstein GANs. In: NIPS, pp. 5767–5777 (2017). http://dblp.uni-trier.de/db/conf/nips/nips2017.html
6. Heusel, M., Ramsauer, H., Unterthiner, T., Nessler, B., Hochreiter, S.: GANs trained by a two time-scale update rule converge to a local nash equilibrium. In: NIPS, December 2017
7. Jack, C., et al.: The Alzheimer's disease neuroimaging initiative (ADNI): MRI methods. J. Magn. Reson. Imaging **27**(4), 685–691 (2008). https://doi.org/10.1002/jmri.21049

8. Jung, E., Chikontwe, P., Zong, X., Lin, W., Shen, D., Park, S.: Enhancement of perivascular spaces using densely connected deep convolutional neural network. IEEE Access **7**(8), 18382–18391 (2019). https://doi.org/10.1109/ACCESS.2019. 2896911

9. Kingma, D.P., Ba, J.: Adam: a method for stochastic optimization. In: 3rd International Conference for Learning Representations (2014)

10. Lei, Y., et al.: MRi-only based synthetic CT generation using dense cycle consistent generative adversarial networks. Med. Phys. **46**(8), 3565–3581 (2019). https://doi.org/10.1002/mp.13617. https://aapm.onlinelibrary.wiley.com/doi/abs/10.1002/mp.13617

11. Mirza, M., Osindero, S.: Conditional generative adversarial nets. arXiv preprint arXiv:1411.1784 (2014)

12. Sohail, M., Riaz, M.N., Wu, J., Long, C., Li, S.: Unpaired multi-contrast MR image synthesis using generative adversarial networks. In: Burgos, N., Gooya, A., Svoboda, D. (eds.) SASHIMI 2019. LNCS, vol. 11827, pp. 22–31. Springer, Cham (2019). https://doi.org/10.1007/978-3-030-32778-1_3

13. Odena, A., Olah, C., Shlens, J.: Conditional image synthesis with auxiliary classifier GANs. In: International Conference on Machine Learning (2017). https://arxiv.org/abs/1610.09585

14. Pan, Y., Liu, M., Lian, C., Zhou, T., Xia, Y., Shen, D.: Synthesizing missing PET from MRI with cycle-consistent generative adversarial networks for Alzheimer's disease diagnosis. In: Frangi, A.F., Schnabel, J.A., Davatzikos, C., Alberola-López, C., Fichtinger, G. (eds.) MICCAI 2018. LNCS, vol. 11072, pp. 455–463. Springer, Cham (2018). https://doi.org/10.1007/978-3-030-00931-1_52

15. Prokopenko, D., Stadelmann, J., Schulz, H., Renisch, S., Dylov, D.: Synthetic CT generation from MRI using improved DualGAN. arXiv:1909.08942, September 2019

16. Pumarola, A., Agudo, A., Martinez, A.M., Sanfeliu, A., Moreno-Noguer, F.: GAN-imation: one-shot anatomically consistent facial animation. Int. J. Comput. Vis. **128**(3), 698–713 (2019). https://doi.org/10.1007/s11263-019-01210-3

17. Romero, A., Arbelaez, P., Van Gool, L., Timofte, R.: SMIT: stochastic multi-label image-to-image translation. In: 2019 IEEE International Conference on Computer Vision (ICCV), December 2018

18. Dar, S.U.H., Yurt, M., Karacan, L., Erdem, A., Erdem, E., Çukur, T.: Image synthesis in multi-contrast MRI with conditional generative adversarial networks. IEEE Trans. Med. Imaging **38**(10), 2375–2388 (2019)

19. Shmelkov, K., Schmid, C., Alahari, K.: How good is my GAN? In: Ferrari, V., Hebert, M., Sminchisescu, C., Weiss, Y. (eds.) ECCV 2018. LNCS, vol. 11206, pp. 218–234. Springer, Cham (2018). https://doi.org/10.1007/978-3-030-01216-8_14

20. Wegmayr, V., Horold, M., Buhmann, J.: Generative aging of brain MRI for early prediction of MCI-AD conversion. In: 2019 IEEE 16th International Symposium on Biomedical Imaging (ISBI 2019), pp. 1042–1046, April 2019. https://doi.org/10.1109/ISBI.2019.8759394

21. Welander, P., Karlsson, S., Eklund, A.: Generative adversarial networks for image-to-image translation on multi-contrast MR images - a comparison of CycleGAN and UNIT. arXiv preprint arXiv:1806.07777, June 2018

22. Wolterink, J.M., Dinkla, A.M., Savenije, M.H.F., Seevinck, P.R., van den Berg, C.A.T., Išgum, I.: Deep MR to CT synthesis using unpaired data. In: Tsaftaris, S.A., Gooya, A., Frangi, A.F., Prince, J.L. (eds.) SASHIMI 2017. LNCS, vol. 10557, pp. 14–23. Springer, Cham (2017). https://doi.org/10.1007/978-3-319-68127-6_2

23. Zhao, Q., Adeli, E., Honnorat, N., Leng, T., Pohl, K.M.: Variational AutoEncoder for regression: application to brain aging analysis. In: Shen, D., et al. (eds.) MIC-CAI 2019. LNCS, vol. 11765, pp. 823–831. Springer, Cham (2019). https://doi.org/10.1007/978-3-030-32245-8_91

24. Zhu, J., Park, T., Isola, P., Efros, A.A.: Unpaired image-to-image translation using cycle-consistent adversarial networks. In: 2017 IEEE International Conference on Computer Vision (ICCV), pp. 2242–2251 (2017). https://doi.org/10.1109/ICCV.2017.244

Inpainting Cropped Diffusion MRI Using Deep Generative Models

Rafi Ayub[1], Qingyu Zhao[1], M. J. Meloy[3], Edith V. Sullivan[1],
Adolf Pfefferbaum[1,2], Ehsan Adeli[1], and Kilian M. Pohl[1,2(✉)]

[1] Stanford University, Stanford, CA, USA
kilian.pohl@stanford.edu
[2] SRI International, Menlo Park, CA, USA
[3] University of California, San Diego, La Jolla, CA, USA

Abstract. Minor artifacts introduced during image acquisition are often negligible to the human eye, such as a confined field of view resulting in MRI missing the top of the head. This cropping artifact, however, can cause suboptimal processing of the MRI resulting in data omission or decreasing the power of subsequent analyses. We propose to avoid data or quality loss by restoring these missing regions of the head via variational autoencoders (VAE), a deep generative model that has been previously applied to high resolution image reconstruction. Based on diffusion weighted images (DWI) acquired by the National Consortium on Alcohol and Neurodevelopment in Adolescence (NCANDA), we evaluate the accuracy of inpainting the top of the head by common autoencoder models (U-Net, VQVAE, and VAE-GAN) and a custom model proposed herein called U-VQVAE. Our results show that U-VQVAE not only achieved the highest accuracy, but also resulted in MRI processing producing lower fractional anisotropy (FA) in the supplementary motor area than FA derived from the original MRIs. Lower FA implies that inpainting reduces noise in processing DWI and thus increases the quality of the generated results. The code is available at https://github.com/RdoubleA/DWI-inpainting.

1 Introduction

Diffusion MRI, or diffusion weighted imaging (DWI), is widely used to investigate white matter integrity and structural connectivity between brain regions. Studies based on DWI have revealed disruption in structural networks associated with stroke, brain tumors, neurodegenerative disorders (such as multiple sclerosis), and neuropsychiatric disorders (e.g., schizophrenia) [1]. Despite its wide usage, DWI is plagued by numerous signal artifacts that require extensive preprocessing, such as eddy currents, susceptibility distortion, signal dropout, and motion artifacts [2]. Additionally, part of the brain can be cut off in the image (as shown in Fig. 1) due to improper positioning of the subject, limitations in slice acquisitions and prescription, or subject repositioning during a scan session. This cropping artifact can frequently occur in prospective longitudinal

© Springer Nature Switzerland AG 2020
I. Rekik et al. (Eds.): PRIME 2020, LNCS 12329, pp. 91–100, 2020.
https://doi.org/10.1007/978-3-030-59354-4_9

studies for investigating neurodevelopment during childhood and adolescence, where imaging acquisition protocols (e.g., field of view) are optimized based on the baseline visits of subjects and then become suboptimal when the head size increases in later visits. The cropping not only results in missing information, but also influences subsequent preprocessing steps such as inter-subject or cross-modality registration that heavily relies on image boundary information [3]. These misalignments can adversely affect the followup group analysis on regional DWI measures leading to spurious findings.

Correcting for cropped brain regions can be addressed by image inpainting methods [4]. The goal of image inpainting is to predict missing data in corrupted regions based on information from the rest of the image. For example, patch-based methods find candidate replacement patches in the undamaged parts of the image to fill in corrupted regions using matrix-based approaches [5–7] and texture synthesis [8]. Other examples are diffusion-based methods propagating information to corrupted regions from its neighboring areas via interpolation [9,10]. While these methods have shown promising results, they rely on local image properties, often resulting in reconstructions that ignore global context and thus produce unrealistic looking MRIs [11].

The global context can be learned by deep learning methods trained on large datasets. For example, fully convolutional networks based on the U-Net architecture [12–14] use skip connections to propagate multiscale features to fix the image appearance in the missing regions [15–18]. The U-Net architecture can be further augmented by deep generative models, such as variational autoencoders (VAE) [19], which first learn a latent distribution explicitly capturing multiscale structures before generating the missing image data. Vanilla VAEs have been implemented for image denoising and inpainting [20], but their low-dimensional latent distribution tend to omit high-frequency features resulting in blurry images [21]. Significant improvement of reconstruction fidelity can be achieved by vector quantized VAEs (VQVAEs) [22,23]. For example, VQVAE (with skip connections similar to U-Net) have accurately reconstructed T1-weighted structural MRIs [24] but their prediction accuracy on cropped image regions still needs to be tested.

Here, we experiment with several deep generative modeling approaches to repair cropping artifacts in DWI acquired by the longitudinal study National Consortium on Alcohol and Neurodevelopment in Adolescence (NCANDA). Based on DWI that were cropped by us (i.e, the ground truth is known), we compare the inpainting accuracy of U-VQVAE, which combines aspects of U-Net and VQVAE, to U-Net, VQVAE and VAE-GAN [25]. VAE-GAN incorporates an adversarial discriminator network and has previously been applied to image reconstruction. On the real data (i.e., image acquisition caused cropping), we then highlight the improvement of processing based on the inpainted DWIs by computing fractional anisotropy (FA) in regions affected by the cropping. Compared to the regional FA from the original DWI, FA derived based on the inpainted DWI were lower, indicating a reduction in noise in the image processing pipeline. These results demonstrate the utility of autoencoder models for repairing cropping artifacts in multishell diffusion MRI and improving signal-to-noise ratio in downstream processing steps. More important, they also provide us with a tool for restoring parts of the brain in MRIs that are cut off due to improper subject positioning or suboptimal field-of-view.

2   Methods

Since the U-Net architecture has been extensively discussed in prior studies, we focus on describing the U-VQVAE architecture. From that, VQVAE and VAE-GAN are derived. After that we introduce the dataset used for training the models and the metrics used for evaluation.

2.1   Model Architecture

U-VQVAE reconstructed cropped DWI by leveraging the generative modeling capabilities of the VAE architecture. VAE [19] consists of an encoder ϕ and a decoder network ψ. The encoder models a posterior distribution $p(\mathbf{z}|\mathbf{x})$ of the latent random variable $\mathbf{z}$ given the input DWI image $\mathbf{x}$, and the decoder models $p(\mathbf{x}|\mathbf{z})$, the likelihood of input image given $\mathbf{z}$. Typically, $\mathbf{z}$ is assumed to be normally distributed $\mathcal{N}(0,1)$, but VQVAEs [22,23] model $\mathbf{z}$ with a collection of embedding vectors $\boldsymbol{E} \in R^{K \times D}$, where K is the predefined number of embedding vectors and D is the predefined dimensionality of each embedding vector $\mathbf{e}_k \in R^D, k \in \{1, 2, \ldots, K\}$. In our model, we set $K = 512$ and $D = 32$. We assume that the encoder first reduces the input $\mathbf{x}$ to a 3D volume of J voxels before entering the latent space, with the jth voxel characterized by a D-dimensional vector $\mathbf{z}_e^j$ (D channels). The encoder ϕ then further incorporates a quantization that maps each $\mathbf{z}_e^j$ to the nearest vector in the embedding space $\boldsymbol{E} = \{\mathbf{e}_0, \ldots, \mathbf{e}_{K-1}\}$. Then the final embedded latent representation $\mathbf{z}^j$ follows a categorical posterior distribution:

$$q(\mathbf{z}^j = \mathbf{e}_\tau | \mathbf{x}) = \begin{cases} 1 & \text{for } \tau = \text{argmin}_k \|\mathbf{z}_e^j - \mathbf{e}_k\|_2 \\ 0 & \text{otherwise} \end{cases} \quad (1)$$

In other words, quantization ensures that the decoder uses discrete vectors from the embedding for a high-resolution reconstruction instead of a fuzzy encoding created by the encoder alone. The embedding space is not predetermined, but instead is learned through back propagation with exponential moving average as described in [22].

The loss function for the U-VQVAE model consisted of an image reconstruction loss, a codebook loss, and a commitment loss. The image reconstruction loss is defined by the Mean Squared Error between the input of the encoder $\mathbf{x}$, i.e, the cropped MRI, and the ground-truth $\mathbf{x}'$, i.e, the MRI without cropping. In other words the loss is $\|\mathbf{x}' - \psi(\phi(\mathbf{x}))\|_2$, which is dependent on both the encoder and decoder networks. The codebook loss uses the l_2 error to encourage the embedding vectors in $\boldsymbol{E}$ to move closer towards the learned features $\mathbf{z}_e^j$; i.e, it ensures

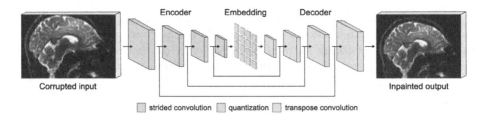

Fig. 1. Architecture of the U-VQVAE model

that the discrete embedding accurately reflects the compressed representation of the image learned by the encoder. Defining $\mathbf{sg}(\cdot)$ as the stop-gradient operation and $\mathbf{e}_\tau^j$ as the final embedded vector that matches $\mathbf{z}_e^j$ (Eq. 1), this loss term is defined by $\sum_{j=1}^{J} \|\mathbf{sg}(\mathbf{z}_e^j) - \mathbf{e}_\tau^j\|_2^2$. The commitment loss also relies on the l_2 error to encourage $\mathbf{z}_e^j$ to converge to the embedding vectors. This loss term is defined by $\sum_{j=1}^{J} \|\mathbf{z}_e^j - \mathbf{sg}(\mathbf{e}_\tau^j)\|_2^2$, which is only dependent on the encoder. Let $\beta = 6$ be the weight associated with the commitment loss and $\alpha = 1$ the weight of the codebook loss, the objective function associated with an input image $\mathbf{x}$ is then defined as

$$\mathcal{L}(\mathbf{x}, E) := \|\mathbf{x}' - \psi(\phi(\mathbf{x}))\|_2 + \sum_{j=1}^{J} \left(\alpha \|\mathbf{z}_e^j - \mathbf{sg}(\mathbf{e}_\tau^j)\|_2^2 + \beta \|\mathbf{z}_e^j - \mathbf{sg}(\mathbf{e}_\tau^j)\|_2^2 \right) \quad (2)$$

The encoder network of the model (see also Fig. 1) consists of four convolutional layers, where each layer downsampls the DWI by a factor of two. The decoder network of the model is defined by four transpose convolutional layers, where each layer upsamples the compressed representation by a factor of two. ReLU activations are used in every layer. All convolutional layers have kernel size $4 \times 4 \times 4$, a stride of 2, and padding of 1.

With regard to the other three models, the U-Net model is implemented as in [13] except with 4 filters in the first convolutional layer as opposed to 64. This modification can effectively reduce the model size so that the batch size can be increased. U-Net uses only the reconstruction loss without the codebook and commitment loss. The VQVAE model removes the skip connections on every level in the U-VQVAE. The VAE-GAN model uses the same U-VQVAE architecture with additional batch normalization layers as a generator and adds a fully convolutional patch-wise discriminator classifier [14] in an adversarial setup. Additionally, it produces less blurry reconstructions by replacing the voxel-wise l_2 reconstruction loss with the l_2 error between real and generated image representations in the third convolutional layer of the discriminator network [25].

2.2   Dataset and Evaluation Metrics

We first trained and tested the model on an artificially cropped dataset, which was based on the b0 and b1000 DWIs of 824 subjects from NCANDA without cropping artifacts (Public Release: NCANDA_PUBLIC_BASE_DIFFUSION_V01) and of 100 subjects from the Human Connectome Project (HCP) [26,27]. Images from HCP were downsampled to $96 \times 96 \times 64$ to match the resolution of NCANDA images. All images were normalized to the range 0–1 to minimize influence from variation in voxel intensities in the training the models. The training data was further augmented by randomly rotating images ten degrees in either direction for every axis and translating 10 voxels in the two directions of the axial plane. This resulted in a dataset of 420,487 MRI, 236,291 MRIs from NCANDA and 184,196 MRIs from HCP. The MRIs consisted of 93,467 b0 volumes and 327,020 b1000 volumes. 80% of the dataset was used for training and 20% for testing.

The optimal model was determined by its capability of inpainting DWI cropped by us. Specifically, training MRIs were cropped eight slices (or 12.5%) from the top before being analyzed by the model. This amount of cropping reflected the average cropping across the real corrupted MRIs of the NCANDA dataset. Models were trained on a single NVIDIA Tesla V100-SXM2 32 GB GPU. The Adam optimizer was used with a learning rate of 0.001. The batch size was set to 128 DWI images for all models. To measure the inpainting accuracy, we applied the models to the artificially cropped MRIs of the testing data and compared the reconstruction to the ground-truth via Structural Similarity [28], Peak Signal-to-Noise Ratio (PSNR), and Mean-Squared Error (MSE). We also computed the average image spatial gradient as an indicator of how well models recreated high-frequency details. Separately, these metrics were calculated confined to the eight cropped slices.

Table 1. Model performance evaluated by various image quality metrics on both the entire image and only the cropped regions. Amount of cropping was fixed to 12.5%, similar to the training data. PSNR is measured in dB.

Model	Whole				Cropped			
	SSIM	PSNR	MSE	Gradient	SSIM	PSNR	MSE	Gradient
U-VQVAE	**0.9973**	**49.8733**	**1.089e−5**	0.0209	**0.9679**	**30.7809**	**8.535e−5**	0.0041
VQVAE	0.8467	32.0512	5.437e−4	0.0064	0.9279	28.4808	1.449e−4	0.0034
U-Net [13]	0.9959	49.4796	1.152e−5	0.0210	0.9638	30.6117	8.723e−5	0.0039
VAE-GAN	0.8074	30.6311	2.919e−3	**0.1206**	0.8036	21.7169	2.348e−3	**0.2033**

Using the optimal model derived by these metrics, we evaluated the impact of inpainting on downstream processing steps. The experiment was based on the DWI sequences of 13 adolescents at their followup visits (from Year 2 to Year 6) of the NCANDA dataset. These DWIs were labelled as 'unusable' by the NCANDA quality assurance protocol [29] due to the field of view not being able to capture the entire head anymore (top of the brain is cut off, see also Fig. 1) as it increased in size compared to the baseline. To show the impact of inpainting, we registered the FA maps of the DWI to the SRI24 atlas space [30] based on either the real b0 volumes with cropping artifacts or the inpainted volumes.

We then analyzed the differences in FA in between those two FA maps to evaluate the influence from the inpainting.

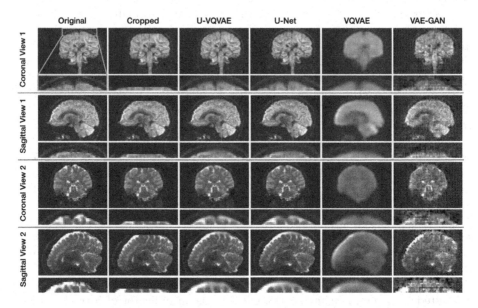

Fig. 2. Example b0 and non-b0 original and inpainted images for each model. Each row is a different view of the image with the bottom half zoomed in on the cropped region.

3 Results and Discussion

3.1 Evaluation on Artificially Cropped B0 MRIs of DWI

The accuracy scores for each model on the artificially cropped dataset are listed in Table 1. While VAE-GAN achieved the highest mean image gradient among the models, it also recorded the lowest PSNR. This is likely due to the relatively high level of noise levels shown in the inpainted images from this model in Fig. 2 (compared to those from U-VQVAE). The increased noise may have been introduced by adversarial training of the generator with the discriminator network, which may have conflicted with reconstruction of intact slices of the image through the generator's skip connections. Across all other metrics, U-VQVAE performed the best. As expected, image quality metrics for U-VQVAE were much better than those for VQVAE, indicating the importance of including skip connections. This is also supported by U-Net's high SSIM and PSNR, which nearly rivals U-VQVAE. To determine whether U-VQVAE had statistically higher reconstruction fidelity than U-Net, we performed a two-sample t-tests on U-Net's and U-VQVAE's mean SSIM and PSNR for both whole image and cropped parts. U-VQVAE's increase in accuracy compared to U-Net was statistically significant in all four cases (i.e, $p < 0.001$; p-values were one-sided and FDR corrected). These results demonstrate that U-VQVAE was the most accurate model for reconstructing cropped regions informed by the image's global structure.

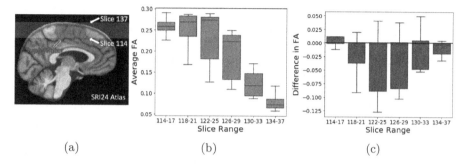

(a)   (b)   (c)

Fig. 3. (a) The Supplementary Motor Area overlaid with the SRI24 atlas; (b) Average FA at different axial slices of the 13 NCANDA DWI sequences with cropping artifacts; (c) Difference in average FA derived by registrations based on either cropped or inpainted b0 volumes

3.2   Impact on Downstream Preprocessing

This section highlights the potential usage of our proposed inpainting method by U-VQVAE in analyzing NCANDA data, which in part studies the white matter microstructural development during adolescence. The DWI sequence of each of the 13 subjects used in this experiment was preprocessed by the publicly available NCANDA image processing pipeline [29], which included bad single shots removal, echo-planar structural distortion correction, eddy-current correction, rigid alignment for motion correction, and skull stripping. The Fractional Anisotropy (FA) map was estimated by CAMINO [31].

Performing population-level analysis on the FA maps requires aligning them to a single template. The alignment was performed by non-rigidly registering the b0 volume to the subject T2w image, which was then non-rigidly registered to the SRI24 atlas [30] (Fig. 3a). This alignment was potentially corrupted at the top of the skull, specifically in the Supplementary Motor Area (SMA, Fig. 3a), due to the cropping artifact. We show this by repeating the registration using the inpainted b0 volumes. Fig. 3c shows the difference in the average FA of SMA at different axial slices (slice 114 to 137) derived by the two registration approaches. We can see that while the two registrations resulted in similar FA in lower axial slices (slice < 118) and outside the brain (slice > 134), the registration based on inpainted b0 volumes generated lower FA at slice 118 to 133. This difference was more pronounced at slice 122 to 129, regions most severely impacted by the cropping, despite the average FA value decreased in magnitude at these slices (Fig. 3b). This indicated that our inpainting could potentially improve the power of group-level analysis on the FA measures as higher FA estimates are generally associated with greater noise or larger artifacts within the data [32].

4 Conclusion

In this study, we presented a vector quantized variational autoencoder architecture that is capable of repairing cropping artifacts in multi-shell diffusion weighted images for the first time. The images inpainted by our model exhibited higher fidelity as measured by various image quality metrics than other landmark models widely used in image reconstruction. Most importantly, images inpainted by our model yielded FA maps with lower FA values in areas previously impacted by the cropping artifact, indicating a reduction in noise in the image processing pipeline and demonstrating that our inpainting can improve the power of group-level analyses. Future directions of our modeling approach could include training with varied levels of cropping to improve model robustness and generalizing the model to other MR imaging modalities.

Acknowledgements. This work was supported by NIH Grants AA021697, AA005965, and AA010723. This work was also supported by the National Science Foundation Graduate Research Fellowship and the 2020 HAI-AWS Cloud Credits Award.

References

1. Soares, J.M., Marques, P., Alves, V., Sousa, N.: A hitchhiker's guide to diffusion tensor imaging. Front. Neurosci. **7**(7), 1–14 (2013). https://doi.org/10.3389/fnins.2013.00031
2. Le Bihan, D., Poupon, C., Amadon, A., Lethimonnier, F.: Artifacts and pitfalls in diffusion MRI. J. Magn. Reson. Imaging **24**(3), 478–488 (2006). https://doi.org/10.1002/jmri.20683
3. Greve, D.N., Fischl, B.: Accurate and robust brain image alignment using boundary-based registration. NeuroImage **48**(1), 63–72 (2009). https://doi.org/10.1016/j.neuroimage.2009.06.060. https://linkinghub.elsevier.com/retrieve/pii/S1053811909006752
4. Elharrouss, O., Almaadeed, N., Al-Maadeed, S., Akbari, Y.: Image inpainting: a review. Neural Process. Lett. **51**(2), 2007–2028 (2020). https://doi.org/10.1007/s11063-019-10163-0. http://link.springer.com/10.1007/s11063-019-10163-0
5. Lu, H., Liu, Q., Zhang, M., Wang, Y., Deng, X.: Gradient-based low rank method and its application in image inpainting. Multimed. Tools Appl. **77**(5), 5969–5993 (2017). https://doi.org/10.1007/s11042-017-4509-0
6. Jin, K.H., Ye, J.C.: Annihilating filter-based low-rank Hankel matrix approach for image inpainting. IEEE Trans. Image Process. **24**(11), 3498–3511 (2015). https://doi.org/10.1109/TIP.2015.2446943
7. Guo, Q., Gao, S., Zhang, X., Yin, Y., Zhang, C.: Patch-based image inpainting via two-stage low rank approximation. IEEE Trans. Vis. Comput. Graph. **24**(6), 2023–2036 (2018). https://doi.org/10.1109/TVCG.2017.2702738

8. Kozhekin, N., Savchenko, V., Senin, M., Hagiwara, I.: An approach to surface retouching and mesh smoothing. Vis. Comput. **19**(7–8), 549–564 (2003). https://doi.org/10.1007/s00371-003-0218-y

9. Chan, T.F., Shen, J.: Nontexture inpainting by curvature-driven diffusions. J. Vis. Commun. Image Represent. **12**(4), 436–449 (2001). https://doi.org/10.1006/jvci.2001.0487

10. Alsalamah, M., Amin, S.: Medical image inpainting with RBF interpolation technique. Int. J. Adv. Comput. Sci. Appl. **7**(8), 91–99 (2016). https://doi.org/10.14569/ijacsa.2016.070814

11. Yan, Z., Li, X., Li, M., Zuo, W., Shan, S.: Shift-net: image inpainting via deep feature rearrangement. In: Ferrari, V., Hebert, M., Sminchisescu, C., Weiss, Y. (eds.) ECCV 2018. LNCS, vol. 11218, pp. 3–19. Springer, Cham (2018). https://doi.org/10.1007/978-3-030-01264-9_1

12. Shelhamer, E., Long, J., Darrell, T.: Fully convolutional networks for semantic segmentation. IEEE Trans. Pattern Anal. Mach. Intell. **39**(4), 640–651 (2017). https://doi.org/10.1109/TPAMI.2016.2572683

13. Ronneberger, O., Fischer, P., Brox, T.: U-Net: convolutional networks for biomedical image segmentation. In: Navab, N., Hornegger, J., Wells, W.M., Frangi, A.F. (eds.) MICCAI 2015. LNCS, vol. 9351, pp. 234–241. Springer, Cham (2015). https://doi.org/10.1007/978-3-319-24574-4_28

14. Isola, P., Zhu, J.Y., Zhou, T., Efros, A.A.: Image-to-image translation with conditional adversarial networks. In: Proceedings of the 30th IEEE Conference on Computer Vision and Pattern Recognition, CVPR 2017, vol. 2017, pp. 5967–5976, January 2017. https://doi.org/10.1109/CVPR.2017.632

15. Armanious, K., Mecky, Y., Gatidis, S., Yang, B.: Adversarial inpainting of medical image modalities. In: ICASSP 2019 – 2019 IEEE International Conference on Acoustics, Speech and Signal Processing (ICASSP), pp. 3267–3271. IEEE, May 2019. https://doi.org/10.1109/ICASSP.2019.8682677. https://ieeexplore.ieee.org/document/8682677/

16. Armanious, K., Kumar, V., Abdulatif, S., Hepp, T., Gatidis, S., Yang, B.: ipA-MedGAN: inpainting of arbitrary regions in medical imaging (2019). http://arxiv.org/abs/1910.09230

17. Armanious, K., Gatidis, S., Nikolaou, K., Yang, B., Kustner, T.: Retrospective correction of rigid and non-rigid MR motion artifacts using GANs. In: Proceedings of the International Symposium on Biomedical Imaging, vol. 2019, pp. 1550–1554, April 2019. https://doi.org/10.1109/ISBI.2019.8759509

18. Sabokrou, M., Pourreza, M., Fayyaz, M., Entezari, R., Fathy, M., Gall, J., Adeli, E.: AVID: adversarial visual irregularity detection. In: Jawahar, C.V., Li, H., Mori, G., Schindler, K. (eds.) ACCV 2018. LNCS, vol. 11366, pp. 488–505. Springer, Cham (2019). https://doi.org/10.1007/978-3-030-20876-9_31

19. Kingma, D.P., Welling, M.: Auto-encoding variational Bayes. In: 2nd International Conference on Learning Representations, ICLR 2014 - Conference Track Proceedings (Ml), pp. 1–14 (2014)

20. Xie, J., Xu, L., Chen, E.: Image denoising and inpainting with deep neural networks. In: Advances in Neural Information Processing Systems, vol. 1, pp. 341–349 (2012)

21. Dosovitskiy, A., Brox, T.: Generating images with perceptual similarity metrics based on deep networks. In: Advances in Neural Information Processing Systems, pp. 658–666 (2016)

22. Van Den Oord, A., Vinyals, O., Kavukcuoglu, K.: Neural discrete representation learning. In: Advances in Neural Information Processing Systems, vol. 2017 (NIPS), pp. 6307–6316, December 2017

23. Razavi, A., van den Oord, A., Vinyals, O.: Generating diverse high-fidelity images with VQ-VAE-2 (2019). http://arxiv.org/abs/1906.00446

24. Tudosiu, P.D., et al.: Neuromorphologicaly-preserving Volumetric data encoding using VQ-VAE, pp. 1–13 (2020). http://arxiv.org/abs/2002.05692

25. Larsen, A.B.L., Sønderby, S.K., Larochelle, H., Winther, O.: Autoencoding beyond pixels using a learned similarity metric. In: 33rd International Conference on Machine Learning, ICML 2016, vol. 4, pp. 2341–2349 (2016)

26. Van Essen, D.C., et al.: The human connectome project: a data acquisition perspective. NeuroImage **62**(4), 2222–2231 (2012). https://doi.org/10.1016/j.neuroimage. 2012.02.018

27. Hodge, M.R., et al.: ConnectomeDB-sharing human brain connectivity data. NeuroImage **124**(3), 1102–1107 (2016). https://doi.org/10.1016/j.neuroimage.2015.04. 046. https://linkinghub.elsevier.com/retrieve/pii/S1053811915003468

28. Wang, Z., Bovik, A.C., Sheikh, H.R., Simoncelli, E.P.: Image quality assessment: from error visibility to structural similarity. IEEE Trans. Image Process. **13**(4), 600–612 (2004). https://doi.org/10.1109/TIP.2003.819861

29. Pohl, K.M., et al.: Harmonizing DTI measurements across scanners to examine the development of white matter microstructure in 803 adolescents of the NCANDA study. NeuroImage **130**, 194–213 (2016). https://doi.org/10.1016/j.neuroimage. 2016.01.061

30. Rohlfing, T., Zahr, N.M., Sullivan, E.V., Pfefferbaum, A.: The SRI24 multichannel atlas of normal adult human brain structure. Hum. Brain Mapp. **31**(5), 798–819 (2010). https://doi.org/10.1002/hbm.20906

31. Cook, P.a., Bai, Y., Seunarine, K.K., Hall, M.G., Parker, G.J., Alexander, D.C.: Camino: open-source diffusion-MRI reconstruction and processing. In: 14th Scientific Meeting of the International Society for Magnetic Resonance in Medicine, vol. 14, p. 2759 (2006)

32. Farrell, J.A.D., et al.: Effects of SNR on the accuracy and reproducibility of DTI-derived fractional anisotropy, mean diffusivity, and principal eigenvector measurements at 1.5T. J. Magn. Reson. **26**(3), 756–767 (2010). https://doi.org/10.1002/ jmri.21053.Effects

Multi-view Brain HyperConnectome AutoEncoder for Brain State Classification

Alin Banka, Inis Buzi, and Islem Rekik$^{(\boxtimes)}$ (iD)

BASIRA Lab, Faculty of Computer and Informatics, Istanbul Technical University, Istanbul, Turkey
irekik@itu.edu.tr
http://basira-lab.com

Abstract. Graph embedding is a powerful method to represent graph neurological data (e.g., brain connectomes) in a low dimensional space for brain connectivity mapping, prediction and classification. However, existing embedding algorithms have two major limitations. *First*, they primarily focus on preserving *one-to-one* topological relationships between nodes (i.e., regions of interest (ROIs) in a connectome), but they have mostly ignored *many-to-many* relationships (i.e., set to set), which can be captured using a *hyperconnectome* structure. *Second*, existing graph embedding techniques cannot be easily adapted to *multi-view* graph data with heterogeneous distributions. In this paper, while cross-pollinating adversarial deep learning with hypergraph theory, we aim to *jointly* learn deep latent embeddings of subject-specific multi-view brain graphs to eventually disentangle different brain states such as Alzheimer's disease (AD) versus mild cognitive impairment (MCI). First, we propose a new simple strategy to build a hyperconnectome for each brain view based on nearest neighbour algorithm to preserve the connectivities across pairs of ROIs. Second, we design a hyperconnectome autoencoder (HCAE) framework which operates directly on the multi-view hyperconnectomes based on hypergraph convolutional layers to better capture the many-to-many relationships between brain regions (i.e., graph nodes). For each subject, we further regularize the hypergraph autoencoding by adversarial regularization to align the distribution of the learned hyperconnectome embeddings with the original hyperconnectome distribution. We formalize our hyperconnectome embedding within a geometric deep learning framework to optimize for a given subject, thereby designing an *individual-based* learning framework. Our experiments showed that the learned embeddings by HCAE yield to better results for AD/MCI classification compared with deep graph-based autoencoding methods.

Keywords: Multi-view brain networks · Brain hyperconnectome · Geometric hyperconnectome autoencoder · Brain state classification · Adversarial learning

GitHub: http://github.com/basiralab.

I. Rekik et al. (Eds.): PRIME 2020, LNCS 12329, pp. 101–110, 2020.
https://doi.org/10.1007/978-3-030-59354-4_10

1   Introduction

Magnetic resonance imaging (MRI) has introduced exciting new opportunities for understanding the brain as a complex system of interacting units in both health and disease and across the human lifespan. Based on MRI data, the brain can be represented as a connectomic graph (i.e., connectome), where the connection between different anatomical regions of interest (ROIs) is modeled. A large body of research work showed how the brain connectome gets altered by neurological disorders, such as mild cognitive impairment (MCI) or Alzheimer's disease (AD) [1,2]. In network neuroscience, the brain connectome, which is typically regarded as a graph encoding the low-order *one-to-one* relationships between pairs of ROIs, presents a macroscale representation of the interactions between anatomical regions at functional, structural or morphological levels [3]. Analyses of either network connectivity or topology for examining variations in the type and strength of connectivity between brain regions, are integral to understanding the connectomics of brain disorders [1] as well as the cross-disorder connectome landscape of brain dysconnectivity [2]. Although graphs enable a powerful interactional representation of the data, they present a reductionist representation of the brain complexity with their simple topology where edges connect at max two nodes. Hence, this limits the learning of representations for complex interactions between brain regions in tasks such as connectome classification, connectomic disease propagation prediction, and holistic brain mapping.

To address this first gap in the connectomics literature [1–4] while drawing inspiration from the hypergraph theory, we present the concept of the brain *hyperconnectome*, which models the high-order *many-to-many* interactions between brain regions. Specifically, in the hyperconnectome, one naturally captures the relationships between *sets* of ROIs, where a hyperedge can link more than two nodes. In other words, the hyperconnectome permits us to overcome the limitations of one-to-one (i.e., low-order) relationships between ROIs in traditional graph-based connectomes [2,4] by introducing many-to-many (i.e., high-order) relationships between nodes. Although compelling, such high-order brain representation introduces more challenges to machine learning in connectomics as it increases the dimensionality of the data. To address the curse of dimensionality, this brings us to deploying dimensionality reduction or data embeddings, which are pivotal for learning-based tasks such as classification between healthy and disordered brains or unsupervised clustering of brain states. However, traditional machine learning techniques such as principle component analysis (PCA) fail to preserve the *topological relationships* between the nodes of the brain connectomes as they operate on vectorized brain connectomes. Recently, the emerging field of geometric deep learning [5–8], aiming to adapt deep learning on Euclidean data such as images to non-Euclidean data including graphs and manifolds, has allowed us not only to generalize deep learning on graphs but also to learn latent representations of graphs in a low-dimensional space. More recently, [9] proposed adversarial connectome embedding (ACE) based on graph convolutional networks [10], which preserves (i) the topological structures of the brain connectomes when generating low-dimensional embeddings, and (ii) enforces the distribution of the learned connectome embeddings to match that of the original connectomes. Although promising, such approaches are not naturally designed to operate on hypergraphs, let alone *multi-view* hypergraphs where each hypergraph encodes the high-order relationship between nodes using a particular data view (e.g., function or morphology in hyperconnectomes). Exceptionally, a recent work [11] cross-pollinated hypergraph theory and deep learning to introduce hypergraph neural networks (HGNN). However, this was primarily designed within a transductive learning setting where inference on hypergraph aims to minimize the label difference among nodes with stronger connections on hypergraph to eventually assign labels to unlabelled nodes. As such, one can learn how to label nodes of testing samples in a hypergraph. However, this stands out from fully unsupervised data autoencoding, where the primary focus is on learning meaningful and representative embeddings of the input data by minimizing its self-reconstruction loss. To the best of our knowledge, hypergraph autoencoding networks are currently absent in the state-of-the-art.

To address these limitations, we propose the first geometric hypergraph autoencoder, named HyperConnectome AutoEncoder (HCAE), for embedding multi-view brain hyperconnectomes derived from multi-view brain connectomes where each individual is represented by a set of brain connectomes, each capturing a particular *view of the brain* (e.g., sulcal depth dissimilarity). *First*, we introduce the definition of the hyperconnectome structure. *Second*, we leverage hypergraph convolutional layers introduced in HGNN [11] to design our HCAE architecture, which preserves the hyperconnectome relationships when learning the latent embeddings. Unlike existing typical graph autoencoders [9,12] which are trained on a population of samples, we formalize our problem as a *subject-specific* loss function to optimize for each individual hyperconnectome. For each subject, to generate a hyperconnectome embedding which is true to the input multi-view brain networks, we further introduce a hyperconnectome adversarial regularization, where we integrate a discriminator network to force the latent representations to match the prior distribution of the subject-specific multi-view hyperconnectome. *Third*, we demonstrate the utility of our architecture in integrating multi-view hyperconnectome by learning a shared embedding exploiting the cross-view relationship between diverse hyperconnectome representation of the same brain. Ultimately, we evaluate the discriminative power of the learned embeddings in distinguishing between different brain states by training a support vector machine classifier using repeated randomized data partition for reproducibility.

2   Proposed HyperConnectome AutoEncoder (HCAE) for Brain State Classification

Problem Statement. Let $\mathcal{G}^s = \{\mathbf{G}_1, \dots, \mathbf{G}_M\}$ denote a set of multi-view brain connectomes of subject s in the population $\mathbb{G}$, comprising M fully-connected brain graphs where $\mathbf{G}_m$ represents the brain graph derived from measurement m (e.g., correlation in neural activity or similarity in morphology). Each brain

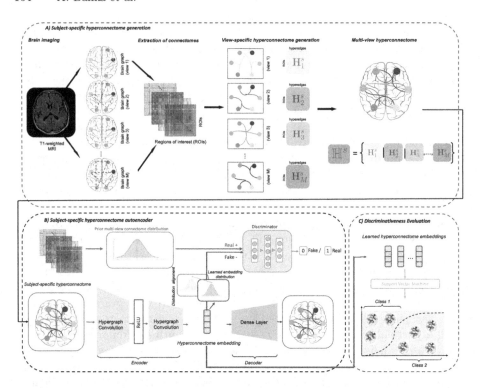

Fig. 1. *Hyperconnectome Autoencoder (HCAE) architecture for multi-view brain network state classification.* **(A)** For each subject, we generate a set of multi-view brain connectomes, each capturing a connectional view of the brain (e.g., function or morphology). From each brain connectome, we construct a view-specific hyperconnectome which consists of hyperedges, built by connecting each node (i.e., an anatomical region of interest (ROI)) to its *k*-nearest neighboring nodes. Ultimately, we stack horizontally the incidence matrices from separate views to create a *multi-view brain hyperconnectome*, which captures the *high-order* connectivity from different complementary brain views. **(B)** HCAE is trained in a *subject-specific* manner, i.e., for each individual independently. The architecture consists of three main components: (1) the encoder, (2) the decoder, and (3) the discriminator. The encoder, consisting of 2 hypergraph convolutional layers and a ReLU activation function in between the layers, embeds the input multi-view hyperconnectome to a low-dimensional space. The decoder reconstructs the subject-specific multi-view brain hyperconnectome from the learned embedding through a single dense layer. The discriminator acts as a regularizer where it enforces the distribution of the learned hyperconnectome embeddings to match that of the original hyperconnectome distribution in an adversarial manner. **(C)** Evaluating the discriminativeness of the learned embeddings in distinguishing between brain states using support vector machines (SVM). We use the encoded multi-view hyperconnectomes to train an SVM classifier to classify two brain states (e.g., AD and MCI).

graph $\mathbf{G}_m = (V, E, \mathbf{X}_m) \in \mathcal{G}^s$ captures a *connectional view* of the brain wiring, where V denotes a set of N brain ROIs, E a set of edges connecting pairs of nodes, and $\mathbf{X}_m \in \mathbb{R}^{N \times N}$ denotes a symmetric brain connectivity matrix encoding the pairwise relationship between brain ROIs. Our goal is to learn *discriminative* and *representative* latent representation of each individual $\mathcal{G}^s$ by capitalizing on hypergraph structure and the nascent field of geometric deep learning.

A-Multi-view Hyperconnectome Definition. Given a brain graph $\mathbf{G}_m = (V, E, \mathbf{X}_m) \in \mathcal{G}^s$ of subject s, we define a hyperconnectome of view m $\mathcal{H}_m^s = \{V, \mathcal{E}_\mathbf{m}, \mathbf{W}_m^s\}$ as a set of nodes V and a set of hyperedges $\mathcal{E}_\mathbf{m}$, where each hyperedge is assigned a unitary weight in the diagonal weight matrix $\mathbf{W}_m \in \mathbb{R}^{|\mathcal{E}| \times |\mathcal{E}|}$. Basically, we construct the hypergraph $\mathcal{H}_m^s$ by connecting each node v in V to its k-nearest neighboring nodes, thereby defining a hyperedge $e \in \mathcal{E}_\mathbf{m}$. Next, we create a view-specific hyperconnectome incidence matrix $\mathbf{H}_m^s \in \mathbb{R}^{|V| \times |\mathcal{E}|}$, the entries of which are defined as:

$$\mathbf{H}_m^s(e, v) = \begin{cases} 1, & \text{if } v \in e. \\ 0, & \text{if } v \notin e. \end{cases} \tag{1}$$

for $v \in V$ and $e \in \mathcal{E}$.

Additionally, each node v_i in $\mathcal{H}_m^s$ stores a set of features, which represent the ith row in the graph connectivity matrix $\mathbf{X}_m^s$ to preserve the relationship between different nodes since our incidence matrix is binary. Ultimately, by constructing a hyperconnectome for each view m, we create a multi-view hyperconnectome $\mathbb{H}^s$ stacking horizontally incidence matrices from different views (Fig. 1):

$$\mathbb{H}^s = \{\mathbf{H}_1^s | \mathbf{H}_2^s |, \dots, | \mathbf{H}_M^s\},$$

In parallel, we also stack the connectivity matrices of all views as follows:

$$\mathbb{X}^s = \{\mathbf{X}_1^s | \mathbf{X}_2^s |, \dots, | \mathbf{X}_M^s\}$$

B-Subject-Specific Hyperconnectome Autoencoder. Next, we construct and train the HCAE model in order to extract low dimensional representations of our hyperconnectome. The model consists of three main components (Fig. 1): (1) the encoder constructed using hypergraph convolutional layers, (2) the decoder constructed using dense layers, and (3) the discriminator, which is utilized for adversarial distribution regularization, and composed of dense layers. The encoder consists of two stacked hypergraph convolutional layers. The two layers utilize the traditional hypergraph convolutional operation [11]. A rectified linear unit (ReLu) activation function is used after the first layer, and a linear activation function is added after the second one.

$$\mathbf{Y}^{(l)} = \phi(\mathbf{D_v}^{-1/2} \mathbb{H}^s \mathbf{W}_m \mathbf{D_e}^{-1} (\mathbb{H}^s)^T \mathbf{D_v}^{-1/2} \mathbf{Y}^{(l-1)} \mathbf{\Theta}^{(l)}),$$

where $d(v) = \sum_{e \in \mathcal{E}} \mathbf{W}_m \mathbb{H}^s(v, e)$ and $\delta(v) = \sum_{v \in V} \mathbb{H}^s(v, e)$ are respectively definitions of the vertex degree and edge degree. $\mathbf{D}_v \in \mathbb{R}^{V \times V}$ and $\mathbf{D}_e \in \mathbb{R}^{|\mathcal{E}| \times |\mathcal{E}|}$ are respectively the diagonal matrices of the vertex degrees and edge degrees. $\mathbf{W}_m$ is the hyperedge weight matrix, $\mathbf{\Theta}^{(l)}$ represents the learned filter (i.e., learned weights of the hypergraph convolutional layers) applied to all hyerconnectome nodes to extract high-order connectional features, and $\mathbf{Y}^{(l-1)}$ represents the input produced by the previous layer. $\mathbf{Y}^{(0)} = \mathbb{X}^s$ denotes the *multi-view* brain connectivity matrix of the subject, and ϕ represents the activation function. The low-dimensional latent embedding is obtained as the output of the second convolutional layer, $\mathbf{Z} = \mathbf{Y}^{(2)} \in \mathbb{R}^N$. Notice that HCAE convolutions are hypergraph convolutions. The purpose of the hypergraph convolutional layer is to take advantage of the high-order correlation among data [11]. It does so by incorporating the node-edge-node transformation. Specifically, the d-dimensional feature is extracted by processing the node feature matrix $\mathbf{Y}^{(0)}$ with the learnable weight matrix $\Theta^{(l)}$. The output extracted is gathered to construct the hyperedge feature through multiplication with $(\mathbb{H}^s)^T$. Finally, the output is received through hyperedge feature aggregation, achieved by multiplying with $\mathbb{H}^s$. $\mathbf{D}_v$ and $\mathbf{D}_e$ are included in the equation for normalization. The reconstruction of the hyperconnectome is done through a dense layer, $\widetilde{\mathbb{H}}^s = \mathbf{Z}\mathcal{W}$, where $\mathcal{W}$ denotes the learned weights of the dense reconstruction layer, and $\widetilde{\mathbb{H}}$ is the reconstructed incidence matrix. The loss is defined as follows:

$$L_0 = E_{q(\mathbf{Z}|\mathbb{X}^s,\mathbb{H}^s)}[\log P(\widetilde{\mathbb{H}}^s|\mathbf{Z})] \tag{2}$$

Drawing inspiration from [12], we utilize adversarial regularization to force the low-dimensional latent embeddings to match the distribution of the input multi-view brain networks (Fig. 1). Specifically, we integrate an adversarial discriminator as a multilayer perceptron (MLP) comprising multiple stacked dense layers. A discriminator D, which is primarily employed in Generative Adversarial Networks (GANs), is commonly trained to discriminate between real samples and fake samples generated by another network known as the generator G. In our case, we integrate the loss of the discriminator into the model in order to force the learned low-dimensional embedding of a hyperconnectome to align better with the prior distribution of the input multi-view brain networks of a single subject:

$$-\frac{1}{2}E_{\mathbf{z}\sim p_Z}[\log D(\mathbf{Z})] - \frac{1}{2}E_{\mathbb{X}^s}[\log (1 - D(G(\mathbb{X}^s, \mathbb{H}^s)))] \tag{3}$$

As such, we create a form of regularization that propels a better autoencoding by solving the following min-max optimization problem:

$$\min_G \max_D E_{\mathbf{Z}\sim p_Z}[\log D(\mathbf{Z})] + E_{\mathbf{Z}\sim p_Z}[\log (1 - D(G(\mathbb{X}^s, \mathbb{H}^s)))] \tag{4}$$

3   Results and Discussion

Dataset, Parameters, and Benchmarking. In our experiments, we evaluated our model with the ADNI GO public dataset [13] over 77 subjects (36 MCI and 41 AD), each with structural T1-w MR image. Each subject has 4 cortical morphological networks derived as explained in [14–16]. Each cortical morphological network is encoded in a symmetric adjacency matrix with size (35×35), generated using a specific cortical attribute: (1) maximum principal curvature, (2) cortical thickness, (3) sulcal depth, and (4) average curvature. We compared our proposed framework with Adversarial Connectome Embedding (ACE) [9], a geometric autoencoder architecture, which captures the region relationships *one-to-one* in a graph structure. It utilizes conventional graph convolutional layers to learn the embeddings and adversarial regularizing network for original-encoded distribution alignment. We evaluated both ACE and HCAE on single-view and multi-view connectomes. Since ACE [9] does not naturally operate on multi-view data, we averaged the multi-view connectomes for evaluating it on multi-view data. HCAE is trained on each subject, independently, using 30 epochs.

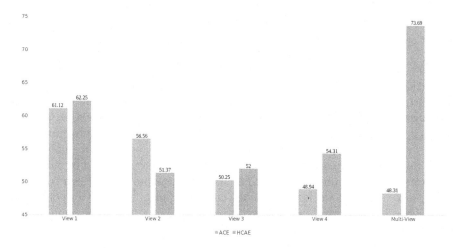

Fig. 2. Comparison of SVM classification accuracies of AD and MCI brain states using low-order embeddings learned by ACE [9] and high-order embeddings learned by our HCAE.

Evaluation of the Discriminativeness of the Learned Hyperconnectome Embeddings. We randomly split our dataset into 80% training samples and 20% testing subjects to train and test an SVM classifier using the learned high-order embeddings by ACE and HCAE. Average classification results over 100 repeated runs are reported in Fig. 2 and cross-entropy reconstruction error in Fig. 3. Remarkably, the AD/MCI classification accuracy was largely boosted from 48.31% to 73.69% when using the multi-view representation of the brain network in comparison with single-view connectomes. Excluding view 2, HCAE achieved the best results. Furthermore, the data reconstruction error was much lower using our HCAE model on both single and multi-view connectomic datasets. This demonstrates that our model better preserves the high-order brain connectivity topology.

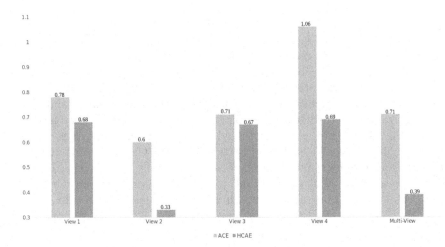

Fig. 3. Comparison of hyperconnectome reconstruction errors by ACE [9] and HCAE.

Limitations and Recommendations for Future Work. Even though our model produced the best results in brain state classification and hyperconnectome autoencoding in both single and multiple brain views, it has a few limitations that could be overcome in future work. *First*, the learned embeddings are learned in a fully unsupervised manner, one possible extension is to integrate a second discriminator to learn *discriminative* embeddings supervised by the input brain states. As such, one needs to adapt HCAE to population-driven training. *Second*, in our model we leverage multi-channel multiplication to operate on a multi-view hyperconnectome. Alternatively, one can add a hyperconnectome fusion block to integrate hyperconnectomes in weighted manner across all views. *Finally*, although our HCAE nicely learns the embeddings capturing many-to-many relationships between brain regions, which was demonstrated to be useful for brain state classification, it cannot handle spatiotemporal multi-view brain connectomes, which are time-dependent. As a future extension of our HCAE, we aim to extend to autoencode evolution trajectories of multi-view brain connectomes leveraging recurrent neural networks in geometric deep learning [17,18] to model the temporal relationships between connectomes acquired at different timepoints.

4   Conclusion

In this paper, we proposed the first hyperconnectome autoencoder framework for brain state classification. Our HCAE operates on multiple brain connectomes, leverages adversarial learning for hyperconnectome autoencoding using hypergraph convolutional layers, and learns representative high-order representation of brain connectivity that was shown to be discriminative in our experiments. This work develops the field of network neuroscience along the hyperconnectivity front, which aims to present a holistic representation of different facets of the brain connectome. This further calls for more scalable applications of the proposed multi-view hyperconnectome representation to unify our understanding of brain structure, function, and morphology, and how these get altered in a wide spectrum of brain disorders.

Acknowledgments. I. Rekik is supported by the European Union's Horizon 2020 research and innovation programme under the Marie Sklodowska-Curie Individual Fellowship grant agreement No 101003403 (http://basira-lab.com/normnets/).

References

1. Fornito, A., Zalesky, A., Breakspear, M.: The connectomics of brain disorders. Nat. Rev. Neurosci. **16**, 159–172 (2015)
2. Van den Heuvel, M.P., Sporns, O.: A cross-disorder connectome landscape of brain dysconnectivity. Nat. Rev. Neurosci. **20**, 435–446 (2019)
3. Bassett, D.S., Sporns, O.: Network neuroscience. Nat. Neurosci. **20**, 353 (2017)
4. Bullmore, E., Sporns, O.: Complex brain networks: graph theoretical analysis of structural and functional systems. Nat. Rev. Neurosci. **10**, 186–198 (2009)
5. Bronstein, M.M., Bruna, J., LeCun, Y., Szlam, A., Vandergheynst, P.: Geometric deep learning: going beyond euclidean data. IEEE Signal Process. Mag. **34**, 18–42 (2017)
6. Zhang, Z., Cui, P., Zhu, W.: Deep learning on graphs: a survey. arXiv preprint arXiv:1812.04202 (2018)
7. Wu, Z., Pan, S., Chen, F., Long, G., Zhang, C., Yu, P.S.: A comprehensive survey on graph neural networks. arXiv preprint arXiv:1901.00596 (2019)
8. Zhou, J., et al.: Graph neural networks: a review of methods and applications. arXiv preprint arXiv:1812.08434 (2018)
9. Banka, A., Rekik, I.: Adversarial connectome embedding for mild cognitive impairment identification using cortical morphological networks. In: International Workshop on Connectomics in Neuroimaging, pp. 74–82 (2019)
10. Kipf, T.N., Welling, M.: Semi-Supervised Classification with Graph Convolutional Networks. arXiv e-prints (2016) arXiv:1609.02907
11. Feng, Y., You, H., Zhang, Z., Ji, R., Gao, Y.: Hypergraph neural networks. arXiv e-prints (2018) arXiv:1809.09401
12. Pan, S., Hu, R., Long, G., Jiang, J., Yao, L., Zhang, C.: Adversarially regularized graph autoencoder for graph embedding. arXiv e-prints (2018) arXiv:1802.04407
13. Mueller, S.G., et al.: The Alzheimer's disease neuroimaging initiative. Neuroimaging Clin. **15**, 869–877 (2005)
14. Mahjoub, I., Mahjoub, M.A., Rekik, I.: Brain multiplexes reveal morphological connectional biomarkers fingerprinting late brain dementia states. Sci. Rep. **8**, 1–14 (2018)
15. Dhifallah, S., Rekik, I., Alzheimer's Disease Neuroimaging Initiative, et al.: Estimation of connectional brain templates using selective multi-view network normalization. Med. Image Anal. **59**, 101567 (2020)

16. Nebli, A., Rekik, I.: Gender differences in cortical morphological networks. Brain Imaging Behav., 1–9 (2019). https://doi.org/10.1007/s11682-019-00123-6
17. Jain, A., Zamir, A.R., Savarese, S., Saxena, A.: Structural-RNN: deep learning on spatio-temporal graphs. In: Proceedings of the IEEE Conference on Computer Vision and Pattern Recognition, pp. 5308–5317 (2016)
18. Hajiramezanali, E., Hasanzadeh, A., Narayanan, K., Duffield, N., Zhou, M., Qian, X.: Variational graph recurrent neural networks. In: Advances in Neural Information Processing Systems, pp. 10700–10710 (2019)

Foreseeing Brain Graph Evolution over Time Using Deep Adversarial Network Normalizer

Zeynep Gürler[1], Ahmed Nebli[1,2]![ORCID], and Islem Rekik[1(✉)]![ORCID]

[1] BASIRA Lab, Faculty of Computer and Informatics, Istanbul Technical University,
Istanbul, Turkey
irekik@itu.edu.tr
[2] National School for Computer Science (ENSI), Mannouba, Tunisia
http://basira-lab.com

Abstract. Foreseeing the brain evolution as a complex highly inter-connected system, widely modeled as a graph, is crucial for mapping dynamic interactions between different anatomical regions of interest (ROIs) in health and disease. Interestingly, brain *graph* evolution models remain almost absent in the literature. Here we design an adversarial brain network normalizer for representing each brain network as a transformation of a fixed centered population-driven connectional template. Such graph normalization with respect to a fixed reference paves the way for reliably identifying the most similar training samples (i.e., brain graphs) to the testing sample at baseline timepoint. The testing evolution trajectory will be then spanned by the selected training graphs and their corresponding evolution trajectories. We base our prediction framework on geometric deep learning which naturally operates on graphs and nicely preserves their topological properties. Specifically, we propose the first *graph-based* Generative Adversarial Network (gGAN) that not only learns how to normalize brain graphs with respect to a fixed connectional brain template (CBT) (i.e., a brain template that selectively captures the most common features across a brain population) but also learns a high-order representation of the brain graphs also called embeddings. We use these embeddings to compute the similarity between training and testing subjects which allows us to pick the closest training subjects at baseline timepoint to predict the evolution of the testing brain graph over time. A series of benchmarks against several comparison methods showed that our proposed method achieved the lowest brain disease evolution prediction error using a single baseline timepoint. Our gGAN code is available at http://github.com/basiralab/gGAN.

Keywords: Adversarial network normalizer · Brain graph evolution prediction · Connectional brain template · Graph generative adversarial network · Sample selection

© Springer Nature Switzerland AG 2020
I. Rekik et al. (Eds.): PRIME 2020, LNCS 12329, pp. 111–122, 2020.
https://doi.org/10.1007/978-3-030-59354-4_11

1   Introduction

Early disease diagnosis using machine learning has become the new essence of modern-day medicine. Studies have shown that predicting the evolution of brain diseases can dramatically change the course of treatment and thus maximizing the chance of improving patient outcome [1]. For instance, [2,3] found that neurodegenerative diseases such as dementia are no longer reversible if diagnosed at a late stage. In this context, several research papers have attempted to combine neuroimaging with the predictive robustness of deep learning frameworks. As such, in one study, [4] used 3D convolutional neural networks to predict the onset of Alzheimer's disease (AD). However, these studies relied on samples that were taken at late disease stages which cannot be useful for prescribing *personalized* treatments for patients. To address this limitation, we are interested in solving a more challenging problem which is predicting the evolution of a brain disease over time given only an initial timepoint.

Previous studies have developed shape-based and image-based prediction frameworks using morphological features derived from brain MRI scans to foresee the brain evolution trajectory [5,6]. For instance, [6] used a representative shape selection method to predict longitudinal development of cortical surfaces and white matter fibers assuming that similar shapes at baseline timepoint will have similar developmental trajectories. Such an assumption has been also adopted in a landmark study [5], demonstrating the reliability of exploring similarities between baseline training and testing samples for predicting the evolution of brain MR image trajectory in patients diagnosed with mild cognitive impairment. Although these works proposed successful predictive frameworks for image-based brain evolution trajectory prediction and classification, these were solely restricted to investigating the brain as a surface or a 3D image. This undeniably overlooks the integral and rich representation of the brain as a *graph*, where the pairwise interconnectedness between pairs of anatomical regions of interest (ROIs) is investigated. To overcome this limitation, [7] proposed a Learning-guided Infinite Network Atlas selection (LINAs) framework, the first study that designed a learning-based atlas-to-atlas similarity estimation to predict brain graph evolution trajectory over time solely from a single observation. Despite its promising prediction accuracy, in the sample selection step, LINAs first vectorized each brain graph by storing the connectivity weights in the graph adjacency matrix in a feature vector. This fails to preserve the brain graph topology since the vectorization step regards the graph as a Euclidean object. A second limitation of these works is that such sample connectomic representation via vectorization might include irrelevant and redundant features that could mislead the training sample selection step.

To address these limitations, we tap into the nascent field of geometric deep learning aiming to learn representations of non-Euclidean objects such as graphs while preserving their geometry. Drawing inspiration from previous brain evolution predictive frameworks [5–7], we also assume the preservation of local sample (i.e., brain graph) neighborhood across different timepoints. As such, by *learning* the similarities between samples at baseline timepoint, one can identify the most similar training brain graphs to a testing brain graph. By integrating the evolution trajectories of the selected training samples, one can then predict the evolution trajectory of the testing brain graph. To this aim, we model each training and testing graph as a deformation or a transformation of a fixed reference, namely a connectional brain template (CBT). Such hypothesis is inspired from the classical deformable theory template widely adopted in Euclidean image-based registration frameworks [8,9], where each sample, in this case an image, is represented as a diffeomorphic transformation of a fixed template.

Specifically, we design the first *graph-based* generative adversarial network (gGAN) [10] that learns how to *normalize* a brain graph with respect to a fixed connectional brain template (CBT). A CBT can be viewed as a center of a population of brain graphs as proposed in [11], selectively capturing the most common features across population brain graphs. Our gGAN is composed of a graph normalizer network that learns a high-order representation of each brain graph as it gets transformed into a fixed CBT, thereby producing a CBT-based *normalized* brain graph. Our gGAN normalizer is also coupled with an adversarial CBT-guided discriminator which learns how to differentiate between a normalized brain network and the reference CBT. We use our trained normalizer's weights to embed both subjects' brain graphs and the fixed CBT. Next, we compute the residual between each training normalized sample embedding and the target testing normalized sample embedding to eventually identify the most similar training samples for the target prediction task. Below, we articulate the main contributions of our work at different levels:

1. We propose to model each brain graph observation as a transformed version of a population graph template. Hence, each brain graph can be normalized with respect to the fixed template, thereby producing a more individualized brain graph capturing its unique and individual connectivity patterns.
2. We propose the first gGAN that learns how to normalize a set of graphs with respect to a fixed biological connectional template (i.e., a CBT).
3. Our prediction framework of brain network evolution trajectory is a generic framework. Hence, it can be used to foresee both healthy and atypical evolution of brain connectivity from a single timepoint.

2   Proposed Method

In this section, we introduce the key steps of our gGAN-based sample selection strategy for predicting brain graph evolution trajectory over time from a single timepoint. Table 1 displays the mathematical notations that we use throughout this paper. We denote the matrices as boldface capital letters, e.g., $\mathbf{X}$, and scalars as lowercase letters, e.g., n. The transpose operator is denoted as $\mathbf{X}^T$. In the following sections, we will detail each of the four key steps of our prediction framework as shown in Fig. 1.

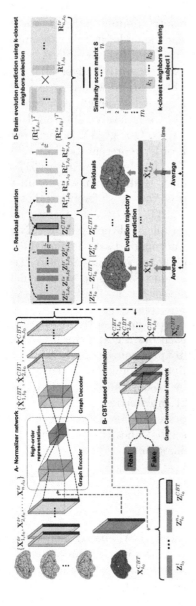

Fig. 1. *Proposed gGAN based sample selection strategy for predicting brain network evolution from baseline timepoint t_0.* (**A**) *Normalizer network.* We develop a gGAN that learns to normalize brain graphs with respect to a fixed connectional brain template (CBT). To do so, we design a three-layer graph convolutional neural network normalizer acting as an encoder and a decoder mimicking a U-net architecture. Our normalizer takes a set of n training subjects $\mathbf{X}_{t_0}^{tr}$ at timepoint t_0 and outputs a set of $\hat{\mathbf{X}}_{t_0}^{CBT}$ that aim to share the same distribution as the population CBT. We use the learned weights from the normalizer's first two layers to embed a set of n_s subjects as well as the CBT $\mathbf{X}_{t_0}^{CBT}$ and the *normalized* brain graph $\hat{\mathbf{X}}_{t_0}^{CBT}$. (**C**) *Residual Generation.* The CBT embedding $\mathbf{Z}_{t_0}^{CBT}$ is subtracted from the testing embeddings $\mathbf{Z}_{t_0}^{ts}$ and training embeddings $\mathbf{Z}_{t_0}^{tr}$, respectively, to generate testing residuals $\mathbf{R}_{t_0}^{ts}$ and training residuals $\mathbf{R}_{t_0}^{tr}$. (**D**) *Brain graph evolution prediction using k-closest neighbors selection.* A similarity score matrix is generated by multiplying the training residuals $\mathbf{R}_{t_0}^{tr}$ by the transpose of the testing residuals $(\mathbf{R}_{t_0}^{ts})^T$ to compute the dot product (similarity) between training subjects $\mathbf{X}^{tr}$ and testing subjects $\mathbf{X}^{ts}$. To predict the brain graph evolution of subject i over timepoints $\{t_1, \ldots, t_T\}$, we select the top k training subjects with the highest similarity scores to the baseline testing subject to predict its evolution trajectory $\{\hat{\mathbf{X}}_{i,t_1}^{ts}, \ldots, \hat{\mathbf{X}}_{i,t_T}^{ts}\}$ by taking the average of these neighboring graphs at $\{t_1, \ldots, t_T\}$.

Connectional Brain Template (CBT) Generation. A CBT is a brain graph template that holds the most shared, representative, and centered brain connectivities across a population of brain graphs. It was first introduced by [11] as an efficient framework to identify discriminative features that help spot out disordered brain connections by comparing healthy and disordered CBTs. Here, we first set out to define the fixed CBT to integrate into our gGAN architecture using an *independent* brain graph dataset composed of n_c subjects.

Let $\mathbf{V}^s_{(i,j)}$ denote the pairwise connectivity between ROIs i and j of a subject s; $1 \leq i, j \leq n_r$. For each pair of ROIs i and j, we define a high-order graph $\mathbf{H}_{(i,j)} \in \mathbb{R}^{n_c \times n_c}$ that holds the pairwise distances across all subjects for each pair of ROIs (i, j) as follows:

$$\mathbf{H}_{(i,j)}(s, s') = \sqrt{(\mathbf{V}^s_{(i,j)} - \mathbf{V}^{s'}_{(i,j)})^2}; \forall 1 \leq s, s' \leq n_c \tag{1}$$

Next, we construct a distance vector $\mathbf{M}_{(i,j)}(s)$ for each subject s that computes the cumulative distance between subject s and other subjects in the independent set for connectivity (i, j). $\mathbf{M}_{(i,j)}(s)$ can be regarded as the topological strength of node s in the high-order graph $\mathbf{H}_{(i,j)}$.

$$\mathbf{M}_{(i,j)}(s) = \sum_{s'=1}^{n_c} \mathbf{H}_{(i,j)}(s, s') = \sum_{s'=1}^{n_c} \sqrt{(\mathbf{V}^s_{(i,j)} - \mathbf{V}^{s'}_{(i,j)})^2}; \forall 1 \leq s, s' \leq n_c \tag{2}$$

Finally, for each brain connectivity (i, j), we select the connectivity weight of the subject achieving the minimum cumulative distance to all other subjects with the assumption that the closest subject's connectivity to all other subjects is indeed the most representative and centered one. Therefore, we define the independent population CBT as follows:

$$\mathbf{X}^{CBT}_{(i,j)} = \mathbf{V}^k_{(i,j)}; \text{ where } k = \min_{1 \leq s \leq n_c} \mathbf{M}_{(i,j)}(s) \tag{3}$$

Overview of CBT-Guided Prediction of Brain Graph Evolution Framework from Baseline. GANs are deep learning frameworks composed of two neural networks: a generator G and a discriminator D [10]. The generator is an encoder and decoder neural network aiming to learn how to generate fake data output that mimics the original data distribution while the discriminator learns how to differentiate between the ground truth data and the fake data produced by the generator. These two networks compete against each other in an adversarial way so that with enough training cycles, the generator learns how to generate more *real-looking* fake samples and the discriminator learns to better discriminate between the real and fake samples. Since this framework has proven its efficiency in translating input data into the desired output domain (e.g., translating T1-MRI to T2-MRI [12]), we propose to modify the generator's task from fake sample production to a *normalization-based* mapping learning from an input space nesting brain graphs to a *fixed* template (i.e., a CBT); and hence, we call

Table 1. Major mathematical notations

Mathematical notation	Definition
n_s	Number of subjects for training and testing our model
n	Total number of training subjects
m	Total number of testing subjects
n_r	Total number of regions of interest in brain
n_c	Total number of independent subjects for CBT generation
$\mathbf{V}^s$	Brain connectivity matrix of subject s
$\mathbf{H}_{(i,j)}$	High-order graph $\in \mathbb{R}^{n_c \times n_c}$ defined for a pair of ROIs i and j
$\mathbf{M}_{(i,j)}(s)$	Node strength of subject s in the high-order graph $\mathbf{H}_{(i,j)}$
$\mathbf{X}^{CBT}$	Connectional brain template connectivity matrix
$\mathbf{X}_{t_0}^{tr} = \{\mathbf{X}_{1,t_0}^{tr}, \dots, \mathbf{X}_{n,t_0}^{tr}\}$	Training brain graph connectivity matrices $\in \mathbb{R}^{n \times n_r \times n_r}$ at t_0
$\mathbf{X}_{t_0}^{ts} = \{\mathbf{X}_{1,t_0}^{ts}, \dots, \mathbf{X}_{m,t_0}^{ts}\}$	Testing brain graph connectivity matrices $\in \mathbb{R}^{m \times n_r \times n_r}$ at t_0
$\hat{\mathbf{X}}_{t_0}^{CBT} = \{\hat{\mathbf{X}}_{1,t_0}^{CBT}, \dots, \hat{\mathbf{X}}_{n,t_0}^{CBT}\}$	CBT-normalized training connectivity matrices $\in \mathbb{R}^{n \times n_r \times n_r}$ at t_0
N	GAN normalizer
D	GAN CBT-guided discriminator
$\mathcal{L}_{full}$	Full loss function
$\mathcal{L}_{adv}$	Adversarial loss function
$\mathcal{L}_{L_1}$	l_1 loss function
λ	Coefficient of l_1 loss
V	A set of n_r nodes
E	A set of m_r directed or undirected edges
l	Index of layer
Y^l	Transformation matrix $\in \mathbb{R}^{n_r \times d_l}$
L	Transformation matrix $\in \mathbb{R}^{m_r \times d_m}$
$\mathcal{N}(i)$	The neighborhood containing all the adjacent nodes of node i
$Y^l(i)$	Filtered signal of node $i \in \mathbb{R}^{d_l}$
F_{ji}^l	Filter generating network
ω^l	Weight parameter
b^l	Bias parameter
$\mathbf{Z}_{t_0}^{tr} = \{\mathbf{Z}_{1,t_0}^{tr}, \dots, \mathbf{Z}_{n,t_0}^{tr}\}$	Training brain graph embeddings $\in \mathbb{R}^{n \times n_r}$ at t_0
$\mathbf{Z}_{t_0}^{ts} = \{\mathbf{Z}_{1,t_0}^{ts}, \dots, \mathbf{Z}_{m,t_0}^{ts}\}$	Testing brain graph embeddings $\in \mathbb{R}^{m \times n_r}$ at t_0
$\mathbf{Z}_{t_0}^{CBT}$	CBT embedding $\in \mathbb{R}^{n_r}$ at t_0
$\mathbf{S}$	Similarity score matrix $\in \mathbb{R}^{m \times n}$
$\mathbf{S}_i$	Similarity score vector of testing subject $i \in \mathbb{R}^n$
$\mathbf{S}_{i,j}$	Similarity score between testing subject i and training subject j
$\mathbf{R}_{t_0}^{tr} = \{\mathbf{R}_{1,t_0}^{tr}, \dots, \mathbf{R}_{n,t_0}^{tr}\}$	Residuals of embedded training subjects at $t_0 \in \mathbb{R}^{n \times n_r}$
$\mathbf{R}_{t_0}^{ts} = \{\mathbf{R}_{1,t_0}^{ts}, \dots, \mathbf{R}_{m,t_0}^{ts}\}$	Residuals of embedded testing subjects at $t_0 \in \mathbb{R}^{m \times n_r}$
$\hat{\mathbf{X}}_{i,t_1}^{ts}$	Predicted test subject i at $t_1 \in \mathbb{R}^{n_r \times n_r}$
$\hat{\mathbf{X}}_{i,t_T}^{ts}$	Predicted test subject i at $t_T \in \mathbb{R}^{n_r \times n_r}$

it the normalizer network N. To the best of our knowledge, our proposed framework is the first gGAN composed of a graph normalizer network, mapping to a fixed output, and a discriminator.

First, we start by training our gGAN to learn how to normalize brain graphs of a set of n training subjects $\mathbf{X}_{t_0}^{tr}$ at timepoint t_0 with respect to a fixed CBT. This will enable us to map each subject's brain graph into a fixed CBT, thereby producing each CBT-normalized brain graph $\hat{\mathbf{X}}_{t_0}^{CBT}$. We use the learned weights from our normalizer's encoding block to embed training subject $\mathbf{X}_{t_0}^{tr}$ and testing subject $\mathbf{X}_{t_0}^{ts}$. We also feed the CBT as an input to the normalizer network to produce a self-normalized embedding $\mathbf{Z}_{t_0}^{CBT}$. Next, for each training subject, we calculate its residual embedding with respect to the CBT by taking the absolute difference between the CBT embedding $\mathbf{Z}_{t_0}^{CBT}$ and the subject normalized embedding $\mathbf{Z}_{t_0}^{tr}$. We also produce similar residual embeddings for the testing subjects. We then use these residual embeddings to define a similarity score matrix computing the dot product between a pair of training and testing residual embeddings $\mathbf{R}_{t_0}^{tr}$ and $\mathbf{R}_{t_0}^{ts}$ (Fig. 1D). Note that this boils down to computing the cosine similarity between two vectors with unitary norms. Finally, for each testing subject, we select the top k training subjects with the highest similarity scores, and predict the evolution trajectory by simply averaging their corresponding training trajectories.

Our gGAN aims to optimize the following loss function:

$$argmin_N max_D \mathcal{L}_{adv} = \mathbb{E}_{x \sim p_{(CBT)}}[log D(x)] + \mathbb{E}_{\hat{x} \sim p_{(\mathbf{X^{tr}})}}[log(1 - D(N(\hat{x})))] \quad (4)$$

To improve the quality of the CBT-normalized brain graph, we propose to preserve each subject's embedding scheme by adding an L_1 loss term that minimizes the distance between each normalized subject $\hat{\mathbf{X}}_{t_0}^{tr}$ and its related ground-truth brain graph $\mathbf{X}_{t_0}^{tr}$. Therefore our full loss function is expressed as follows:

$$\mathcal{L}_{full} = \mathcal{L}_{adv} + \lambda \mathcal{L}_{L1}(N) \quad (5)$$

The Normalizer Network. As shown in Fig. 1A, our proposed normalizer network is composed of three-layer graph convolutional neural network (GCN) inspired by the dynamic edge convolution operation introduced in [13] and mimicking a U-net architecture [14] with skip connections that enhance brain graph normalization and thus improve the quality of our normalized graph embeddings [15]. The normalizer takes a set of $\mathbf{X}_{t_0}^{tr}$ training subjects as input and outputs a set of $\hat{\mathbf{X}}_{t_0}^{CBT}$ which share the same distribution as the fixed CBT. Hence, our normalizer's encoder not only learns a deep non-linear mapping between any subject's brain graph and the fixed reference graph (i.e., CBT) but also a high-order embedding of the input with regard to the CBT.

Our normalizer contains three graph convolutional neural network layers regularized using batch normalization [16] and dropout [17] to the output of each layer. These two operations undeniably help simplify and optimize the network training. For instance, batch normalization was proven to accelerate network training through a rapid convergence of the loss function while dropout was proven to eliminate the risk of overfitting.

CBT-Guided Discriminator. We display the architecture of the discriminator in Fig. 1B. The discriminator is also a graph neural network inspired by [13]. Our proposed discriminator is a two-layer graph neural network that takes as input a concatenation of the normalizer's output $\hat{\mathbf{X}}_{t_0}^{CBT}$ and the CBT. The discriminator outputs a value between 0 and 1 characterizing *the realness* of the normalizer's output. To improve our discriminator's ability to differentiate between the fixed CBT and CBT-normalized samples, we design our gGAN's loss function so that it maximizes the discriminator's output value for the CBT and minimize it for each $\hat{\mathbf{X}}_{t_0}^{CBT}$.

Dynamic Graph-Based Edge Convolution. Each of the graph convolutional layers of our gGAN architecture uses a dynamic graph-based edge convolution operation proposed by [13]. In particular, let $G = (V, E)$ be a directed or undirected graph where V is a set of n_r ROIs and $E \subseteq V \times V$ is a set of m_r edges. Let l be the layer index in the neural network. We define $Y^l : V \to \mathbb{R}^{d_l}$ and $L : E \to \mathbb{R}^{d_m}$ which can be respectively considered as two transformation matrices (i.e., functions) where $Y^l \in \mathbb{R}^{n_r \times d_l}$ and $L \in \mathbb{R}^{m_r \times d_m}$. d_m and d_l are dimensionality indexes. We define by $\mathcal{N}(i) = \{j; (j, i) \in E\} \cup \{i\}$ of a node i the neighborhood containing all the adjacent ROIs.

$$Y^l(i) = \frac{1}{\mathcal{N}(i)} \sum_{j \in \mathcal{N}(i)} \Theta_{ji}^l Y^{l-1}(j) + b^l,$$

where $\Theta_{ji}^l = F^l(L(j, i); \omega^l)$. We note that $F^l : \mathbb{R}^{d_m} \to \mathbb{R}^{d_l \times d_l - 1}$ is the filter generating network, ω^l and b^l are model parameters that are updated only during training.

Embedding the Training, Testing Subjects and the CBT. We recall that our gGAN's main purpose is to (i) learn how to normalize brain graphs with respect to a fixed CBT and (ii) learn a CBT-normalized embedding. As shown in Fig. 1A, once we train the normalizer network using our training set, we produce the embeddings of the training subjects, testing subjects, and the CBT (i.e., self-embedding). We define $\mathbf{Z}_{t_0}^{tr}$ and $\mathbf{Z}_{t_0}^{ts}$ as the results of our embedding operation of training and testing data, respectively. Given that our normalizer encodes brain graphs and extracts their high-order representative features in a low-dimensional space with respect to the CBT, we assume that such embeddings might be better representations of the brain graphs as they capture individual traits that distinguish them from the population 'average'.

Residual Computation and Sample Similarity Estimation. As shown in Fig. 1C, we obtain the residuals between the embedding of each brain graph and the CBT embedding by calculating their absolute differences. Next, we use these residuals to define the similarity score matrix $\mathbf{S} \in \mathbb{R}^{n \times m}$, where each element $\mathbf{S}_{i,j}$ expresses the pairwise similarity between a row-wise testing subject $\mathbf{X}_i^{ts}$ and a column-wise training subject $\mathbf{X}_j^{tr}$. Specifically, to obtain the similarity matrix, we calculate the dot product of the matrix composed of the vertically stacked transposed residual embeddings of testing subjects and the matrix composed of the vertically stacked residuals of training subjects. As stated in [18], the dot product of two normalized matrices provides the similarity between them. As a result, the greater the value of the element of the similarity matrix is, the most similar the related subjects are. We note the training and testing residuals as $\mathbf{R}_{t_0}^{tr}$ and $\mathbf{R}_{t_0}^{ts}$, respectively, and we define them as follows:

$$\mathbf{R}_{t_0}^{tr} = |\mathbf{Z}_{t_0}^{tr} - \mathbf{Z}_{t_0}^{CBT}| \tag{6}$$

$$\mathbf{R}_{t_0}^{ts} = |\mathbf{Z}_{t_0}^{ts} - \mathbf{Z}_{t_0}^{CBT}| \tag{7}$$

Brain Graph Evolution Prediction Using Top k-Closest Neighbor Selection. Assuming that the top k-closest neighbors of the testing subjects will remain neighbors at the following timepoints $t \in \{t_1, \ldots, t_T\}$ [5,6], we predict the brain graph evolution by selecting its most similar k training subjects at baseline. Next, we predict the testing subject's brain evolution by averaging its corresponding training subjects' graphs (i.e., neighbors) at follow-up timepoints. We select the top k subjects for each testing subject using their highest corresponding elements in the similarity score matrix. To predict the evolution of a baseline testing brain graph i, we sort its derived row $\mathbf{S}_i$ vector in the similarity score matrix $\mathbf{S}$ and select the top k-samples with the highest similarity scores. Given a baseline testing brain graph $\mathbf{X}_{i,t_0}^{ts}$, we foresee the evolution of its connectivity $\hat{\mathbf{X}}_{i,t}^{ts}$ at later timepoints $t \in \{t_1, \ldots, t_T\}$ by averaging the k selected training brain graphs at each timepoint t.

3   Results and Discussion

Evaluation Dataset. We used 114 subjects from the OASIS-2[1] longitudinal dataset [19]. This set consists of a longitudinal collection of 150 subjects aged 60 to 96. Each subject was scanned on two or more visits, separated by at least one year. For each subject, we construct a cortical morphological network derived from cortical thickness measure using structural T1-w MRI as proposed in [20]. Each cortical hemisphere is parcellated into 35 ROIs using Desikan-Killiany cortical atlas. We built our gGAN with PyTorch Geometric library [21] and trained it using 3-fold cross-validation applied on $n = 91$ training subjects. We randomly selected $n_c = 23$ subjects from the OASIS-2 dataset [19] to generate a CBT using the netNorm [11].

Parameter Setting. We varied the number of selected neighboring samples k from $\{2, \ldots, 10\}$ for the target prediction task. In Table 2, we report prediction mean absolute error averaged across k. We set the normalizer's loss hyperparameter to 100 which is $\times 100$ the adversarial loss. Also, we chose ADAM [22] as our default optimizer and set the learning rate at 0.001 for the normalizer and 0.01 for the discriminator. We set the exponential decay rate for the first moment estimates (i.e., beta 1) to 0.5, and the exponential decay rate for the second-moment estimates (i.e., beta 2) to 0.999 for the ADAM optimizer. Finally, we trained our gGAN for 700 epochs using NVIDIA Tesla V100 GPU.

---

[1] https://www.oasis-brains.org/.

Comparison Methods and Evaluation. We benchmarked our framework against three comparison methods for neighboring sample selection (SS) using: (i) the original graph features (OF) which is a baseline method that computes the dot product similarities between *vectorized* connectivity matrices of testing and training graphs as in [7]. (ii) CBT-based residuals (SS-CR), which is a variation of SS-OF where we first produce residuals by computing the absolute difference between the *vectorized* brain graphs and the *vectorized* CBT, then compute the dot product between the produced residuals of training and testing subjects. Note that in these two variants, we are not producing any embeddings of the brain graphs. (iii) CBT-normalized embeddings (SS-CE), which is a variant of our method that discards the residual generation step (Fig. 1C) and predicts the brain graph evolution by computing the dot product between the embeddings of the training graphs and the testing graphs by gGAN.

All benchmarks were performed by calculating the mean absolute error (MAE) between the ground-truth and predicted brain graphs of the testing subjects at t_1 and t_2 timepoints and varying the number of selected training samples k in the range of $\{2, \ldots, 10\}$ for a better evaluation. Table 2 shows the results of MAE-based prediction accuracy for t_1 and t_2 timepoints.

Table 2. Prediction accuracy using mean absolute error (MAE) of our proposed method and comparison methods at t_1 and t_2 timepoints. We report the MAE averaged across $k \in \{2, \ldots, 10\}$.

	t_1		t_2	
Method	Mean MAE ± std	Best MAE	Mean MAE ± std	Best MAE
SS-OF	0.04469 ± 0.00247	0.04194	0.05368 ± 0.00449	0.04825
SS-CR	0.04417 ± 0.002026	0.04225	0.05045 ± 0.000942	0.04939
SS-CE	0.04255 ± 0.001835	**0.04064**	0.04948 ± 0.002480	0.04707
Ours	**0.04237 ± 0.001679**	0.04075	**0.04882 ± 0.002517**	**0.04624**

Our proposed brain graph framework integrating both CBT-based normalization and CBT-based residual computation steps outperformed baseline methods at both timepoints. Our method also achieved the best MAE in foreseeing the brain graph evolution at t_2. However, the best MAE for prediction at t_1 was achieved by SS-CE, which uses the gGAN normalizer network and discards the residual computation with respect to the CBT. This might be due to the fact that subjects are more likely to be more divergent from the center at t_2 than t_1. Overall, our sample selection using CBT-guided embedded residuals achieved the best performance in foreseeing brain graph evolution trajectory and showed that normalizing brain graphs with respect to a fixed graph template such as a CBT is indeed a successful strategy outperforming methods using the original brain graphs.

Limitations and Future Work. Although our graph prediction framework achieved the lowest average MAE against benchmarking methods in predicting brain graph evolution trajectory from a single observation, it has a few limitations. So far, the proposed method only handles uni-modal brain graphs with a single edge type. In our future work, we aim to generalize our gGAN normalizer to handle brain multigraphs. In a multigraph representation of the brain wiring, the interaction between two anatomical regions of interest, namely the multigraph nodes, is encoded in a set of edges of multiple types. Each edge type is defined using a particular measure for modeling the relationship between brain ROIs such as functional connectivity derived from resting state functional MRI or morphological similarity derived from structural T1-weighted MRI. Furthermore, our framework can only operate on undirected and positive brain graphs. Extending our framework to handle directed and signed networks would constitute a big leap in generalizing our approach to different biological and connectomic datasets.

4   Conclusion

In this paper, we proposed a novel brain graph evolution trajectory prediction framework based on a gGAN architecture comprising a normalizer network with respect to a fixed connectional brain template (CBT) to first learn a topology-preserving (using graph convolutional layers) brain graph representation. We formalized the prediction task as a sample selection task based on the idea of using the residual distance of each sample from a fixed population center (CBT) to capture the unique and individual connectivity patterns of each subject in the population. Our results showed that our brain graph prediction framework from baseline can remarkably boost the prediction accuracy compared to the baseline methods. Our framework is generic and can be used in predicting both typical and disordered brain evolution trajectories. Hence, in our future work we will evaluate our framework on large-scale connectomic datasets with various brain disorders such as brain dementia. We will investigate the potential of *predicted* evolution trajectories in boosting neurological disordered diagnosis.

Acknowledgement. I. Rekik is supported by the European Union's Horizon 2020 research and innovation programme under the Marie Sklodowska-Curie Individual Fellowship grant agreement No 101003403 (http://basira-lab.com/normnets/).

References

1. Querbes, O., et al.: Early diagnosis of Alzheimer's disease using cortical thickness: impact of cognitive reserve. Brain **132**, 2036 (2009)
2. Leifer, B.P.: Early diagnosis of Alzheimer's disease: clinical and economic benefits. J. Am. Geriatr. Soc. **51**, S281–S288 (2003)
3. Grober, E., Bang, S.: Sentence comprehension in Alzheimer's disease. Dev. Neuropsychol. **11**, 95–107 (1995)
4. Payan, A., Montana, G.: Predicting Alzheimer's disease: a neuroimaging study with 3d convolutional neural networks. arXiv preprint arXiv:1502.02506 (2015)

5. Gafuroğlu, C., Rekik, I., et al.: Joint prediction and classification of brain image evolution trajectories from baseline brain image with application to early dementia. In: International Conference on Medical Image Computing and Computer-Assisted Intervention, pp. 437–445 (2018)

6. Rekik, I., Li, G., Yap, P., Chen, G., Lin, W., Shen, D.: Joint prediction of longitudinal development of cortical surfaces and white matter fibers from neonatal MRI. Neuroimage **152**, 411–424 (2017)

7. Ezzine, B.E., Rekik, I.: Learning-guided infinite network atlas selection for predicting longitudinal brain network evolution from a single observation. In: Shen, D., et al. (eds.) MICCAI 2019. LNCS, vol. 11765, pp. 796–805. Springer, Cham (2019). https://doi.org/10.1007/978-3-030-32245-8_88

8. Allassonnière, S., Trouvé, A., Younes, L.: Geodesic shooting and diffeomorphic matching via textured meshes. In: Rangarajan, A., Vemuri, B., Yuille, A.L. (eds.) EMMCVPR 2005. LNCS, vol. 3757, pp. 365–381. Springer, Heidelberg (2005). https://doi.org/10.1007/11585978_24

9. Trouvé, A.: An approach of pattern recognition through infinite dimensional group action (1995)

10. Goodfellow, I.J., et al.: Generative adversarial networks (2014)

11. Dhifallah, S., Rekik, I.: Estimation of connectional brain templates using selective multi-view network normalization. Med. Image Anal. **59**, 101567 (2020)

12. Yang, Q., et al.: MRI cross-modality image-to-image translation. Sci. Rep. **10**, 1–18 (2020)

13. Simonovsky, M., Komodakis, N.: Dynamic edge-conditioned filters in convolutional neural networks on graphs. CoRR abs/1704.02901 (2017)

14. Ronneberger, O., Fischer, P., Brox, T.: U-Net: convolutional networks for biomedical image segmentation. CoRR abs/1505.04597 (2015)

15. Mao, X., Shen, C., Yang, Y.B.: Image restoration using very deep convolutional encoder-decoder networks with symmetric skip connections. In: Advances in Neural Information Processing Systems, pp. 2802–2810 (2016)

16. Ioffe, S., Szegedy, C.: Batch normalization: accelerating deep network training by reducing internal covariate shift. arXiv preprint arXiv:1502.03167 (2015)

17. Xiao, T., Li, H., Ouyang, W., Wang, X.: Learning deep feature representations with domain guided dropout for person re-identification. In: Proceedings of the IEEE Conference on Computer Vision And Pattern Recognition, pp. 1249–1258 (2016)

18. Ding, C.H.: A similarity-based probability model for latent semantic indexing. In: Proceedings of the 22nd Annual International ACM SIGIR Conference on Research and Development in Information Retrieval, pp. 58–65 (1999)

19. Marcus, D.S., Fotenos, A.F., Csernansky, J.G., Morris, J.C., Buckner, R.L.: Open access series of imaging studies: longitudinal MRI data in nondemented and demented older adults. J. Cogn. Neurosci. **22**, 2677–2684 (2010)

20. Mahjoub, I., Mahjoub, M.A., Rekik, I.: Brain multiplexes reveal morphological connectional biomarkers fingerprinting late brain dementia states. Sci. Rep. **8**, 4103 (2018)

21. Fey, M., Lenssen, J.E.: Fast graph representation learning with PyTorch geometric. CoRR abs/1903.02428 (2019)

22. Kingma, D.P., Ba, J.: Adam: a method for stochastic optimization (2014)

Longitudinal Prediction of Radiation-Induced Anatomical Changes of Parotid Glands During Radiotherapy Using Deep Learning

Donghoon Lee, Sadegh Alam, Saad Nadeem, Jue Jiang, Pengpeng Zhang, and Yu-Chi Hu[✉]

Department of Medical Physics, Memorial Sloan Kettering Cancer Center, New York, USA
huj@mskcc.org

Abstract. During a course of radiotherapy, patients may have weight loss and radiation induced anatomical changes. To avoid delivering harmful dose to normal organs, the treatment may need adaptation according to the change. In this study, we proposed a novel deep neural network for predicting parotid glands (PG) anatomical changes by using the displacement fields (DFs) between the planning CT and weekly cone beam computed tomography (CBCT) acquired during the treatment. Sixty three HN patients treated with volumetric modulated arc therapy of 70 Gy in 35 fractions were retrospectively studied. We calculated DFs between week 1–3 CBCT and the planning CT by a B-spline deformable image registration algorithm. The resultant DFs were subsequently used as input to a novel network combining convolutional neural networks and recurrent neural networks for predicting the DF between the Week 4–6 CBCT and the planning CT. Finally, we reconstructed the warped PG contour using the predicted DF. For evaluation, we calculated DICE coefficient and mean volume difference by comparing the predicted PG contours, and manual contours at weekly CBCT. The average DICE was 0.82 (week 4), 0.81 (week 5), and 0.80 (week 6) and the average of volume difference between predict contours and manual contours was 1.85 cc (week 4), 2.20 cc (week 5) and 2.51 cc (week 6). In conclusion, the proposed deep neural network combining CNN and RNN was capable of predicting anatomical and volumetric changes of the PG with clinically acceptable accuracy.

Keywords: Parotid gland · Displacement vector field · Deep neural network

1 Introduction

Radiation therapy (RT) is one of the standard therapeutic modalities for head and neck (HN) cancer patients. It is technically challenging, requiring delivery of high tumoricidal dose to target while minimizing the dose to adjacent critical structures and organ at risk (OAR) [1, 2]. Intensity modulated radiotherapy (IMRT) and volumetric modulated arch therapy (VMAT) are considered standard external beam RT methods for treating HN cancer [1–5]. These methods enable delivering high radiation dose to tumor volumes while minimizing dose to adjacent structures, such as parotid gland (PG) and spinal cord, with resultant reduction in toxicities to patients [6].

© Springer Nature Switzerland AG 2020
I. Rekik et al. (Eds.): PRIME 2020, LNCS 12329, pp. 123–132, 2020.
https://doi.org/10.1007/978-3-030-59354-4_12

However, the OARs and the target may change their shape and volume over the course of treatment, resulting in clinically relevant deviations of delivered dose from the planning dose [7–9]. Especially, PG, which is extremely sensitive to radiation, shows significant volume reduction due to patient weight loss [10–13]. For examples, Ricchetti et al. [11] concluded that, among the OARs which underwent volume reduction, the PGs changed the most with implications for daily dose distribution, and Nishimaru et al. [12] reported the volume decrease of about 30% ($p < 0.001$) for the PGs in the third week of 4-week course of IMRT.

To overcome clinical uncertainty regarding anatomical changes during RT, treatment procedures are predominantly adopting a cone-beam computed tomography (CBCT) based image guided radiotherapy (IGRT). Fast online setup corrections can be performed immediately after image acquisition prior to irradiation [12–15]. However, dealing with deformations is an on-going challenge which is mostly compensated by re-planning, since deformations cannot be corrected by simple treatment couch shifts.

When deciding re-planning, the deformation of OARs and targets is one of the main factors. Reasonable deformation prediction of an organ with possibly large changes can be of great help in developing a treatment strategy. Therefore, this study aims to develop a technique that can help in establishing an overall treatment strategy by predicting the longitudinal PG anatomical changes, which is one of the largest uncertainties during the HN RT, from a relatively early treatment stage.

2 Related Works

Recently, longitudinal image frame prediction by deep learning has attracted great interest in the field of medical imaging as well as computer vision. For example, Zhang et al. and Wang et al. presented approaches to predict lung tumor anatomical changes by deep learning models combining CNN and RNN [16, 17]. Shi et al. applied CNN and RNN for predicting rainfall intensity [18]. CNN and RNN models were also used for predicting video sequences [18, 20, 21]. Moreover, attempts were also made to predict image frames using the generative adversarial network (GAN) [22]. The research in this field was mainly dominated by deep learning models such as convolutional long short-term memory (LSTM) and auto encoder. Convolution LSTM has the advantage of preserving spatial structure in both the input-to-state and state-to-state transitions [16–19]. Encoder-decoder network has been commonly used for image-to-image translation [16]. Since the encoder-decoder model can extract features representing the non-linear relationship between input and output, many attempts have been made to apply it to longitudinal prediction [16–20]. However, it is difficult to train time series of spatial data, in which the geometry of input and output differs greatly, by using conventional encoder-decoder model only. Therefore, recently, studies have been conducted to integrate convolutional LSTM and encoder-decoder models for training successful longitudinal prediction [20, 21]. To this end, GANs have also been incorporated to alleviate the blur phenomenon that usually occurs in convolutional LSTM and auto-encoder [16, 22].

In contrast to previous work, we focused on improving longitudinal prediction by applying deep learning to displacement fields (DFs). Rather than using the noisy and artifact ridden CBCT images for this purpose, we believe it is feasible to analyze clearer patterns of anatomical changes in sequential DFs which represent the regularized smooth movements of tissues. The predicted DF can be further used for other RT tasks such as dose accumulation, contour, and image prediction. To the best of our knowledge, this is the first attempt at using DF for end-to-end training and prediction in longitudinal medical image analysis.

3 Materials and Methods

3.1 Dataset

Sixty-three HN cancer patients treated with VMAT of 70 Gy in 35 fractions were retrospectively studied. Each patient's data contained the planning CT, planning contours and weekly CBCTs. Among the 63 patients, 53 had up to week 4 CBCT, 43 had up to week 5 and 33 had up to week 6. We used 10 patients with up to week 6 CBCT as the testing set and the rest of the data was used for training. We calculated DF between week 1–6 CBCT (moving) and the planning CT (fixed) by a multi resolution B-spline deformable image registration (DIR) algorithm. DIR was performed using Plastimatch, an open source software for DIR [23]. In the initial stage of DIR, the CBCT and planning CT images are aligned by matching the geometric center of images. Next, a single stage of rigid registration was performed to ensure that CBCT and planning CT images are in the same position. Finally, three stages of multi resolution B-spline registration were performed, where the image resolution was 4, 2, and 1 mm^3 and the B-spline grid spacing was 40 20 and 10 mm at each stage respectively. To improve efficiency and accuracy of predicting future PG deformation during the RT, we focused on the DF of PG regions during the training proposed model. We extracted regions of interest (ROI) of DFs in PG regions by masking DFs with morphologically dilated PG contours to contain enough DF information surrounding the PG region. Figure 1 described data processing including DFs calculation and ROI extracting process.

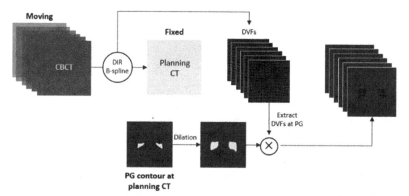

Fig. 1. Schematic image for DFs calculation and Extracting DFs of PG regions. We used multi resolution B-spline DIR algorithms and applying morphological dilation to PG contour data to including enough DFs information for PG regions.

DFs between the planning CT and week 1–3 CBCT were used for input of a novel neural network combining convolutional neural networks (CNNs) and recurrent neural networks (RNNs) to predict the DF between week 4–6 CBCT and the planning CT.

3.2 Deep Learning Model

The proposed model, depicted in Fig. 2, is composed of 3D CNNs and RNNs. The role of CNNs is to extract features of weekly volumetric DFs by the convolutional encoder, and to restore the predicted DF by a convolutional decoder. CNN model contains residual building blocks based on the residual network [24]. The RNNs built with Gated Recurrent Unit (GRU) analyzes the longitudinal sequential features embeddings from the CNN [25]. The output of the RNN then is fed to the decoder to predict DF of a future week. In the case of week 4 prediction, Output features from the first GRU were fed to the convolutional decoder to restore the predicted week 4 DFs. In case of prediction of a later week (5 or 6) predicted DF of the previous week and embedding features from the previous GRU were cascading down to the next GRU block for further analysis. Mathematically, the cascading network part can be written as

$$\hat{y}_t = g_t\left(\hat{y}_{t-1}, h(x_{1,\ldots,k})\right), \text{ for } t > k+1$$

where $h(x_{1,\ldots,k})$ is the feature embeddings from week 1 to week k (k = 3 in this study) g_t is the encoder, GRU, and decoder for predicting week t DF, $\hat{y}_t$.

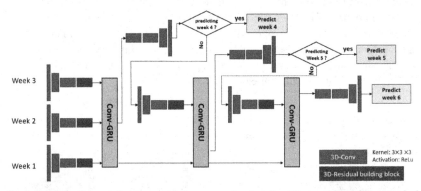

Fig. 2. Schematic diagram for proposed deep neural networks. We combined 3D convolutional encoder and decoder structures and GRU. For precise feature extraction of weekly DFs, we added residual building block to convolutional encoder part. Longitudinal sequential features of weekly DFs were analyzed through GRUs

The kernel size for convolution was $3 \times 3 \times 3$ and the stride was $2 \times 2 \times 2$. The number of feature channels at first convolution encoder layer was 16 and doubled at each convolution layer.

Conventional recurrent unit including GRU and LSTM are designed for processing text data rather than images. Using them on multi-dimensional data such as 3D images and DFs, without any modification causes difficulties in training due to memory issues.

Therefore, we used convolutional GRU, which is characterized by substituting matrix multiplication to convolution operation for training multidimensional sequential data such as DFs [26].

Equation (1–2) are loss functions for the proposed model. Equation (1) is a loss function for the week 4 DFs prediction. L2 loss and Jacobian regularization between the predicted week 4 DF and actual week 4 DF were used. For predicting week 5 and 6 DFs, we ensemble loss functions of the week 4, 5 and 6 as described at Eq. (2). To focused on week 5 and 6 prediction, we used weighting factor. In case of week 5 prediction, the weighting factors, λ_q, were 0.2 (q = 4), and 0.8 (q = 5) and for week 6 predictions, λ_q were 0.1 (q = 4, 5) and 0.8 (q = 6).

$$Loss_t = \frac{1}{N} \sum_{i=1}^{N} \left(\left\| y_t(i) - \hat{y}_t(i) \right\|_2^2 + \left| J(y_t(i)) - J(\hat{y}_t(i)) \right| \right), \text{for } t = k + 1 \quad (1)$$

$$Loss_t = \sum_{q=k+1}^{t} \lambda_q \left(\frac{1}{N} \sum_{i=1}^{N} \left(\left\| y_q(i) - \hat{y}_q(i) \right\|_2^2 + \left| J(y_q(i)) - J(\hat{y}_q(i)) \right| \right) \right), \text{for } t > k + 1$$

$$(2)$$

Where, $J(\cdot)$ is the determinant of voxel-wise Jacobian matrix [27]. We trained proposed model up to 600 epochs with adaptive momentum estimation (ADAM) optimizer and the learning rate was 0.001. Finally, we reconstructed the warped PG contour using the predicted DFs and invert warp function.

3.3 Evaluation

To evaluate results, we used the dice similarity coefficient (DICE) and volume difference (ΔV) for accuracy of predicting anatomical and volumetric changes of PG. We compared the predictions from the proposed method to the extrapolated predictions from linear regression. Voxel-specific linear regression models [17] of the voxel displacements were trained with week 1 to week 3 DFs to extrapolate week 4 to week 6 DFs. We performed DIR for the testing cases to obtain the reference DFs for the comparison. For DICE evaluations, manual contours from clinical experts at weekly CBCT were considered as the ground truth (GT). ΔV between the manual contours and the propagated contours by DIR, by the extrapolated DFs, and by the predicted DFs.

4 Results

Figure 3 shows two examples of predicted contours derived from the predicted DFs. Background images are planning CT. Predicted and GT contours of week 4, 5 and 6 are shown in the first, second, and third columns respectively. Green contours are the PG contour at the planning CT as the reference to the initial PG before the treatment, the red contour is the manual contour at the weekly CBCT. Yellow contours are the propagated contour by DIR. Blue contours are the predicted contours by the proposed method for the given week. For comparison, contours predicted by a linear regression model of DF are shown in Cyan. The DICE of the proposed method was indicated at the upper left of Fig. 3. As shown in the results, the shape and volume of PG are significantly changed during the RT. Linear regression (cyan contour) was to some extent possible to predict the tendency of volume changes of the PG, but could not accurately predict the irregular PG deformation for each patient. Further, linear regression can misplace the location of the PG as demonstrated in the first example of Fig. 3. As shown in the sagittal and coronal view of the first example, the prediction by linear regression was overlaid with bony structures. On the other hand, the proposed method generated PG anatomical shape closely resembling the GT as well as tendency of volume changes.

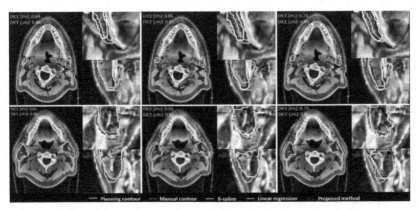

Fig. 3. Two examples of testing cases. Green contour is the planning PG contour at the planning CT (displayed), the red contour is the manual contour from weekly CBCT, and yellow, cyan and blue contour is the predicted contoured by the DIR, linear regression, and proposed method, respectively. (Color figure online)

Figure 4 shows the box plots of DICE results. Red, blue, yellow and green boxes indicated results of planning contours, propagated contours by linear regression and propagated contours from the proposed method, and propagated contours by DIR, respectively. Average DICE and p value of ipsilateral PG (iPG) of the proposed method were 0.81 ± 0.04, 0.80 ± 0.05, and 0.78 ± 0.07, for week 4, 5, and 6 respectively, and contralateral PG (cPG) were 0.84 ± 0.02, 0.8 3± 0.03, and 0.80 ± 0.04. The results of the proposed method were significantly better than linear regression (p = 0.013 for week 5, p = 0.009 for week 6), and there was no significant difference (p = 0.11 for week5, p = 0.28 for week6) between our proposed method and results from DIR with real weekly images. The lower DICE of planning contours confirmed PG anatomical changes during the treatment. We observed that DICE accuracy of linear regression decreased as we predicted further into future. On the contrast, the proposed method consistently achieved relatively high DICE value with smaller variation.

Table 1 is the mean and standard deviation of ΔV. The ΔV of the proposed method was less than 3 cc, and ΔV of iPG, which have large deformation due to high radiation exposure, was larger than cPG. The ΔV of PG was slightly increased as the prediction time point increased from week 4 to 6. The ΔV derived by linear regression showed relatively worse ΔV compared to proposed method.

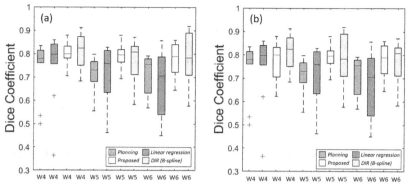

Fig. 4. Results of the dice coefficient. (a) DICE of ipsilateral PGs and (b) DICE of contralateral PGs. Red box indicated results of planning contours, blue box indicated results of linear regression and yellow box is the result of the proposed method. Each graph has three groups including results of week 4, 5 and 6 predictions. (Color figure online)

Table 1. Mean, standard deviation and *p-value* of volume difference (cc) between manual contours and propagated contours by DIR, linear regression and the proposed method

	DIR		Linear regression		Proposed	
	iPG	cPG	iPG	cPG	iPG	cPG
Week 4	1.95 ± 1.14	1.09 ± 0.94	2.74 ± 1.69	1.80 ± 1.63	2.06 ± 1.64	1.64 ± 0.86
Week 5	2.13 ± 1.88	1.53 ± 1.52	3.47 ± 2.47	2.70 ± 1.70	2.28 ± 2.50	2.12 ± 1.71
Week 6	2.06 ± 1.68	1.77 ± 1.49	3.74 ± 2.84	3.34 ± 2.19	2.82 ± 2.19	2.20 ± 1.58

5 Discussion

According to previous studies, one of the most common toxicities of HN RT is Xerostomia and hyposalivation, including difficulties in swallowing, speaking and loss of taste and caries with therefore a direct impact on patient quality of life [28, 29]. Approximately 70% of patients receiving HN cancer RT develop hyposalivation with significant alternation in volume [28]. The degree of xerostomia is largely dependent on radiation dose and the volume of the salivary gland that is in the radiation field. For these reasons, early prediction of the PG anatomical shape is important for minimizing side effects result from excessive radiation exposure to PG. In this study, we developed a deep learning model for longitudinal prediction of the PG anatomical changes during the RT. Our deep learning model is composed of three stages depending on the prediction DF's time point. As the time point of DFs to be predicted increases from week 4 to 6, the network becomes deeper through cascading a series of convolutional GRU for the analysis of sequential DFs. The reason why the model was designed in multiple stages is that the availability of weekly CBCT for each patient is different.

The loss function at a given time point is constructed to give higher weight to the loss from the time point of prediction and less weights for loss from previous time points.

Optimization of the weighting factor requires more investigation. We used Jacobian as a regularization of the loss function with respect to volume change. Since DF can be used to derive other valuable information in the course of radiotherapy, we used DFs alone for end-to-end training and prediction so that the predicted DF has similar magnitude and direction to the DF obtained from registration of real images.

Our proposed technique achieved high DICE and low ΔV between the predicted PG contours and the manual contours. As the prediction time point changed from week 4 to 6, the reduction in DICE, which occurred significantly in linear regression, did not appear to be severe in the proposed method.

Furthermore, it is expected that better prediction will be possible if advanced DIR algorithms are used for DFs calculation for training the proposed deep neural networks.

6 Conclusion

The proposed method can effectively predict anatomical changes of the parotid glands, which is commonly considered as an organ at risk exhibiting significant shrinkage for head and neck cancer patients undergoing radiotherapy. The prediction of anatomical changes of parotid glands was clinically acceptable thus, it is expected that the proposed method can contribute to establishing a treatment strategy such as re-planning to reduce radiation-induced toxicities and improve treatment outcomes.

References

1. Johnston, M., Clifford, S., Bromley, R., Back, M., Oliver, L., Eade, T.: Volumetric-modulated arc therapy in head and neck radiotherapy: a planning comparison using simultaneous integrated boost for nasopharynx and oropharynx carcinoma. Clin. Oncol. **23**(8), 503–511 (2011)
2. Baskar, R., Kuo Lee, K.A., Yeo, R., Yeoh, K.-W.: Cancer and radiation therapy: current advances and future directions. Int. J. Med. Sci. **9**(3), 193–199 (2012)
3. Alvarez-Moret, J., Pohl, F., Koelbl, O., Dobler, B.: Evaluation of volumetric modulated arc therapy (VMAT) with Oncentra MasterPlan n® for the treatment of head and neck cancer. Radiat. Oncol. **5**, 110 (2010)
4. Bhide, S.A., Nutting, C.M.: Advances in radiotherapy for head and neck cancer. Oral Oncol. **46**(6), 439–441 (2010)
5. Brown, E., Owen, R., Harden, F., et al.: Predicting the need for adaptive radiotherapy in head and neck cancer. Radiother. Oncol. **116**(1), 57–63 (2015)
6. Alam, S., et al.: Quantification of accumulated dose and associated anatomical changes of esophagus using weekly Magnetic Resonance Imaging acquired during radiotherapy of locally advanced lung cancer. J. Phys. Imaging Radiat. Oncol. Accepted for publication (2020)
7. Stoll, M., Giske, K., Debus, J., Bendl, R., Stoiber, E.M.: The frequency of re-planning and its variability dependent on the modification of the re-planning criteria and IGRT correction strategy in head and neck IMRT. Radiat. Oncol. **9**, 175 (2014)
8. Giske, K., et al.: Local setup errors in image-guided radiotherapy for head and neck cancer patients immobilized with a custom-made device. Int. J. Radiat. Oncol. Biol. Phys. **80**(2), 582–589 (2011)

9. Craig, T., Battista, J., Van Dyk, J.: Limitation of a convolution method for modeling geometric uncertainties in radiation therapy I. The effect of shift invariance. Med. Phys. **30**(8), 2001–2011 (2003)

10. Fiorentino, A., et al.: Parotid gland volumetric changes during intensity-modulated radiotherapy in head and neck cancer. Br. J. Radiol. **85**(1018), 1415–1419 (2012)

11. Ricchetti, F., et al.: Volumetric change of selected organs at risk during IMRT for oropharyngeal cancer. Int. J. Radiat. Oncol. Biol. Phys. **80**(1), 161–168 (2011)

12. Nishimaura, Y., Nakamatsu, K., Shibata, T., Kanamori, S., Koike, R., Okumura, M.: Importance of the initial volume of parotid glands in xerostomia for patients with head and neck cancer treated with IMRT. Jpn. J. Clin. Oncol. **35**(3), 375–379 (2005)

13. Zhang, L., et al.: Multiple regions-of-interest analysis of setup uncertainties for head-and-neck cancer radiotherapy. Int. J. Radiat. Oncol. Biol. Phys. **64**(5), 1559–1569 (2006)

14. Ploat, B., Wilbert, J., Baier, K., Flentje, M., Guckenberger, M.: Nonrigid patient setup errors in the head-and-neck region. Strahlenther. Onkol. **183**(9), 506–511 (2007)

15. Elstrom, U.V., Wysocka, B.A., Muren, L.P., Petersen, J.B., Grau, C.: Daily kV cone-beam CT and deformable image registration as a method for studying dosimetric consequences of anatomic changes in adaptive IMRT of head and neck cancer. Acta Oncol. **49**(7), 1101–1108 (2010)

16. Zang, L., et al.: Spatio-temporal convolutional LSTMs for tumor growth prediction by learning 4D longitudinal patient data. IEEE Trans. Med. Imaging (Early Access) (2019). https://doi.org/10.1109/TMI.2019.2943841

17. Wang, C., Rimner, A., Hu, Y.C., et al.: Toward predicting the evolution of lung tumors during radiotherapy observed on a longitudinal MR imaging study via a deep learning algorithm. Med. Phys. **46**(10), 4699–4707 (2019)

18. Srivastava, N., Mansimov, E., Salakhudinov, R.: Unsupervised learning of video representation using LSTMs. In: International Conference on Machine Learning, Lille, France, vol. 37, pp. 843–852 (2015)

19. Shi, X., Chen, H., Wna, D.Y., Yeung, W., Wong, K., Woo, W.C.: Convolutional LSTM network: a machine learning approach for precipitation nowcasting. In: Neural Information Processing Systems, Montreal, Canada, pp. 802–810 (2015)

20. Patraucean, V., Handa, A., Cipolla, R.: Spatio-temporal video autoencoder with differentiable memory. In: International Conference on Machine Learning, New York, USA (2016)

21. Villegas, R., Yang, J., Hong, S., Lin, X., Lee, H.: Decomposing motion and content for natural video sequence prediction. In: International Conference on Machine Learning, Sydney, Australia (2017)

22. Liang, X., Lee, L., Dai, W., Xing, P.E.: Dual motion GAN for future flow embedded video prediction. In: International Conference on Computer Vision, Seoul, South Korea, pp. 1744–1752. IEEE (2017)

23. Plastimatch. https://www.plastimatch.org/. Accessed 17 Mar 2020

24. Tai, Y., Yang, J., Liu, X.: Image super-resolution via deep recursive residual network. In: Conference on Computer Vision and pattern Recognition, Honolulu, HI, USA, pp. 3147–3155. IEEE (2017)

25. Cho, K., Merrienboer, B.V., Bahdanau, D., Bengio, Y.: On the properties of neural machine translation: encoder-decoder approaches. In: Proceeding of Eighth Workshop on Syntax, Semantics and Structures in Statistical Translation, Doha, Qatar, pp. 103–111 (2014)

26. Mennatulah, S., Sepehr, V., Martin, J., Nilanjan, R.: Convolutional gated recurrent networks for video segmentation. In: International Conference on Image Processing, Beijing, China. IEEE (2017)

27. Riyahi, S., Choi, W., Liu, C.-J., Zhong, H., Wu, A.J.: Quantifying local tumor morphological changes with Jacobian map for prediction of pathologic tumor response to chemo-radiotherapy in locally advanced esophageal cancer. Phys. Med. Biol. **63**(14), 145020 (2018)

28. Jaguar, G.C., Prado, J.D., Campanhã, D., Alves, F.A.: Clinical features and preventive therapies of radiation-induced xerostomia in head and neck cancer patient: a literature review. Appl. Cancer Res. **37**(31), 1–8 (2017)
29. Keiko, T., et al.: Radiation-induced parotid gland changes in oral cancer patients: correlation between parotid volume and saliva production. Jpn. J. Clin. Oncol. **40**(1), 42–46 (2009)

Deep Parametric Mixtures for Modeling the Functional Connectome

Nicolas Honnorat[1], Adolf Pfefferbaum[1,2], Edith V. Sullivan[2],
and Kilian M. Pohl[1,2(✉)]

[1] Center for Health Sciences, SRI International, Menlo Park, CA, USA
[2] Department of Psychiatry and Behavioral Sciences, Stanford University School of
Medicine, Stanford, CA, USA
kilian.pohl@stanford.edu

Abstract. Functional connectivity between brain regions is often estimated by correlating brain activity measured by resting-state fMRI in
those regions. The impact of factors (e.g., disorder or substance use) are
then modeled by their effects on these correlation matrices in individuals. A crucial step in better understanding their effects on brain function could lie in estimating connectomes, which encode the correlation
matrices across subjects. Connectomes are mostly estimated by creating a single average for a specific cohort, which works well for binary
factors (such as sex) but is unsuited for continuous ones, such as alcohol consumption. Alternative approaches based on regression methods
usually model each pair of regions separately, which generally produces
incoherent connectomes as correlations across multiple regions contradict
each other. In this work, we address these issues by introducing a deep
learning model that predicts connectomes based on factor values. The
predictions are defined on a simplex spanned across correlation matrices, whose convex combination guarantees that the deep learning model
generates well-formed connectomes. We present an efficient method for
creating these simplexes and improve the accuracy of the entire analysis by defining loss functions based on robust norms. We show that our
deep learning approach is able to produce accurate models on challenging
synthetic data. Furthermore, we apply the approach to the resting-state
fMRI scans of 281 subjects to study the effect of sex, alcohol, and HIV
on brain function.

1   Introduction

One popular way of measuring the impact of factors such as neurodevelopment
[4,5] and alcohol consumption on brain function is to correlate the BOLD signal
captured by rs-fMRI of different brain regions [1,18]. The resulting correlation
matrices are then analyzed by regression models to identify regional connectivity
patterns significantly predicting factor values [13,20]. However, the impact of
factors on regions omitted from those patterns is unknown. This task requires
the opposite approach of using parametric and generative models to predict
connectomes, i.e., correlation matrices across a population [14].

© Springer Nature Switzerland AG 2020
I. Rekik et al. (Eds.): PRIME 2020, LNCS 12329, pp. 133–143, 2020.
https://doi.org/10.1007/978-3-030-59354-4_13

The most common approach for computing connectomes consists of creating a single average for a specific cohort, where the cohort is confined to specific factor values, e.g., adolescents or adults [5]. While this approach works well for binary factors, such as sex, it cannot accurately model continuous ones, such as alcohol consumption [3] or age [4]. The state-of-the art is to replace the average with computing the regression between factors and regional functional separately for each pair of regions [19, 21]. As a result, a large number of parameters need to be estimated and overfitting might happen. In addition, the resulting connectome generally is not a correlation matrix [16]. This issue was partly mitigated by modeling distributions in the space of covariance matrices [16], which are, however, not necessarily correlation matrices either.

In this work, we propose to build functional connectomes taking into account the effects of factors. This new approach, called deep parametric mixtures (DPM), encodes these factor-dependent connectomes on a simplex defined by correlation matrices so that DPM learns to predict their coordinates on the simplex based on the corresponding factor values. By doing so, DPM can capture non-linear effects of factors and is guaranteed to generate realistic connectomes. We validate our optimization methods using synthetic data. Then, we show that DPM performs better than standard pairwise polynomial models for a set of 281 restingtate fMRI scans.

2   Methods

Our *deep parametric model* (DPM) aims to infer factor-dependent connectomes from a data set, where each subject 'i' is encoded by its functional correlation matrix X_i and the set of factor values F_i. To derive connectomes corresponding to realistic correlation matrices, we assume that any connectome lies inside a simplex defined by a set of basis correlation matrices $\{Y^1, \ldots, Y^J\}$ so that their convex combination can be used to approximate correlation matrices such as

$$X_i \sim \sum_j w_{ij} Y^j \text{ where } w_{ij} \geq 0 \text{ and } \sum_j w_{ij} = 1. \tag{1}$$

DPM then learns the relation between the input F_i and 'output weights $w_i :=(w_{i1}, \ldots, w_{iJ})$ (see Fig. 1). Once learned, our model can produce a connectome for any given factor value, which we call factor-dependent connectome. Note, the connectome must be well-formed as the outputs generated by our model strictly remain inside the simplex and a convex combination of correlation matrices is a correlation matrix. The remainder of this section introduces the deep learning model before presenting an algorithm for selecting the optimal basis matrices.

2.1   Deep Parametric Mixtures

DPM (see Fig. 1) consists of a stack of fully connected layers followed by leaky ReLu and batch normalization [11]. The dimension of the output is then set by a fully connected layer and the output is applied to a softmax function to generate

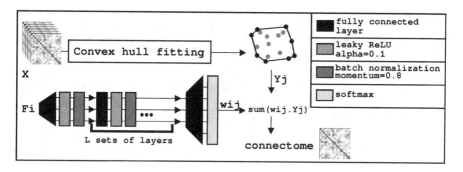

Fig. 1. Design of our deep parametric mixture model. The last two layers contain J nodes, one node per basis Y^j. Other layers contain M nodes. We set the number of layers L and their number of nodes M by cross-validation.

non-negative weights w_i summing to one. In our experiments, the number of fully connected layers L and their number of nodes M were set by Monte-Carlo cross-validation (within range 1 to 4), which aims to minimize the following loss function based on the squared Euclidean distance during training (Fig. 1):

$$||X_i - \sum_{j=1,...,J} w_{ij}Y^j||_2^2 \text{ where } w_{ij} \geq 0 \text{ and } \sum_{j=1,...,J} w_{ij} = 1 \quad (2)$$

To reduce the computational burden, we reformulate the loss by defining the rows of matrix X by X_i, the rows of Y by Y^j, and introduce $L(x) := x$ and the Gramian matrices [8] $K := XX^T$, $K_{XY} := XY^T$, and $K_{YY} := XY^T$ so that

$$\sum_i ||X_i - \sum_j w_{ij}Y^j||_2^2 = Trace\left(L\left(K + wK_{YY}w^T - 2K_{XY}w^T\right)\right). \quad (3)$$

The squared Euclidean loss is known to be sensitive to outliers, such as matrices severely corrupted by motion. For the DPM to be more robust, we experiment with two alternative norms. The loss function for *robust* DPM is based on the L₂-norm (omitting squaring in Eq. 3) so that $L(\cdot)$ changes to the element-wise square root $L(x) := \sqrt{x}$ while other than that the trace remains the same. The *Huber* DPM instead relies on the element-wise Huber loss [9]

$$||x||_H := \delta^2\left(\sqrt{1 + \frac{x^2}{\delta^2}} - 1\right) \quad (4)$$

so that $L(x) := ||\sqrt{x}||_H$. In our experiments, the parameter δ was set by first computing the entry-wise median across all training subjects, computing the squared Euclidean distance between the median and each X_i, and then setting δ to the value of the lower quintile.

2.2   Selecting Optimal Basis Y

The simplest choice for the basis $\{Y^1, \ldots Y^J\}$ would be the correlation matrices $\{X_1, \ldots, X_n\}$ of the training set. This strategy would increase the risk of

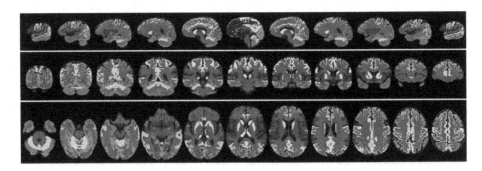

Fig. 2. The 17 brain areas determined by Louvain method.

overfitting and be computationally expensive, especially with large numbers of training samples. To avoid these issues, we propose to combine the correlation matrices of the training data set to generate a smaller set that can accurately approximate the training data by convex combination. We do so by defining that set as $Y := BX$ where B is obtained by solving the non-negative optimization (Fig. 2):

$$min_{A,B}||X - ABX||_2^2 \text{ such that } \begin{cases} \forall (i,j) \ A_{ij} \geq 0 \text{ and } \forall i \sum_j A_{i,j} = 1 \\ \forall (j,k) \ B_{j,k} \geq 0 \text{ and } \forall j \sum_k B_{j,k} = 1 \end{cases} \quad (5)$$

We initialized A and B by randomly sampling for each matrix entry from a Gaussian distribution with zero mean and unit variance, taking the absolute value of A and B components, adding 0.1 to avoid null entries, and finally normalizing the rows of A and B by dividing them by their sum. We then estimate the solution to Eq. (5) by alternating between estimating the minimum via multiplicative update [12] and matrix row normalization:

```
Algorithm 1
```
$$K^+ = max(K, 0) \quad \text{\# see Eq. 4 for definition of K}$$
$$K^- = max(-K, 0)$$
```
for N iterations
```
$$\left| \begin{array}{l} G_A \leftarrow \left[(ABK^- + K^+) B^T \right] \oslash max \left(\epsilon, (ABK^+ + K^-) B^T \right) \\ A \leftarrow \lambda A + (1 - \lambda) A \odot G_A \\ \text{Normalize } A \text{ by dividing each row of } A \text{ by its sum} \end{array} \right.$$

$$\left| \begin{array}{l} G_B \leftarrow \left[A^T (ABK^- + K^+) \right] \oslash max \left(\epsilon, A^T (ABK^+ + K^-) \right) \\ B \leftarrow \lambda B + (1 - \lambda) B \odot G_B \\ \text{Normalize } B \text{ by dividing each row of } B \text{ by its sum} \end{array} \right.$$

where $\odot$ denotes the Hadamard product (entry-wise matrix multiplication) and $\oslash$ denotes the entry-wise matrix division. We set the stabilizer λ to 0.05, $\epsilon = 10^{-16}$, and N = 5000 as our approach always converged before that.

In Sect. 2.1, we derived a robust version of the algorithm by omitting squaring the L_2-norm. Applying the same strategy to Eq. (5) and turning the optimiza-

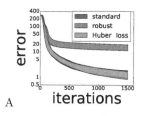 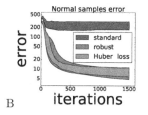 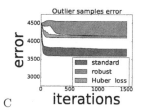

A   B   C

Fig. 3. (A) Squared Euclidean error (see Eq. 5) when fitted on the normal samples only, (B) error in fitting normals when the fitting was based on 25% of the samples being outliers, and (C) the error associated with the outliers.

tion into an iteratively re-weighted least-square optimization [7] changes the definition of G_A and G_B in the previous algorithm to

$$G_A \leftarrow \left[S \left(ABK^- + K^+ \right) B^T \right] \oslash max \left(\epsilon, S \left(ABK^+ + K^- \right) B^T \right) \qquad (6)$$

$$G_B \leftarrow \left[A^T S \left(ABK^- + K^+ \right) \right] \oslash max \left(\epsilon, A^T S \left(ABK^+ + K^- \right) \right) \qquad (7)$$

where the weight matrix S is initialized by the identity I and updated via

$$S \leftarrow Diag \left(\left((X - ABX)(X - ABX)^T \right)_{i,i}^{-1/2} \right) \qquad (8)$$

at each iteration. Using instead the Huber norm in Eq. (5), the previous computation of G_A and G_B stay the same but the update rule for S changes to

$$S \leftarrow Diag \left(\frac{\left\| \left((X - ABX)(X - ABX)^T \right)_{i,i} \right\|_H}{\left((X - ABX)(X - ABX)^T \right)_{i,i}} \right). \qquad (9)$$

We greatly reduced the computational cost associated with Eq. (8) and (9) by reformulating them like Eq. (3) to use Gramian matrices in our implementation.

3 Experiments

3.1 Data Pre-processing

The analysis focused on resting-state fMRI scans acquired for 281 individuals part of a study investigating the effects of alcohol consumption on the brain [14]. Preprocessing of each scan included motion correction [10], band-passed filtering between 0.01 and 0.1 Hz, registering to an atlas [17], and applying spatial Gaussian smoothing of 5.0 mm FWHM. The 111 regions of interest of the atlas [17] were used to define an average connectivity matrix, which was further reduced to correlations among the 17 brain areas shown in Fig. 2 by applying the Louvain method [2]. These areas were used to define the final functional correlations that were z-transformed [6]. For each study participant, the total alcohol consumption during life was determined based on self-reported consumption and ranged between 0 and 4718 kg. We also considered sex and HIV status, which are known to impact brain structure significantly [14,15] (Fig. 4).

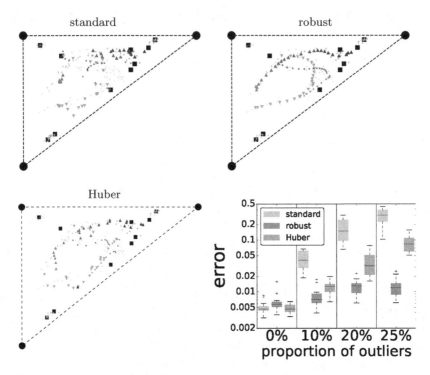

Fig. 4. Predictions of standard, robust and Huber DPM for a data set with 25% of outliers. Large markers are DPM predictions, small ones are training samples, the black dots are the 3 selected real matrices, and the convex hull is shown with black squares. Color brightness increases along the splines. All the results are displayed in the 2-simplex coordinates. The plot to the right summarizes the median prediction error.

3.2   Synthetic Experiments

The synthetic data set was generated from three real correlation matrices and was used to a) compare standard, robust, and Huber loss implementations of the convex hull optimization (Sect. 2.2) and b) test the ability of the three different DPM implementations to fit challenging nonlinear trends (Sect. 2.1).

The first synthetic data set consists of 75 *normal* matrices, which are generated by randomly and uniformly sampling from the 2D-simplex formed by the 3 selected matrices. Each of the three implementations is applied to this data set 10 times, where each time the methods use a different random initialization. For each run and iteration, the Squared Euclidean error (see Eq. (5)) is recorded, which is summarized in Fig. 3A showing that all three implementations converged by 1500 iterations. Next, we repeat the entire analysis adding 25 *outlier* matrices to the data set. An outlier is created by the convex combination of a normal matrix (with weight 0.2) and the correlation matrix (weight: 0.8) obtained for random time series of two time points sampled from $N(0, 1)$. We then report the error separately for the normal (Fig. 3B) and the outlier matrices (Fig. (3C)). As expected, the standard approach performs very well when just trained on normal matrices (Fig. 3A), but the reconstruction error for normal matrices greatly increases when including outliers (Fig. 3B) as it also optimizes the loss function for them (Fig. 3C). In contrast, robust and Huber loss implementations largely ignore outliers. The Huber loss implementation is the only one that generates optimal convex hulls on datasets with and without outliers.

To test the abilities of the DPM implementations to fit nonlinear trends, we generated 4 different data sets. Each data set contained three groups of normal matrices. For each group, we randomly sampled three locations in the 2D simplex to define a quadratic B-spline. For each B-spline, we generated 50 correlation matrices by randomly sampling locations along the curve and computing the convex combination accordingly. The resulting matrices were corrupted by adding Gaussian noise $N(0, 0.1)$ and projecting them back onto the simplex. The factors describing each matrix were then the group assignment and the relative location on the B-spline (between 0 and 1). After creating four data sets containing normal samples, we derived from each data set one corrupted by 10%, 20%, and 25%. For each group, a cluster of outliers was created around a random location on the 2D simplex by selecting a fraction of the normal samples at random and then replacing their matrices with the one generated with respect to that location. The three DPM variants were then applied to the resulting 16 datasets. For each data set and implementation, DPM was run using the previously described factors as input, 10000 iterations, and a convex hull of 5,10,15,20, or 25 basis matrix. The resulting error scores of the 80 runs per DPM implementation were then summarized in the plot of Fig. 4. As in the previous experiment, robust DPM demonstrated good robustness to outliers compared to the standard approach, and the approach that provided a trade-off between the two was the implementation based on the Huber loss. This quantitative finding is also supported by the 2D simplexes shown in Fig. 4, which reveal that for the dataset with 25% outliers standard DPM was not able to recover the shape of the 3 B-Splines, Huber DPM was better at it, while robust DPM achieved the best results.

4   Connectomes Specific to Sex, HIV, and Alcohol

We applied the 3 DPM implementations (dimension of convex hull: [5, 10, 25, 50, 100]) to the entire data set with the continuous factor alcohol consumption and

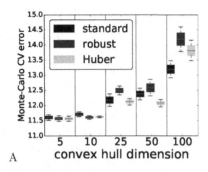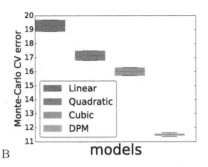

Fig. 5. (A) DPM cross-validation error for all the convex hulls and all DPM variants. (B) comparison between DPM and component-wise polynomial regressions.

the binary factors sex and HIV status as input. We measured the accuracy of each implementation via Monte-Carlo cross-validation. More specifically, we randomly split our data set into sets of 224 and 57 scans twenty-five times. For each split, we trained the methods using the large set, and we measured the squared Euclidean distance between the matrices in the small set and matrices predicted by the trained models. The results are summarized in Fig. 5A, which revealed that the best DPM was obtained for a convex hull of 5 basis correlation matrices and the Huber loss. The best DPM implementation was also much better than linear, quadratic, and cubic regression models (Fig. 5B), which predicted the values of the correlation matrices independently for each matrix element.

Figure 6 shows the connectome generated by DPM and quadratric regression for women with and without HIV that did no drink any alcohol (baseline). The connectomes of both methods agree that the effect of HIV is rather minor in comparison to that of alcohol consumption, whose difference to the baseline is shown in the images to the right. Furthermore, the effect of alcohol consumption is stronger in women with HIV compared to those without HIV and seems to strengthen as alcohol consumption increases; findings echoed by the clinical literature [15]. Disagreement among the methods is about the strength of alcohol consumption effects on brain function, which are more subtle according to connectomes generated by DPM. These more subtle effects also seem more realistic based on the error plots of Fig. 5B. Cubic regression models (not shown here for the sake of simplicity) predicted unrealistic alcohol effects that were diverging even faster than the quadratic models (Fig. 6).

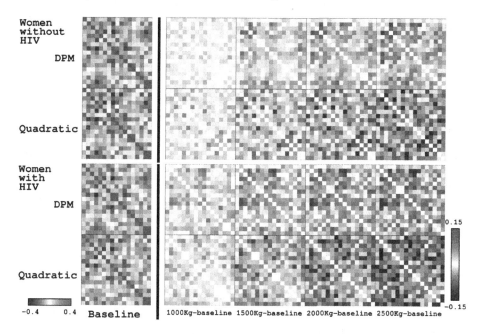

Fig. 6. Functional connectivity changes induced by alcohol consumption predicted in women with and without HIV, as a function of total lifetime alcohol consumption (in kg). Baseline functional connectivity is shown on the left. Functional connectivity changes induced by alcohol are shown on the right.

5   Conclusion

In this paper, we introduced a new approach to model non-linear changes of the functional connectome with respect to factors, such as brain disorders and alcohol consumption. We described the connectome as a convex combination of basis correlation matrices modeled by deep neural networks. We established the validity of our approach via synthetic experiments. Applied to rs-fMRIs of 281 subjects, we showed that our approach is more accurate than simpler regression approaches and results in factor-dependent connectomes that reveal an effect of alcohol-HIV comorbidity on brain function.

Acknowledgement. This work was supported by the National Institute on Alcohol Abuse and Alcoholism (NIAAA) under the grants AA005965, AA010723, AA017347 and the 2020 HAI-AWS Cloud Credits Award.

References

1. Biswal, B., Zerrin Yetkin, F., Haughton, V., Hyde, J.: Functional connectivity in the motor cortex of resting human brain using echo-planar MRI. Magn. Reson. Med. **34**(4), 537–541 (1995)

2. Blondel, V., Guillaume, J.L., Lambiotte, R., Lefebvre, E.: Fast unfolding of communities in large networks. J. Stat. Mech. Theory Exp. **2008**(10), P10008 (2008)
3. Chanraud, S., Pitel, A.L., Pfefferbaum, A., Sullivan, E.: Disruption of functional connectivity of the default-mode network in alcoholism. Cereb. Cortex **21**(10), 2272–2281 (2011)
4. Fair, D.A., et al.: Functional brain networks develop from a "local to distributed" organization. PLoS Comput. Biol. **5**(5), e1000381 (2009)
5. Fair, D.A., et al.: Development of distinct control networks through segregation and integration. Proc. Nat. Acad. Sci. (PNAS) **104**(33), 13507–13512 (2007)
6. Fisher, R.: Frequency distribution of the values of the correlation coefficient in samples of an indefinitely large population. Biometrika **10**(4), 507–521 (1915)
7. Green, P.: Iteratively reweighted least squares for maximum likelihood estimation, and some robust and resistant alternatives. J. Roy. Stat. Soc. B (Methodol.) **46**(2), 149–192 (1984)
8. Hofmann, T., Schölkopf, B., Smola, A.: Kernel methods in machine learning. Ann. Stat. **36**(3), 1171–1220 (2008)
9. Huber, P.: Robust estimation of a location parameter. Ann. Stat. **53**(1), 73–101 (1964)
10. Jenkinson, M., Bannister, P., Brady, J., Smith, S.: Improved optimisation for the robust and accurate linear registration and motion correction of brain images. NeuroImage **17**(2), 825–841 (2002)
11. Krizhevsky, A., Sutskever, I., Hinton, G.: Imagenet classification with deep convolutional neural networks. In: Advances in Neural Information Processing Systems, vol. 25 (2012)
12. Lee, D., Seung, H.: Algorithms for non-negative matrix factorization. In: Proceedings of the 2000 Advances in Neural Information Processing Systems Conference, pp. 556–562 (2001)
13. Lundervold, A., Lundervold, A.: An overview of deep learning in medical imaging focusing on MRI. Zeitschrift für Medizinische Physik **29**(2), 102–127 (2019)
14. Pfefferbaum, A., et al.: Accelerated aging of selective brain structures in human immunodeficiency virus infection. Neurobiol. Aging **35**(7), 1755–1768 (2014)
15. Pfefferbaum, A., Zahr, N., Sassoon, S., Kwon, D., Pohl, K., Sullivan, E.: Accelerated and premature aging characterizing regional cortical volume loss in human immunodeficiency virus infection: contributions from alcohol, substance use, and hepatitis C coinfection. Biol. Psychiatr. Cogni. Neurosci. Neuroimaging **3**(10), 844–859 (2018)
16. Rahim, M., Thirion, B., Varoquaux, G.: Population shrinkage of covariance (PoSCE) for better individual brain functional-connectivity estimation. Med. Image Anal. **54**, 138–148 (2019)
17. Rohlfing, T., Zahr, N., Sullivan, E., Pfefferbaum, A.: The SRI24 multichannel atlas of normal adult human brain structure. Hum. Brain Mapp. **31**(5), 798–819 (2014)
18. Smith, S.M., et al.: Network modelling methods for fMRI. NeuroImage **54**, 875–891 (2011)

19. Vergara, V., Liu, J., Claus, E., Hutchison, K., Calhoun, V.: Alterations of resting state functional network connectivity in the brain of nicotine and alcohol users. NeuroImage **151**, 45–54 (2017)
20. Wen, D., Wei, Z., Zhou, Y., Li, G., Zhang, X., Han, W.: Deep learning methods to process fMRI data and their application in the diagnosis of cognitive impairment: a brief overview and our opinion. Front. Neuroinformatics **12**, Article 23 (2018)
21. Zhu, X., Cortes, C., Mathur, K., Tomasi, D., Momenan, R.: Model-free functional connectivity and impulsivity correlates of alcohol dependence: a resting-state study. Addict. Biol. **22**(1), 206–217 (2017)

Deep EvoGraphNet Architecture for Time-Dependent Brain Graph Data Synthesis from a Single Timepoint

Ahmed Nebli[1,2] (ID), Uğur Ali Kaplan[1], and Islem Rekik[1](✉) (ID)

[1] BASIRA Lab, Faculty of Computer and Informatics, Istanbul Technical University, Istanbul, Turkey
irekik@itu.edu.tr
[2] National School for Computer Science (ENSI), Mannouba, Tunisia
http://basira-lab.com

Abstract. Learning how to predict the brain connectome (i.e. graph) development and aging is of paramount importance for charting the future of within-disorder and cross-disorder landscape of brain dysconnectivity evolution. Indeed, predicting the *longitudinal* (i.e., *time-dependent*) brain dysconnectivity as it emerges and evolves over time from a single timepoint can help design personalized treatments for disordered patients in a very early stage. Despite its significance, evolution models of the brain *graph* are largely overlooked in the literature. Here, we propose EvoGraphNet, the first *end-to-end* geometric deep learning-powered *graph*-generative adversarial network (gGAN) for predicting time-dependent brain graph evolution from a single timepoint. Our EvoGraphNet architecture cascades a set of time-dependent gGANs, where each gGAN communicates its predicted brain graphs at a particular timepoint to train the next gGAN in the cascade at follow-up timepoint. Therefore, we obtain each next predicted timepoint by setting the output of each generator as the input of its successor which enables us to predict a given number of timepoints using only one single timepoint in an end-to-end fashion. At each timepoint, to better align the distribution of the predicted brain graphs with that of the ground-truth graphs, we further integrate an auxiliary Kullback-Leibler divergence loss function. To capture time-dependency between two consecutive observations, we impose an l_1 loss to minimize the sparse distance between two serialized brain graphs. A series of benchmarks against variants and ablated versions of our EvoGraphNet showed that we can achieve the lowest brain graph evolution prediction error using a single baseline timepoint. Our EvoGraphNet code is available at http://github.com/basiralab/EvoGraphNet.

Keywords: Time-dependent graph evolution prediction · KL divergence loss · Graph generative adversarial network · Cascaded time-dependent generators

---

A. Nebli and U. A. Kaplan—Co-first authors.

© Springer Nature Switzerland AG 2020
I. Rekik et al. (Eds.): PRIME 2020, LNCS 12329, pp. 144–155, 2020.
https://doi.org/10.1007/978-3-030-59354-4_14

1   Introduction

Recent findings in neuroscience have suggested that providing personalized treatments for brain diseases can significantly increase the chance of a patient's recovery [1]. Thereby, it is vital to undertake an early diagnosis of brain diseases [2], especially for neurodegenerative diseases such as dementia which was found to be irreversible if discovered at a late stage [3]. In this context, recent landmark studies [4,5] have suggested using the robust predictive abilities of machine learning to predict the time-dependent (i.e., longitudinal) evolution of both the healthy and the disordered brain. However, such works only focus on predicting the brain when modeled as an image or a surface, thereby overlooking a wide spectrum of brain dysconnectivity disorders that can be pinned down by modeling the brain as a graph (also called connectome) [6], where the connectivity weight between pairs of anatomical regions of interest (ROIs) becomes the feature of interest.

In other works, [7,8] have proposed to use deep learning frameworks aiming to utilize hippocampal magnetic resonance imaging (MRI) to predict the onset of Alzheimer's disease (AD). However, these studies have only focused on a single brain region overlooking other brain regions' engagement in predicting AD. To overcome this limitation, [9,10] proposed to use brain MRI to predict AD across all brain regions, yet such experiments focused on MRI samples collected at the late stages of the illness which are inadequate for administering patient's personalized treatments at *baseline observation*. Here, we set out to solve a more difficult problem which is forecasting the evolution of the brain graph over time from an initial timepoint. Despite the lack of studies in this direction, [11] has attempted to solve this challenge by suggesting the Learning-guided Infinite Network Atlas selection (LINAs) framework, a first-ever study that developed a learning-based sample similarity learning framework to forecast the progression of brain disease development over time from a single observation only. This study reflects a major advancement in brain disease evolution trajectory prediction since it considered using the brain as a set of interconnected ROIs, instead of performing image-based prediction which is agnostic to the nature of the complex wiring of the brain as a graph.

Regardless of the fact that the aforementioned techniques were aiming to address the issue of early diagnosis of brain diseases, all of these approaches share the same *dichotomized* aspect of the engineered learning framework, each composed of independent blocks that cannot co-learn together to better solve the target prediction problem. For instance, [11] first learns the data manifold, then learns how to select the best samples before performing the prediction step independently. These sub-components of the framework do not interact with each other and thus there is no feedback passed on to earlier learning blocks.

To address these limitations and while drawing inspiration from the compelling generative adversarial network (GAN) architecture introduced in [12], we propose EvoGraphNet, a framework that first generalizes the GAN architecture, originally operating on Euclidean data such as images, to non-Euclidean graphs by designing a *graph-based* GAN (gGAN) architecture. Second and more importantly, our EvoGraphNet chains a set of gGANs, each specialized in learning how to generate a brain graph at follow-up timepoint from the predicted brain graph (output) of the previous gGAN in the *time-dependent* cascade. We formalize our brain graph prediction task from baseline using a single loss function to optimize with a backpropagation process throughout our EvoGraphNet architecture, trained in an end-to-end fashion. Our framework is inspired by the works of [13,14] where we aim to perform an *assumption free* mapping from an initial brain graph to its consecutive time-dependent representations using a stack of m paired generators and discriminators at m follow-up timepoints. Each generator inputs the output of its predecessor generator making the framework work in an end-to-end fashion. We further propose to enhance the quality of the evolved brain graphs from baseline by maximizing the alignment between the predicted and ground-truth brain graphs at each prediction timepoint by integrating a Kullback-Leibler (KL) divergence. To capture time-dependency between two consecutive observations, we impose an l_1 loss to minimize the sparse distance between two serialized brain graphs. We also explore the effect of adding a graph-topology loss where we enforce the preservation of the topological strength of each ROI (graph node) strength over time.

Below, we articulate the main contributions of our work:

1. *On a conceptual level.* EvoGraphNet is the first geometric deep learning framework that predicts the time-dependent brain graph evolution from a single observation in an end-to-end fashion.
2. *On a methodological level.* EvoGraphNet is a unified prediction framework stacking a set of time-dependent graph GANs where the learning of the current gGAN in the cascade benefits from the learning of the previous gGAN.
3. *On clinical level.* EvoGraphNet can be used in the development of a more personalized medicine for the early diagnosis of brain dysconnectivity disorders.

2   Proposed Method

In this section, we explain the key building blocks of our proposed EvoGraphNet architecture for time-dependent brain graph evolution synthesis from a single baseline timepoint. Table 1 displays the mathematical notations used throughout our paper.

Overview of EvoGraphNet for Time-Dependent Brain Graph Evolution Prediction from a Single Source Timepoint. GANs [15] are deep learning models consisting of two neural networks competing in solving a target learning task: a generator G and a discriminator D. The generator is an encoder and decoder neural network aiming to learn how to generate fake samples that mimics a given original data distribution while the discriminator learns how to discriminate between the ground-truth data and the fake data produced by the generator. These two networks are trained in an adversarial way so that with enough training cycles, the generator learns how to better generate fake samples that look real and the discriminator learns how to better differentiate between

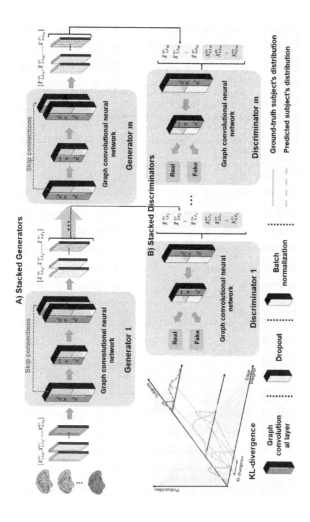

Fig. 1. *Proposed EvoGraphNet architecture for predicting the longitudinal brain graph evolution from baseline timepoint t_0.* **(A)** *Stacked generators network.* We develop a graph GAN (gGAN) that learns how to map an input brain graph measured at t_{i-1} to a follow-up timepoint t_i. For m timepoints, we design m identical graph generators each composed of a three-layer graph convolutional neural network acting as an encoder-decoder network that mimics a U-net architecture with skip connections. For each t_i, $i > 0$, each generator G_i in the chain takes a set of predicted training brain graphs $\hat{\mathbf{X}}_{t_{i-1}}^{tr}$ by the previous generator and outputs a set of $\hat{\mathbf{X}}_{t_i}$. **(B)** *Stacked discriminator network.* For each generator G_i, we associate a discriminator D_i aiming to distinguish the ground-truth brain graphs $\mathbf{X}_{t_i}^{tr}$ from the predicted brain graphs $\hat{\mathbf{X}}_{t_i}^{tr}$ by generator G_i. Hence, we design m identical discriminators each composed of a two-layer graph convolutional neural network, each outputting a single score in the range of $[0, \ldots, 1]$ expressing the *realness* of $\hat{\mathbf{X}}_{t_i}^{tr}$. To enhance the generation quality at each follow-up timepoint t_i, we further integrate a Kullback-Leibler divergence loss to better align the distribution of the predicted brain graphs with that of the ground-truth graphs.

Table 1. Major mathematical notations

Mathematical notation	Definition
m	Number of timepoints to predict
n_s	Number of training subjects
n_r	Number of regions of interest in the brain
m_r	Number of edges in a brain graph
μ_k	Mean of the connected edge weights for node k in a ground-truth brain graph
σ_k	Standard deviation of the connected edge weights for node k in a ground-truth brain graph
$\hat{\mu}_k$	Mean of the connected edge weights for node k in a predicted brain graph
$\hat{\sigma}_k$	Standard deviation of the connected edge weights for node k in a predicted brain graph
p_k	Normal distribution of the connected edge weights for a node k in a ground-truth brain graph
p_k	Normal distribution of the connected edge weights for a node k in the ground-truth brain graph
$\mathbf{X}_{t_i}^{tr}$	Training brain graph connectivity matrices $\in \mathbb{R}^{n \times n_r \times n_r}$ at t_i
$\hat{\mathbf{X}}_{t_i}^{tr}$	Predicted brain graph connectivity matrices $\in \mathbb{R}^{n \times n_r \times n_r}$ at t_i
G_i	GGAN generator at timepoint t_i
D_i	GGAN discriminator at timepoint t_i
$\mathcal{L}_{full}$	Full loss function
$\mathcal{L}_{adv}$	Adversarial loss function
$\mathcal{L}_{L_1}$	l_1 loss function
$\mathcal{L}_{KL}$	KL divergence loss function
λ_1	Coefficient of adversarial loss
λ_2	Coefficient of l_1 loss
λ_3	Coefficient of KL divergence loss
V	A set of n_r nodes
E	A set of m_r directed or undirected edges
l	Index of layer
$\mathbf{L}$	Transformation matrix $\in \mathbb{R}^{m_r \times s}$
$\mathcal{N}(k)$	The neighborhood containing all the adjacent nodes of node k
$\mathbf{Y}^l(k)$	Filtered signal of node (ROI) $i \in \mathbb{R}^{d_l}$
$\mathbf{F}_{k'k}^l$	Filter generating network
ω^l	Weight parameter
b^l	Bias parameter

ground-truth samples and generator's produced samples. We draw inspiration from the work of [16] which successfully translated a T1-weighted magnetic resonance imaging (MRI) to T2-weighted MRI using GAN and the work of [17] which proposed to use a stacked form of generators and discriminators for image synthesis. Therefore, as shown in Fig. 1 our proposed EvoGraphNet is a chain of gGANs composed of m generators and discriminators aiming to map a subject's brain graph measured at timepoint t_0 onto m sequential follow-up timepoints. Excluding the baseline gGAN trained to map ground-truth baseline graphs at t_0 to the ground-truth brain graphs at timepoint t_1, a gGAN at time t_i is trained to map the generated graphs by the previous gGAN at t_{i-1} onto the ground-truth brain graphs at timepoint t_i. Below is our adversarial loss function for one pair of generator G_i and discriminator D_i composing our gGAN at timepoint t_i:

$$argmin_{G_i}max_{D_i}\mathcal{L}_{adv}(G_i, D_i) = \mathbb{E}_{G_i(\mathbf{X}_{t_i})}[\log(D_i(G_i(\mathbf{X}_{t_i})))] \tag{1}$$

$$+ \mathbb{E}_{G_i(\hat{\mathbf{X}}_{t_{i-1}})}[\log(1 - D_i(G_i(\hat{\mathbf{X}}_{t_{i-1}})))]$$

$\hat{\mathbf{X}}_{t_{i-1}}$ denotes the predicted brain graph connectivity matrix by the previous generator G_{i-1} in the chain, and which is inputted to the generator G_i for training. $\mathbf{X}_{t_i}^{tr}$ denotes the target ground-truth brain connectivity matrix at timepoint t_i. G_i is trained to learn a non-linear mapping from the previous prediction $\hat{\mathbf{X}}_{t_{i-1}}$ to the target ground truth $\mathbf{X}_{t_i}^{tr}$.

Since the brain connectivity changes are anticipated to be sparse over time, we further impose that the l_1 distance between two consecutive timepoints t_{i-1} and t_i to be quite small for $i \in \{1, \ldots, m\}$. This acts as a time-dependent regularizer for each generator G_i in our EvoGraphNet architecture. Thus, we express the proposed $l1$ loss for each subject tr using the predicted brain graph connectivity matrix $\hat{\mathbf{X}}_{t_{i-1}}^{tr}$ by the previous generator G_{i-1} and the ground-truth brain graph connectivity matrix to predict by generator G_i as follows:

$$\mathcal{L}_{l1}(G_i, tr) = ||\hat{\mathbf{X}}_{t_{i-1}}^{tr} - \mathbf{X}_{t_i}^{tr}||_1 \tag{2}$$

In addition to the $l1$ loss term introduced for taking into account time-dependency between two consecutive predictions, we further enforce the alignment between the ground-truth and predicted brain graph distribution at each timepoint t_i. Precisely, we use the Kullback-Leibler (KL) divergence between both ground-truth and predicted distributions. KL divergence is a metric indicating the ability to discriminate between two given distributions. Thereby, we propose to add the KL divergence as a loss term to minimize the discrepancy between ground-truth and predicted connectivity weight distributions at each timepoint t_i. To do so, first, we calculate the mean μ_k and the standard deviation σ_k of connected edge weights for each node in each brain graph.

We define the normal distributions as follows:

$$p_k = N(\hat{\mu}_k, \hat{\sigma}_k) \tag{3}$$

$$q_k = N(\mu_k, \sigma_k), \tag{4}$$

where p_k is the normal distribution for node k in the predicted graph $\hat{\mathbf{X}}_{t_i}^{tr} = G_i(\hat{\mathbf{X}}_{t_{i-1}}^{tr})$ and q_k is the normal distribution defined for the same node k in $\mathbf{X}_{t_i}^{tr}$.

Thus, the KL divergence between the previously calculated normal distributions for each subject is expressed as follows:

$$\mathcal{L}_{KL}(t_i, tr) = \sum_{k=1}^{n_r} KL(p_k||q_k), \tag{5}$$

where each node's KL divergence is equal to:

$$KL(p_k||q_k) = \int_{-\infty}^{+\infty} p_k(x) log \frac{p_k(x)}{q_k(x)} dx \tag{6}$$

Full Loss. By summing up over all training n_s subjects and all m timepoints to predict, we obtain the full loss function to optimize follows:

$$\mathcal{L}_{Full} = \sum_{i=1}^{m} \left(\lambda_1 \mathcal{L}_{Adv}(G_i, D_i) + \frac{\lambda_2}{n_s} \sum_{tr=1}^{n_s} \mathcal{L}_{l1}(G_i, tr) + \frac{\lambda_3}{n_s} \sum_{tr=1}^{n_s} \mathcal{L}_{KL}(t_i, tr) \right) \tag{7}$$

where λ_1, λ_2, and λ_3 are hyperparameters controlling the significance of each loss function in the overall objective to minimize.

The Generator Network Design. As shown in Fig. 1A, our proposed Evo-GraphNet is composed m generators aiming to predict the subject's brain graphs at m follow-up timepoints. Since all generators are designed identically and for the sake of simplicity, we propose to detail the architecture of one generator G_i aiming to predict subjects' brain graphs at timepoint t_i.

Our proposed generator G_i consists of a three-layer encoder-decoder graph convolutional neural network (GCN) leveraging the dynamic edge convolution process implemented in [18] and imitating a U-net architecture [19] with skip connections which enhances the decoding process with respect to the encoder's embedding. For each t_i, $i > 0$, each generator G_i in the chain takes a set of predicted training brain graphs $\hat{\mathbf{X}}_{t_{i-1}}^{tr}$ by the previous generator and outputs a set of $\hat{\mathbf{X}}_{t_i}$. Hence, our generator G_i contains three graph convolutional neural network layers to which we apply batch normalization [20] and dropout [21] to the output of each layer. These two operations undeniably contribute to simplifying and optimizing the network training. For instance, batch normalization was proven to accelerate network training while dropout was proven to eliminate the risk of overfitting.

The Discriminator Network Design. We display the architecture of our discriminator in Fig. 1B. Similar to the above sub-section, all discriminators share the same design, thus we propose to only detail one discriminator D_i trained at timepoint t_i. We couple each generator G_i with its corresponding discriminator D_i which is also a graph neural network inspired by [18]. Our proposed discriminator is a two-layer graph neural network that takes as input a concatenation of the generator's output $\hat{\mathbf{X}}_{t_i}^{tr}$ and the ground-truth subjects' brain graphs $\mathbf{X}_{t_i}^{tr}$. The discriminator outputs a value in the range of $[0, \ldots, 1]$ measuring *the realness* of the synthesized brain graph $\hat{\mathbf{X}}_{t_i}^{tr}$ at timepoint t_i. As reflected by our adversarial loss function, we design our gGAN's loss function so that it maximizes the discriminator's output score for $\mathbf{X}_{t_i}^{tr}$ and minimizes it for $\hat{\mathbf{X}}_{t_i}^{tr}$, which is the output of the previous generator in the chain $G_i(\hat{\mathbf{X}}_{t_{i-1}}^{tr})$.

Dynamic Graph-Based Edge Convolution. Each of the graph convolutional layers of our gGAN architecture uses a dynamic graph-based edge convolution operation proposed by [18]. In particular, let $G = (V, E)$ be a directed or undirected graph where V is a set of n_r ROIs and $E \subseteq V \times V$ is a set of m_r edges. Let l be the layer index in the neural network. We define $\mathbf{Y}^l : V \to \mathbb{R}^{d_l}$ and $\mathbf{L} : E \to \mathbb{R}^{d_m}$ which can be respectively considered as two transformation matrices (i.e., functions) where $\mathbf{Y}^l \in \mathbb{R}^{n_r \times d_l}$ and $\mathbf{L} \in \mathbb{R}^{m_r \times d_m}$. d_m and d_l are dimensionality indexes. We define by $\mathcal{N}(k) = \{k'; (k', k) \in E\} \cup \{k\}$ the neighborhood of a node k containing all its adjacent ROIs.

The goal of each layer in each generator and discriminator in our EvoGraphNet is to output the graph convolution result which can be considered as a filtered signal $\mathbf{Y}^l(k) \in \mathbb{R}^{d_l}$ at node k's neighborhood $k' \in \mathcal{N}(k)$. $\mathbf{Y}^l$ is expressed as follows:

$$\mathbf{Y}^l(k) = \frac{1}{\mathcal{N}(k)} \sum_{k' \in \mathcal{N}(k)} \mathbf{\Theta}^l_{k'k} \mathbf{Y}^{l-1}(k') + b^l, \tag{8}$$

where $\mathbf{\Theta}^l_{k'k} = \mathbf{F}^l(\mathbf{L}(k', k); \omega^l)$. We note that $\mathbf{F}^l : \mathbb{R}^{d_m} \to \mathbb{R}^{d_l \times d_l - 1}$ is the filter generating network, ω^l and b^l are model parameters that are updated only during training.

3   Results and Discussion

Evaluation Dataset. We used 113 subjects from the OASIS-2[1] longitudinal dataset [22]. This set consists of a longitudinal collection of 150 subjects aged 60 to 96. Each subject has 3 visits (i.e., timepoints), separated by at least one year. For each subject, we construct a cortical morphological network derived from cortical thickness measure using structural T1-w MRI as proposed in [23–25]. Each cortical hemisphere is parcellated into 35 ROIs using Desikan-Killiany cortical atlas. We program our EvoGraphNet using PyTorch Geometric library [26].

Parameter Setting. In Table 2, we report the mean absolute error between ground-truth and synthesized brain graphs at follow-up timepoints t_1 and t_2. We set each pair of gGAN's hyperparameter as follows: $\lambda_1 = 2$, $\lambda_2 = 2$, and $\lambda_3 = 0.001$. Also, we chose AdamW [27] as our default optimizer and set the learning rate at 0.01 for each generator and 0.0002 for each discriminator. We set the exponential decay rate for the first moment estimates to 0.5, and the exponential decay rate for the second-moment estimates to 0.999 for the AdamW optimizer. Finally, we trained our gGAN for 500 epochs using a single Tesla V100 GPU (NVIDIA GeForce GTX TITAN with 32 GB memory).

Comparison Method and Evaluation. To evaluate the reproducibility of our results and the robustness of our EvoGraphNet architecture to training and testing sample perturbation, we used a 3-fold cross-validation strategy for training and testing. Due to the lack of existing works on brain graph evolution

---

[1] https://www.oasis-brains.org/.

prediction using geometric deep learning, we proposed to evaluate our method against two of its variants. The first comparison method (i.e., base EvoGraphNet) is an ablated of our proposed framework where we remove the KL divergence loss term while for the second comparison method (i.e., EvoGraphNet (w/o KL) + Topology), we replace our KL-divergence loss with a graph topology loss. Basically, we represent each graph by its node strength vector storing the topological strength of each of its nodes. The node strength is computed by adding up the weights of all edges connected to the node of interest. Next, we computed the L_2 distance between the node strength vector of the ground-truth and predicted graphs. Table 2 shows the MAE results at t_1 and t_2 timepoints.

Table 2. Prediction accuracy using mean absolute error (MAE) of our proposed method and comparison methods at t_1 and t_2 timepoints.

Method	t_1		t_2	
	Mean MAE ± std	Best MAE	Mean MAE ± std	Best MAE
Base EvoGraphNet (w/o KL)	0.05626 ± 0.00446	**0.05080**	0.13379 ± 0.01385	0.11586
EvoGraphNet (w/o KL) + Topology	0.05643 ± 0.00307	0.05286	0.11194 ± 0.00381	0.10799
EvoGraphNet	$\mathbf{0.05495 \pm 0.00282}$	0.05096	$\mathbf{0.08048 \pm 0.00554}$	**0.07286**

Clearly, our proposed EvoGraphNet outperformed the comparison methods in terms of mean (averaged across the 3 folds) and the best MAE for prediction at t_2. It has also achieved the best mean MAE for brain graph prediction at t_1. However, the best MAE for prediction at t_1 was achieved by base EvoGraphNet which used only a pair of loss functions (i.e., adversarial loss and $l1$ loss). This might be due to the fact that our objective function is highly computationally expensive compared to the base EvoGraphNet making it less prone to learning flaws such as overfitting. Also, we notice that the prediction error at t_1 is lower than t_2, which indicates that further observations become more challenging to predict from the baseline timepoint t_0. Overall, our EvoGraphNet architecture with an additional KL divergence loss has achieved the best performance in foreseeing brain graph evolution trajectory and showed that stacking a pair of graph generator and discriminator for each predicted timepoint is indeed a promising strategy in tackling our time-dependent graph prediction problem.

Limitations and Future Work. While our graph prediction framework reached the lowest average MAE against benchmark methods in predicting the evolution of brain graphs over time from a single observation, it has a few limitations. So far, the proposed method only handles brain graphs where a single edge connects two ROIs. In our future work, we aim to generalize our stacked gGAN generators to handle brain hypergraphs, where a hyperedge captures high-order relationships between sets of nodes. This will enable us to better model and capture the complexity of the brain as a highly interactive network with different topological properties. Furthermore, we noticed that the joint integration of KL divergence loss and the topological loss produced a negligible improvement in the brain graph evolution prediction over time. We intend to investigate this point in depth in our future work. Besides, we aim to use a population network atlas as introduced in [28] to assist EvoGraphNet training in generating biologically sound brain networks.

4   Conclusion

In this paper, we proposed a first-ever geometric deep learning architecture, namely EvoGraphNet, for predicting the longitudinal evolution of a baseline brain graph over time. Our architecture chains a set of gGANs where the learning of each gGAN in the chain depends on the output of its antecedent gGAN. We proposed a time-dependency loss between consecutive timepoints and a distribution alignment between predicted and ground-truth graphs at the same timepoint. Our results showed that our time-dependent brain graph generation framework from the baseline timepoint can notably boost the prediction accuracy compared to its ablated versions. Our EvoGraphNet is generic and can be trained using any given number of prediction timepoints, and thus can be used in predicting both typical and disordered changes in brain connectivity over time. Therefore, in our future research, we will be testing our designed architecture on large-scale connectomic datasets of multiple brain disorders such as schizophrenia by exploring the ability of the *synthesized* brain graphs at later timepoints to improve neurological and neuropsychiatric disorder diagnosis from baseline.

Acknowledgement. This project has been funded by the 2232 International Fellowship for Outstanding Researchers Program of TUBITAK (Project No: 118C288, http://basira-lab.com/reprime/) supporting I. Rekik. However, all scientific contributions made in this project are owned and approved solely by the authors.

References

1. Mukherjee, A., Srivastava, R., Bhatia, V., Mohanty, S., et al.: Stimuli effect of the human brain using EEG SPM dataset. In: Pattnaik, P., Mohanty, S., Mohanty, S. (eds.) Smart Healthcare Analytics in IoT Enabled Environment, pp. 213–226. Springer, Cham (2020). https://doi.org/10.1007/978-3-030-37551-5_14
2. Lohmeyer, J.L., Alpinar-Sencan, Z., Schicktanz, S.: Attitudes towards prediction and early diagnosis of late-onset dementia: a comparison of tested persons and family caregivers. Aging Mental Health 1–12 (2020)
3. Stoessl, A.J.: Neuroimaging in the early diagnosis of neurodegenerative disease. Transl. Neurodegeneration **1**, 5 (2012)
4. Rekik, I., Li, G., Yap, P., Chen, G., Lin, W., Shen, D.: Joint prediction of longitudinal development of cortical surfaces and white matter fibers from neonatal MRI. Neuroimage **152**, 411–424 (2017)
5. Gafuroğlu, C., Rekik, I., et al.: Joint prediction and classification of brain image evolution trajectories from baseline brain image with application to early dementia. In: International Conference on Medical Image Computing and Computer-Assisted Intervention, pp. 437–445 (2018)

6. van den Heuvel, M.P., Sporns, O.: A cross-disorder connectome landscape of brain dysconnectivity. Nat. Rev. Neurosci. **20**, 435–446 (2019)

7. Li, H., Habes, M., Wolk, D.A., Fan, Y.: A deep learning model for early prediction of Alzheimer's disease dementia based on hippocampal MRI. arXiv preprint arXiv:1904.07282 (2019)

8. Liu, M., et al.: A multi-model deep convolutional neural network for automatic hippocampus segmentation and classification in Alzheimer's disease. NeuroImage **208**, 116459 (2020)

9. Zhang, Y., et al.: Detection of subjects and brain regions related to Alzheimer's disease using 3D MRI scans based on eigenbrain and machine learning. Front. Comput. Neurosci. **9**, 66 (2015)

10. Islam, J., Zhang, Y.: A novel deep learning based multi-class classification method for Alzheimer's disease detection using brain MRI data. In: Zeng, Y., et al. (eds.) BI 2017. LNCS (LNAI), vol. 10654, pp. 213–222. Springer, Cham (2017). https://doi.org/10.1007/978-3-319-70772-3_20

11. Ezzine, B.E., Rekik, I.: Learning-guided infinite network atlas selection for predicting longitudinal brain network evolution from a single observation. In: Shen, D., et al. (eds.) MICCAI 2019. LNCS, vol. 11765, pp. 796–805. Springer, Cham (2019). https://doi.org/10.1007/978-3-030-32245-8_88

12. Goodfellow, I.J., et al.: Generative adversarial networks (2014)

13. Isola, P., Zhu, J., Zhou, T., Efros, A.A.: Image-to-image translation with conditional adversarial networks. CoRR abs/1611.07004 (2016)

14. Welander, P., Karlsson, S., Eklund, A.: Generative adversarial networks for image-to-image translation on multi-contrast MR images-a comparison of CycleGAN and unit. arXiv preprint arXiv:1806.07777 (2018)

15. Goodfellow, I., et al.: Generative adversarial nets. In: Ghahramani, Z., Welling, M., Cortes, C., Lawrence, N.D., Weinberger, K.Q. (eds.) Advances in Neural Information Processing Systems, vol. 27, pp. 2672–2680. Curran Associates, Inc. (2014)

16. Yang, Q., et al.: MRI cross-modality image-to-image translation. Sci. Rep. **10**, 1–18 (2020)

17. Zhang, H., et al.: StackGAN: text to photo-realistic image synthesis with stacked generative adversarial networks. CoRR abs/1612.03242 (2016)

18. Simonovsky, M., Komodakis, N.: Dynamic edge-conditioned filters in convolutional neural networks on graphs. CoRR abs/1704.02901 (2017)

19. Ronneberger, O., Fischer, P., Brox, T.: U-Net: convolutional networks for biomedical image segmentation. CoRR abs/1505.04597 (2015)

20. Ioffe, S., Szegedy, C.: Batch normalization: accelerating deep network training by reducing internal covariate shift. arXiv preprint arXiv:1502.03167 (2015)

21. Xiao, T., Li, H., Ouyang, W., Wang, X.: Learning deep feature representations with domain guided dropout for person re-identification. In: Proceedings of the IEEE Conference on Computer Vision And Pattern Recognition, pp. 1249–1258 (2016)

22. Marcus, D.S., Fotenos, A.F., Csernansky, J.G., Morris, J.C., Buckner, R.L.: Open access series of imaging studies: longitudinal MRI data in nondemented and demented older adults. J. Cogn. Neurosci. **22**, 2677–2684 (2010)

23. Mahjoub, I., Mahjoub, M.A., Rekik, I.: Brain multiplexes reveal morphological connectional biomarkers fingerprinting late brain dementia states. Sci. Rep. **8**, 4103 (2018)

24. Soussia, M., Rekik, I.: Unsupervised manifold learning using high-order morphological brain networks derived from T1-w MRI for autism diagnosis. Front. Neuroinformatics **12**, 70 (2018)

25. Lisowska, A., Rekik, I.: ADNI: pairing-based ensemble classifier learning using convolutional brain multiplexes and multi-view brain networks for early dementia diagnosis. In: International Workshop on Connectomics in Neuroimaging, pp. 42–50 (2017)

26. Fey, M., Lenssen, J.E.: Fast graph representation learning with PyTorch geometric. CoRR abs/1903.02428 (2019)

27. Loshchilov, I., Hutter, F.: Fixing weight decay regularization in adam. CoRR abs/1711.05101 (2017)

28. Mhiri, I., Rekik, I.: Joint functional brain network atlas estimation and feature selection for neurological disorder diagnosis with application to autism. Med. Image Anal. **60**, 101596 (2020)

Uniformizing Techniques to Process CT Scans with 3D CNNs for Tuberculosis Prediction

Hasib Zunair[1], Aimon Rahman[2(✉)], Nabeel Mohammed[2], and Joseph Paul Cohen[3]

[1] Concordia University, Montreal, Canada
hasibzunair@gmail.com
[2] North South University, Dhaka, Bangladesh
irsnigdha@gmail.com, nabeel.mohammed@northsouth.edu
[3] Mila, University of Montreal, Montreal, Canada
joseph@josephpcohen.com

Abstract. A common approach to medical image analysis on volumetric data uses deep 2D convolutional neural networks (CNNs). This is largely attributed to the challenges imposed by the nature of the 3D data: variable volume size, GPU exhaustion during optimization. However, dealing with the individual slices independently in 2D CNNs deliberately discards the depth information which results in poor performance for the intended task. Therefore, it is important to develop methods that not only overcome the heavy memory and computation requirements but also leverage the 3D information. To this end, we evaluate a set of volume uniformizing methods to address the aforementioned issues. The first method involves sampling information evenly from a subset of the volume. Another method exploits the full geometry of the 3D volume by interpolating over the z-axis. We demonstrate performance improvements using controlled ablation studies as well as put this approach to the test on the ImageCLEF Tuberculosis Severity Assessment 2019 benchmark. We report 73% area under curve (AUC) and binary classification accuracy (ACC) of 67.5% on the test set beating all methods which leveraged only image information (without using clinical meta-data) achieving 5-th position overall. All codes and models are made available at https://github.com/hasibzunair/uniformizing-3D.

Keywords: 3D data processing · CT images · Convolutional neural networks

1 Introduction

To learn the geometric properties of volumetric data, there are challenges imposed by the data itself [1]. One major challenge is fitting the data in GPU memory during optimization. Furthermore, complicacy also arises when dealing

© Springer Nature Switzerland AG 2020
I. Rekik et al. (Eds.): PRIME 2020, LNCS 12329, pp. 156–168, 2020.
https://doi.org/10.1007/978-3-030-59354-4_15

with the variable depth size in the data. Hence, the data preparation scheme plays a vital role to build robust systems comprising volumetric image data. In the context of medical imaging, deep learning [22] has been widely used in a variety of tasks and domains [2,14,21,26,30]. While many of these medical image modalities are two dimensional (2D), computed tomography (CT) volumes are three dimensional (3D) and require more computational expense which can be an insurmountable obstacle in the case of limited GPU memory.

This necessitates the use of 2D CNN architectures [7,8,12,13,19,33,35] where the 3D data is treated as a set of independent *slices*. However, there is evidence that better results are achievable when using the full volumetric data [12,15, 18,23,28]. An observation is that 2D approaches discard information along the depth dimension/z-axis and prevents to preserve 3D context [39] leading to non-optimal performance. On the other hand, memory challenges are also experienced due to the nature of 3D data. It is also noteworthy to mention that 3D datasets exist which are annotated at the slice level, where it is justified to use 2D CNN approaches [7] but it is not the case when the data is annotated at the volume level [4,17].

In this work, we evaluate a set of volume uniformizing methods in the 3D image domain. First, we explore sampling a subset of the slices using a spacing factor to evenly sample from the sequence of slices to construct the desired volumetric output. However, deliberately losing information likely prevents learning robust representations from the data with the risk of adding artifacts. We explore interpolating over the z-axis to capture information from multiple slices which turns out to be a very reasonable solution and provides good performance and at the same time satisfy GPU memory requirements. We put our technique to the test using 3D medical images originating from the Computed Tomography (CT) domain with annotations at the CT/volume level. This is evaluated on the ImageCLEF Tuberculosis Severity Assessment 2019 test set which outperforms all methods leveraging only image information and achieves 5-th position overall. We summarize our contributions as follows:

1. We evaluate Even Slice Selection (ESS) and Spline Interpolated Zoom (SIZ) which exploit the full geometry of the 3D CT data based on improvements upon SSS [40].
2. We develop a 17-layer 3D convolutional neural network inspired by [27] with major modifications.
3. We perform controlled ablation studies and show superior performance and reliability for SIZ, both qualitatively and quantitatively.
4. We evaluate our best approach on the ImageCLEF Tuberculosis Severity Assessment 2019 benchmark which outperforms all methods leveraging only image information achieving 5-th position overall.

2   Related Work

2D Approaches. To mimic the 3-channel image representation (i.e., RGB), prior works follow multi-slice representation of 3D images as 2D inputs [9].

UUIP_BioMed [24] proposes a CNN using 2D projections of 3D CT scans which provide a probability score. HHU [3] demonstrates a multi-stage approach where they first assess the CT-findings for another task and then apply linear regression to obtain the final predictions. A hybrid 2D CNN was trained by creating 2D derived images by concatenating sagittal and coronal CT slices by CompElecEngCU [29]. Ensembling of 2D CNNs was also demonstrated by SD VA HCS/UCSD [8] for tuberculosis (TB) prediction. MedGIFT [6] used a graph-based approach by dividing the lung fields into several subregions (different for each patient) and considered these subregions as nodes of a graph. These graphs were transformed into lung descriptor vectors and then classified. UniversityAlicante [25] proposed to use each CT volume as a time series and used optical flow on the 3 directions. MostaganemFSEI [13] first selected relevant axial CT slices manually. Features are extracted using a 2D CNN which is followed by a long short term memory (LSTM) to obtain the final predictions. SSN CoE [19] manually selected a subset of slices for each patient and then used a 2D CNN for classification. FIIAugt [35] performed a random sampling of pixels of the CT volumes and used a combination of decision trees and weak classifiers.

3D Approaches. Instead of regarding the 3D spatial information as the input channel in 2D based methods, studies based on 3D convolutions for 3D medical image analysis have been demonstrated [11,37,38]. These methods are capable of capturing the 3D context in any axis and mitigates the limited 3D context along a certain axis (depth/z-axis) in 2D approaches. Hence, the 3D methods are generally better when the 3D context is required (e.g., locating nodules). A related study is UUIP [20], where they use 3D CNN as an autoencoder followed by a random forest classifier. Before training the autoencoder, the downsampling was performed at the volume level to preserve the 3D context. UoAP [40] used a 3D CNN (VoxNet) with either 16 or 32 slices that were selected from the top, middle, and bottom of the volume.

3   Methods

In this section, we describe the main components and the algorithmic steps of the methods employed for the task of TB prediction. Our goal is to learn a discriminative function $f(\mathbf{X}) \in \{0, 1\}$, where 1 indicates high TB severity and 0 otherwise. $\mathbf{X}$ represents a CT scan volume of size $W \times H \times D$, where W, H, and D represent the width, height, and depth of the volume respectively.

3.1   Uniformizing Techniques

We discuss the techniques in detail which we use to prepare the data before learning $f(.)$, the discriminative function. We talk about the algorithmic step of each technique and show qualitative results. It is important to mention that readers should not be confused when we refer to the term *slices*, it means that the sampling is done at the slice level to acquire the desired output *volume*.

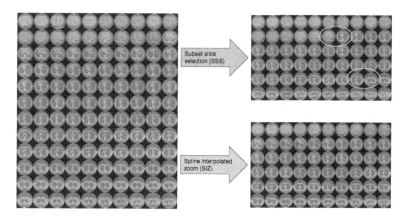

Fig. 1. Visualization of raw CT slices from an arbitrary 3D CT scan from ImageCLEF Tuberculosis Severity Assessment 2019 (left), qualitative comparison of SSS and SIZ (right) which shows SSS changes the semantic meaning of the volumetric data as a subset of the *slices* are being discarded, variations marked in red circles. This results in information loss where SIZ on the other hand maintains. (Color figure online)

Slice Selection. Depth variability of the 3D CT scans motivate the concept of sampling from *slice* level to construct the desired *volume* and balance between model performance and GPU memory constraints [7,12,15,18,23,40].

Subset Slice Selection (SSS): In this technique originally proposed in [40], *slices* are sampled from the first, middle and last position of the entire volume. The middle slices are sampled by indexing from half of the input volume depth to ensure consistency due to the depth variability. A depthwise stack is then performed over the subsets to attain the desired input volume. An illustration is shown in Fig. 1.

Even Slice Selection (ESS): A major drawback of SSS is that it prevents us from using the remaining subset of the data which causes the processed volume not to be representative of the original volume. We show qualitative evidence in Fig. 1 which is indicated by red circles. ESS can be considered as an improved version of SSS which provides good performance compared to SSS. In ESS, a target depth N and a scan depth of size D is computed. A spacing factor is then determined by the equation $F = \frac{D}{N}$. Sampling is done at the slice level by maintaining the spacing factor F between the sequence of slices in the volumetric data. This gives a better representation compared to the SSS technique as we show experimentally in later sections. The algorithmic steps are shown in Algorithm 1.

Spline Interpolated Zoom (SIZ). Even though ESS preserves the representation to an extent, the desired volume is still acquired from a subset of the data. Therefore, to discard the concept of sampling from independent *slices*, an alternative solution is Spline Interpolated Zoom (SIZ) which enables even better representation of the volumetric data. Similar techniques have been used in the other studies [11,20,37,38]. In this technique, instead of manually selecting a subset of slices, a constant target depth size of N is pre-determined. We then take each volume, calculate its depth D, and zoom it along the z-axis by a factor of $\frac{1}{D/N}$ using spline interpolation [5], where the interpolant is an order of three. Here, the input volume is zoomed or squeezed by replicating the nearest pixel along the depth/z-axis. A visual representation of this can be seen in Fig. 1 along with the algorithm summarized in Algorithm 2. As it uses spline interpolation to squeeze or expand the z-axis to the desired depth, it retains a substantial level of information from original 3D volume as opposed to the aforementioned techniques, SSS and ESS, which discarded a part of the volumetric data.

Algorithm 1. Even Slice Selection (ESS) data processing method	**Algorithm 2.** Spline Interpolated Zoom (SIZ) data processing method
Require: A 3D volumetric image I of size $W \times H \times depth$.	**Require:** A 3D volumetric image I of size $W \times H \times depth$.
Ensure: I is a rank 3 tensor.	**Ensure:** I is a rank 3 tensor.
1: Set constant target depth of size N	1: Set constant target depth of size N
2: Compute *depth* denoted as D	2: Calculate the *depth* denoted as D
3: Compute depth factor by $F = \frac{D}{N}$	3: Compute depth factor by $\frac{1}{D/N}$ denoted as DF
4: Sample slices from the volume by maintaining the depth factor F	4: Zoom I using spline interpolation [5] by the factor DF
5: Output processed volume I' of dimension $W \times H \times N$	5: Output processed volume I' of dimension $W \times H \times N$

3.2 Three-Dimensional (3D) CNN Architecture

Inspired from [27], we design a 17 layer 3D CNN which comprises four 3D convolutional (CONV) layers with two layers consisting of 64 filters followed by 128 and 256 filters all with a kernel size of $3 \times 3 \times 3$. Each CONV layer is followed by a max-pooling (MAXPOOL) layer with a stride of 2 and ReLU activation which ends with batch normalization (BN) layer [16]. Essentially, our feature extraction block consists of four CONV-MAXPOOL-BN modules. The final output from the feature extraction block is flattened and passed to a fully connected layer with 512 neurons. We use an effective dropout rate of 60% similar to [31]. Due to a coding error, we implement this using two dropout layers [34]. The output is then carried to a dense layer of 2 neurons with softmax activation for the binary classification problem. The network architecture is shown in Fig. 2.

We consider keeping the network relatively simple to avoid overparameterization [32] problems with only 10,658,498 learnable parameters. This is also motivated by the fewer number of training samples and the memory challenges associated with it.

4   Experiments

4.1   Dataset

The dataset is provided by ImageCLEF Tuberculosis 2019 [4,17], intended for the task of severity scoring (SVR). It consists of a total 335 chest 3D CT scans with annotation of high and low provided by a medical doctor and also lung segmentation masks, in addition to clinically relevant metadata was also available which includes the following binary measures: disability, relapse, symptoms of TB, comorbidity, bacillary, drug resistance, higher education, ex-prisoner, alcoholic, smoking. From the dataset, 218 individual chest CT scans are provided for training, and the remaining 117 were held out for the final evaluation in the ImageCLEF evaluation platform. The CT images each have a dimension of 512×512 pixels and the depth size varying from about 50 to 400 which store raw voxel intensity in Hounsfield units (HU). Figure 1 shows an instance of this.

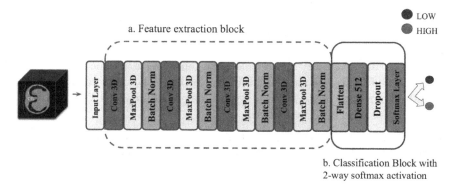

Fig. 2. Our proposed 17-layer 3D convolutional neural network architecture which consist of several modules of 3D conv, maxpool and batch normalization layers.

4.2   Baseline and Implementation Details

We consider SSS [40] as the baseline. Each configuration embodies a different type of processing discussed in Sect. 3.1. All configurations are based on the network described in Sect. 3.2 and trained on a machine with NVIDIA 1050Ti with 4 GB memory. We used Stochastic Gradient Descent(SGD) optimizer with a learning rate of 10^{-6} and a momentum of 0.99, parameters found from multiple trials. Weight is initialized using the Glorot initialization method [10] and minimize the Mean average error [36] during training. During training, the network accepts input of size $128 \times 128 \times 64$ with a batch size of 2. We tried increasing the depth size to more than 64 but resulted in GPU memory error. For our experiments with ESS, we found four CT scans which had a depth of less than 64 with a minimum being 47. In these cases, we first apply ESS and then calculate the difference with the target depth, 64, and repeatedly add the last slice until the target depth is reached. We resize to 128×128 on the slice level and then use techniques discussed in Sect. 3.1 to get the desired volume. To ensure a fair comparison between the uniformizing methods, we keep the desired input size of $128 \times 128 \times 64$ for all our experiments. We provide code and model to reproduce our experiments at https://github.com/hasibzunair/uniformizing-3D.

4.3 Metrics

As per challenge rules, the task is evaluated as a binary classification problem. The evaluation metrics are Area Under the ROC Curve (AUC) and accuracy (ACC), prioritizing the former by the challenge organizers. We refrain from using other evaluation metrics since it would limit our comparison with the approaches proposed in the challenge.

4.4 Results

In this section, extensive experiments are conducted to evaluate the performance of the uniformizing methods. First, we compare our methods with the baseline on the ImageCLEF Tuberculosis Severity Assessment 2019 benchmark. Since the dataset is small, we also perform cross-validation tests to estimate the general effectiveness and reliability of the methods, ensuring a balance between bias and variance. Finally, we show ablations of orthogonal preprocessing and how our method performs related to other methods on the ImageCLEF Tuberculosis Severity Assessment 2019 benchmark.

Comparison with Baseline. We believe SIZ better represents the 3D CT when downsampled compared to SSS and ESS. This is depicted in Fig. 3, which shows that SIZ yields better performance in both metrics by a margin of 9% and 8% compared to SSS and is of significance. We further validate this by showing the qualitative comparison in Fig. 1 in which we show visual evidence that slice selection methods do not leverage information from full 3D CT scans which SIZ does. It is also observed that ESS yields slightly better results than SSS. This is because even though ESS samples from half of the volume, the sampling is carried out in a sequential process. This approach results in a better representation of the 3D CT scan compared to SSS where a subset of slices is sampled from predefined points. Thus, selecting specific *slices* does not preserve the semantic meaning of volumetric data as it is not the proper representation of the 3D CT scan which is also intuitive. Even though ESS is downsampling the volume from a subset, this still results in better performance as the sampling is done throughout the entire volume. In particular, ESS increases the probability of sampling the TB affected slices compared to SSS. Since TB infection can affect any part of the lung, it is also not possible to determine which *slices* are to be discarded without looking at the scans individually. As the annotations are provided at the volume level and not at the slice level, it is crucial to retrieve information from the entire volume.

Cross Validation. We also report the cross-validation results as shown in Fig. 4a. It can be seen that SIZ not only has a higher mean accuracy than

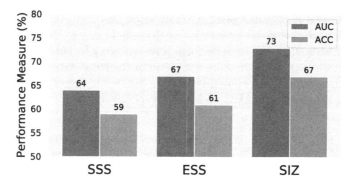

Fig. 3. Performance measures reported are evaluated on the test set provided by Image-CLEF Tuberculosis Severity Assessment 2019 consisting of 117 chest 3D CT scans.

the baselines but also has a lower standard deviation owing to more reliability. Figure 4b displays the ROC curve, which shows better performance of the method SIZ compared to the baselines. It is to be noted that the ROC curves reported are from the best performing results on the validation set. Each point on ROC represents a different trade-off between false positives and false negatives. A ROC curve that is closer to the upper right indicates better performance (TPR is higher than FPR). Even though during the early and last stages, the ROC curve of SIZ seems to highly fluctuate at certain points, the overall performance is much higher than the baselines, as indicated by the AUC value. This better performance demonstrates that 3D context plays a crucial role and enables the model to learn effective representations.

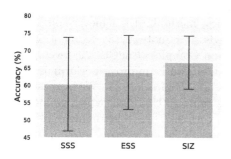

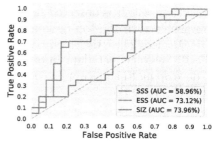

(a) Mean accuracy and standard deviation of cross validation results over 10 trials with randomly separated 80% training and 20% test images.

(b) ROC curves for SSS, ESS and SIZ, along with the corresponding AUC values from best weights for each configuration.

Fig. 4. Performance measures reported from 10 runs of the cross-validation.

Ablation Study. Table 1 illustrates the ablations on orthogonal preprocessing. For all configurations SSS, ESS, and SIZ we observe performance improvements on both AUC and ACC after pixel normalization and zero-centering. Since the 3D CT scans have raw voxel intensities in Hounsfield units (HU), we normalize the values between [0,1]. We then perform zero-centering by subtracting the total mean value from each pixel, making the mean of the total dataset zero. For SIZ, the increase in performance compared to baseline is the larger with an increase of 11% and 14% margin in AUC and ACC respectively.

Table 1. Ablations of orthogonal preprocessing evaluated on the final test set provided by ImageCLEF Tuberculosis Severity Assessment 2019 consisting of 117 chest CT scans.

Method	Normalize	Zero center	AUC	ACC
SSS	No	No	0.626	0.538
SSS	Yes	No	0.635	0.573
SSS	Yes	Yes	0.640	0.598
ESS	No	No	0.639	0.607
ESS	Yes	No	0.667	0.598
ESS	Yes	Yes	0.670	0.611
SIZ	No	No	0.648	0.581
SIZ	Yes	No	0.652	0.607
SIZ	Yes	Yes	**0.730**	**0.675**

ImageCLEF Tuberculosis Severity Assessment 2019 Benchmark. We summarize the results in Table 2 which report the performance evaluation on the final test set. It is observed that our best method, SIZ, achieves comparable performance with the top-ranking methods. It is noteworthy to mention that UUIP_Biomed [24], UUIP [20], HHU [3] and CompElecEngCU [29] leverage the clinically relevant metadata in order to significantly improve performance and also develop multi-stage approaches which adds complexity [4]. We increased the input volume to the $128 \times 128 \times 128$, the same as UUIP[20] which results in a model almost three times larger than ours with 29,532,866 learnable parameters and led to a memory error. Even with using only image information, our method performs better than SD VA HCS/UCSD [8] where they used an ensemble of 2D CNNs and the relevant meta-data. It also performed better than the 3D CNN method by UoAP [40]. Our best method also outperforms several 2D approaches such as MedGIFT [13], SSN CoE [19] and FIIAugt [35].

From Table 2 it is also seen that among the top-ranking results which only use image information (no meta-data), our method achieves the best results. Even though MedGIFT [6] did not use any meta-data, they were the only team that used the lung segmentation masks.

Table 2. Performance metric results compared with previous top ranking approaches on ImageCLEF Benchmark. The results reported on each of the metrics are on the ImageCLEF test set which consists of 117 3D CT scans. Boldface indicates our best method

Group name	Method type	Input volume	AUC	ACC	Meta-data
UIIP_BioMed [24]	2D	None	0.7877	0.7179	Yes
UIIP [20]	3D - None	$(128 \times 128 \times 128)$	0.7754	0.7179	Yes
HHU [3]	2D	None	0.7695	0.6923	Yes
CompElecEngCU [29]	2D	None	0.7629	0.6581	Yes
Ours	3D - SIZ	$(128 \times 128 \times 64)$	**0.7300**	**0.6750**	No
SD VA HCS/UCSD [8]	2D	None	0.7214	0.6838	Yes
MedGIFT [6]	2D	None	0.7196	0.6410	No
UniversityAlicante [25]	2D	None	0.7013	0.7009	No
MostaganemFSEI [13]	2D	None	0.6510	0.6154	No
SSN CoE [19]	2D	None	0.6264	0.6068	No
UoAP [40]	3D - SSS	$(128 \times 128 \times 32)$	0.6111	0.6154	No
FIIAugt [35]	2D	None	0.5692	0.5556	No

5   Discussion and Conclusion

We address the problem of variable volume size and heavy computation requirements during optimization when dealing with 3D image data. In particular, we evaluate a set of volume uniformizing methods applied to 3D medical images in the CT domain for the task of TB prediction. We hypothesize that analyzing 3D images in a per slice (2D) basis is a sub-optimal approach that can be improved by 3D context if computational challenges can be overcomed. We systematically evaluate different ways of uniformizing CT volumes so that they fit into memory and determine interpolating over the z-axis to be the best. We further validate this approach on the ImageCLEF benchmark obtaining 5th place and beat all methods which operate on the CT image alone without patient metadata.

References

1. Ahmed, E., et al.: A survey on deep learning advances on different 3D data representations. arXiv preprint arXiv:1808.01462 (2018)
2. Becker, A., et al.: Detection of tuberculosis patterns in digital photographs of chest x-ray images using deep learning: feasibility study. Int. J. Tuberc. Lung Dis. **22**(3), 328–335 (2018)
3. Bogomasov, K., Braun, D., Burbach, A., Himmelspach, L., Conrad, S.: Feature and deep learning based approaches for automatic report generation and severity scoring of lung tuberculosis from CT images. In: CLEF 2019 Working Notes, vol. 2380, pp. 9–12 (2019)

4. Cid, Y.D., Liauchuk, V., Klimuk, D., Tarasau, A., Kovalev, V., Müller, H.: Overview of imagecleftuberculosis 2019-automatic CT-based report generation and tuberculosis severity assessment. In: CLEF 2019 Working Notes. CEUR Workshop Proceedings, pp. 09–12 (2019)

5. De Boor, C.: Bicubic spline interpolation. J. Math. Phys. **41**(1–4), 212–218 (1962)

6. Diecente Cid, Y., Müller, H.: Lung graph-model classiffication with SVM and CNN for tuberculosis severity assessment and automatic CT report generation. In: Proceedings of CLEF (Conference and Labs of the Evaluation Forum) 2019 Working Notes. No. CONFERENCE, 9–12 September 2019 (2019)

7. Gao, X.W., Hui, R., Tian, Z.: Classification of CT brain images based on deep learning networks. Comput. Methods Programs Biomed. **138**, 49–56 (2017)

8. Gentili, A.: ImageCLEF 2019: tuberculosis-severity scoring and CT report with neural networks, transfer learning and ensembling. IN: CLEF2019 Working Notes vol. 2380, pp. 9–12 (2019)

9. Gerard, S.E., Herrmann, J., Kaczka, D.W., Musch, G., Fernandez-Bustamante, A., Reinhardt, J.M.: Multi-resolution convolutional neural networks for fully automated segmentation of acutely injured lungs in multiple species. Med. Image Anal. **60**, 101592 (2020)

10. Glorot, X., Bengio, Y.: Understanding the difficulty of training deep feedforward neural networks. In: Proceedings of the Thirteenth International Conference on Artificial Intelligence and Statistics, pp. 249–256 (2010)

11. Gordaliza, P.M., Vaquero, J.J., Sharpe, S., Gleeson, F., Munoz-Barrutia, A.: A multi-task self-normalizing 3D-CNN to infer tuberculosis radiological manifestations. arXiv preprint arXiv:1907.12331 (2019)

12. Grewal, M., Srivastava, M.M., Kumar, P., Varadarajan, S.: RadNet: radiologist level accuracy using deep learning for hemorrhage detection in CT scans. In: 2018 IEEE 15th International Symposium on Biomedical Imaging (ISBI 2018), pp. 281–284. IEEE (2018)

13. Hamadi, A., Cheikh, N.B., Zouatine, Y., Menad, S.M.B., Djebbara, M.R.: Image-CLEF 2019: deep learning for tuberculosis CT image analysis. In: CLEF2019 Working Notes, vol. 2380, pp. 9–12 (2019)

14. Hua, K.L., Hsu, C.H., Hidayati, S.C., Cheng, W.H., Chen, Y.J.: Computer-aided classification of lung nodules on computed tomography images via deep learning technique. OncoTargets Therapy **8**, 2015–2022 (2015)

15. Huang, X., Shan, J., Vaidya, V.: Lung nodule detection in CT using 3D convolutional neural networks. In: 2017 IEEE 14th International Symposium on Biomedical Imaging (ISBI 2017), pp. 379–383. IEEE (2017)

16. Ioffe, S., Szegedy, C.: Batch normalization: accelerating deep network training by reducing internal covariate shift. arXiv preprint arXiv:1502.03167 (2015)

17. Ionescu, B., et al.: ImageCLEF 2019: multimedia retrieval in medicine, lifelogging, security and nature. In: Crestani, F., et al. (eds.) CLEF 2019. LNCS, vol. 11696, pp. 358–386. Springer, Cham (2019). https://doi.org/10.1007/978-3-030-28577-7_28

18. Ji, S., Xu, W., Yang, M., Yu, K.: 3D convolutional neural networks for human action recognition. IEEE Trans. Pattern Anal. Mach. Intell. **35**(1), 221–231 (2012)

19. Kavitha, S., Nandhinee, P., Harshana, S., Jahnavi Srividya S., Harrinei, K.: Image-CLEF 2019: A 2D convolutional neural network approach for severity scoring of lung tuberculosis using CT images. In: CLEF 2019 Working Notes, vol. 2380, pp. 9–12 (2019)

20. Kazlouski, S.: ImageCLEF 2019: CT image analysis for TB severity scoring and CT report generation using autoencoded image features. In: CLEF2019 Working Notes, vol. 2380, pp. 9–12 (2019)
21. Lakhani, P., Sundaram, B.: Deep learning at chest radiography: automated classification of pulmonary tuberculosis by using convolutional neural networks. Radiology **284**(2), 574–582 (2017)
22. LeCun, Y., Bengio, Y., Hinton, G.: Deep learning. Nature **521**(7553), 436 (2015)
23. Li, B., Zhang, T., Xia, T.: Vehicle detection from 3D lidar using fully convolutional network. arXiv preprint arXiv:1608.07916 (2016)
24. Liauchuk, V.: ImageCLEF 2019: projection-based CT image analysis for TB severity scoring and CT report generation. In: CLEF 2019 Working Notes, vol. 2380, pp. 9–12 (2019)
25. Llopis, F., Fuster, A., Azorın, J., Llopis, I.: Using improved optical flow model to detect tuberculosis. In: CLEF 2019 Working Notes, vol. 2380, pp. 9–12 (2019)
26. Lopes, U., Valiati, J.F.: Pre-trained convolutional neural networks as feature extractors for tuberculosis detection. Comput. Biol. Med. **89**, 135–143 (2017)
27. Maturana, D., Scherer, S.: VoxNet: a 3D convolutional neural network for real-time object recognition. In: 2015 IEEE/RSJ International Conference on Intelligent Robots and Systems (IROS), pp. 922–928. IEEE (2015)
28. Milletari, F., Navab, N., Ahmadi, S.A.: V-Net: fully convolutional neural networks for volumetric medical image segmentation. In: 2016 Fourth International Conference on 3D Vision (3DV), pp. 565–571. IEEE (2016)
29. Mossa, A.A., Yibre, A.M., Çevik, U.: Multi-view CNN with MLP for diagnosing tuberculosis patients using CT scans and clinically relevant metadata. In: CLEF2019 Working Notes, vol. 2380, pp. 9–12 (2019)
30. Pan, S.J., Yang, Q.: A survey on transfer learning. IEEE Trans. Knowl. Data Eng. **22**(10), 1345–1359 (2009)
31. Pattnaik, A., Kanodia, S., Chowdhury, R., Mohanty, S.: Predicting tuberculosis related lung deformities from CT scan images using 3D CNN. In: CLEF2019 Working Notes, vol. 2380, pp. 9–12 (2019)
32. Raghu, M., Zhang, C., Kleinberg, J., Bengio, S.: Transfusion: understanding transfer learning for medical imaging. In: Advances in Neural Information Processing Systems, pp. 3342–3352 (2019)
33. Ronneberger, O., Fischer, P., Brox, T.: U-Net: convolutional networks for biomedical image segmentation. In: Navab, N., Hornegger, J., Wells, W.M., Frangi, A.F. (eds.) MICCAI 2015. LNCS, vol. 9351, pp. 234–241. Springer, Cham (2015). https://doi.org/10.1007/978-3-319-24574-4_28
34. Srivastava, N., Hinton, G., Krizhevsky, A., Sutskever, I., Salakhutdinov, R.: Dropout: a simple way to prevent neural networks from overfitting. J. Mach. Learn. Res. **15**(1), 1929–1958 (2014)
35. Tabarcea, A., Rosca, V., Iftene, A.: ImageCLEFmed tuberculosis 2019: predicting CT scans severity scores using stage-wise boosting in low-resource environments. In: CLEF2019 Working Notes, vol. 2380, pp. 9–12 (2019)
36. Willmott, C.J., Matsuura, K.: Advantages of the mean absolute error (MAE) over the root mean square error (RMSE) in assessing average model performance. Clim. Res. **30**(1), 79–82 (2005)
37. Wu, W., et al.: A deep learning system that generates quantitative CT reports for diagnosing pulmonary tuberculosis. arXiv preprint arXiv:1910.02285 (2019)
38. Yang, J., Huang, X., Ni, B., Xu, J., Yang, C., Xu, G.: Reinventing 2D convolutions for 3D images. arXiv-1911 (2019)

39. Zou, L., Zheng, J., Miao, C., Mckeown, M.J., Wang, Z.J.: 3D CNN based automatic diagnosis of attention deficit hyperactivity disorder using functional and structural MRI. IEEE Access **5**, 23626–23636 (2017)
40. Zunair, H., Rahman, A., Mohammed, N.: Estimating severity from CT scans of tuberculosis patients using 3d convolutional nets and slice selection. In: CLEF2019 Working Notes, vol. 2380, pp. 9–12 (2019)

mr²NST: Multi-resolution and Multi-reference Neural Style Transfer for Mammography

Sheng Wang[1,2], Jiayu Huo[1,2], Xi Ouyang[1,2], Jifei Che[2], Zhong Xue[2], Dinggang Shen[2], Qian Wang[1], and Jie-Zhi Cheng[2(✉)]

[1] Shanghai United Imaging Intelligence Co., Ltd., Shanghai, China
wang.qian@sjtu.edu.cn
[2] Institute for Medical Imaging Technology, School of Biomedical Engineering, Shanghai Jiao Tong University, Shanghai, China
jiezhi.zheng@united-imaging.com

Abstract. Computer-aided diagnosis with deep learning techniques has been shown to be helpful for the diagnosis of the mammography in many clinical studies. However, the image styles of different vendors are very distinctive, and there may exist domain gap among different vendors that could potentially compromise the universal applicability of one deep learning model. In this study, we explicitly address style variety issue with the proposed multi-resolution and multi-reference neural style transfer (mr²NST) network. The mr²NST can normalize the styles from different vendors to the same style baseline with very high resolution. We illustrate that the image quality of the transferred images is comparable to the quality of original images of the target domain (vendor) in terms of NIMA scores. Meanwhile, the mr²NST results are also shown to be helpful for the lesion detection in mammograms.

Keywords: Mammography · Neural style transfer · Style normalization

1 Introduction

The mammography is a widely used screening tool for breast cancer. It has been shown in many studies [2,5] that the incorporation of CAD softwares in the reading workflow of mammography can be helpful to improve the diagnostic workup. Equipped with the deep learning (DL) techniques, the CAD scheme was shown to further outperform radiologists from multiple centers across several western countries [7]. Although promising CAD performances for mammography have been shown in many previous studies, there is still an essential issue that is not well and explicitly addressed in previous DL works. As shown in Fig. 1, the image styles, like image contrast, edge sharpness, etc., of different vendors are quite different. Accordingly, one DL based CAD scheme may not always perform well on mammograms from different vendors, unless sufficient large and diverse training data are

© Springer Nature Switzerland AG 2020
I. Rekik et al. (Eds.): PRIME 2020, LNCS 12329, pp. 169–177, 2020.
https://doi.org/10.1007/978-3-030-59354-4_16

provided. Because the collection of large mammograms from various vendors can be very difficult and expensive, we here propose a mammographic style transfer (mST) scheme to normalize the image styles of different vendors to the same style baseline. It will be shown that style normalization step with the mST scheme can further boost the robustness of the classic Faster-RCNN detector [6] to the mammograms of different vendors and improve the detection performance for masses and microcalcification, denoted as μC for short throughout this paper.

The direct use of the off-the-shell neural style transfer (NST) methods for the mST scheme may encounter two major issues. First, the style transfer of very subtle but important abnormalities like μC or calcification is very challenging. It is because the ST for the μC, which could be depicted in less than 20 pixels, may need to be carried out in high resolution. However, to our best knowledge, most classic NST methods only support images with resolution less than 1000 × 1000, whereas the dimensionality of nowadays mammography is usually larger than 2000 × 2000. Therefore, the step of image downsize is inevitable in our problem and hence the quality of subtle abnormalities like μC after transfer may be compromised. Second, for most classic NST methods, a style reference image is usually needs to be manually selected as network input. However, in our context, an automatic selection scheme for style reference images is needed to facilitate the style normalization process. Meanwhile, the appearance variety of mammography is large and also depends on the category of breast density and the subject's figure. The consideration of only one style reference image may not be sufficient to yield a plausible transfer results.

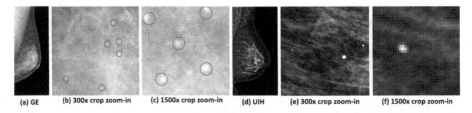

Fig. 1. The comparison of image styles from different vendors. Red circles highlight calcifications and μCs. (Color figure online)

To address the two issues, the mST scheme is realized with a new multiresolution and multi-reference neural style transfer (mr^{2}NST) network in this study. By considering multi-resolution, the details of subtle abnormalities like μC or calcification can be better preserved in the transfer process. With the multiple reference images, our mr^{2}NST network can deal with wide variety of mammography and integrate the style transfer effects from the reference images for more plausible style normalization results. Our mr^{2}NST network also takes into account the similarities between the input image to be transferred and reference images for the integration of multiple style transfer effects. To our best knowledge, this is the first study that explicitly explores the style transfer technique to mitigate the style variation problem, which may compromise the detection performance for breast lesions.

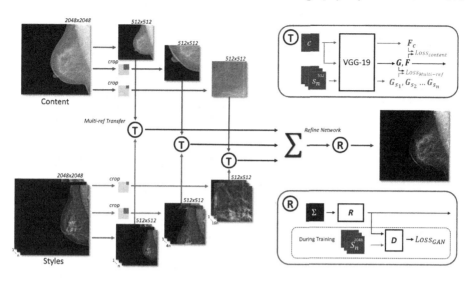

Fig. 2. The pipeline of the proposed mr^{2}NST for mST. **T** denote the multi-resolution operation; **R** stands for the refiner network.

We perform the style transfer experiments by comparing with the classic cycleGAN [11] and the conventional exact histogram matching (EHM) [1], and test the style normalization, i.e., mST, results on the detection tasks of masses and μCs in mammograms. The experimental results suggest that the mST results from our mr^{2}NST network are more plausible and can mitigate the problem of style differences from distinctive vendors for better detection results.

2   Method

In this section, we will briefly introduce the concept of NST and then discuss the details of our mr^{2}NST network. The network of our mr^{2}NST network is shown in Fig. 2, and the backbone is VGG19 [8].

2.1   Neural Style Transfer

The NST, which was first introduced by Gatys et al. [3], commonly requires two input images of a content image x_C to be transferred and a style reference image x_S, and then performs feature learning of the feature representatives of $F_l(x_C)$ and $F_l(x_S)$ in layer l of a NST network. Each column of $F_l(x)$, $F_l \in R^{M_l(x) \times N_l}$, is a feature map, whereas N_l is the number of feature maps in layer l and $M_l(x) = H_l(x) \times W_l(x)$ is the product of height and width of each feature map. The output of NST is the style transferred image, denoted as $\hat{x}$, by minimizing the loss function:

$$L_{total} = L_{content} + L_{style}, \tag{1}$$

where the content term $L_{content}$ compares feature maps from the $\hat{x}$ and x_S of each single layer l_C:

$$L_{content} = \frac{1}{N_{l_c} M_{l_c}(x_C)} \sum_{ij} (F_{l_c}(\hat{x}) - F_{l_c}(x_C))_{ij}^2, \tag{2}$$

and the style term L_{style} compares a set of summary statistics:

$$L_{style} = \sum_l w_l E_l;$$
$$E_l = \frac{1}{4N_l^2} \sum_{ij} (G_l(\hat{x}) - G_l(x_S))_{ij}^2, \tag{3}$$

where $G_l(x) = \frac{1}{M_l(x)} F_l(x)^T F_l(x)$ is the gram matrix of the feature maps of the layer l in response to image x.

2.2   Multiple Reference Style Images

The mr^{2}NST network takes multiple reference style images for better accommodate the appearance variety of mammography. Different regions in a mammography may need distinctive reference images to be transferred. For example the dense breast image to be transferred may be more suitable to take reference of images with denser glandular tissues. To attain this goal, a quantitative measurement for style similarity is needed.

The gram matrix in the Eq. 3 computes the co-variance statistics of features at one layer as the quantification of style similarity of the corresponding perceptual level. A higher value in the gram matrix suggests more similar of the corresponding paired feature maps in style. Accordingly, with the multiple n reference style images, we can compute the corresponding gram matrices with each style image and integrate of the gram matrices with the max operation. Specifically, A simple but effective multi-reference style term is defined as

$$L_{Multi-ref} = \sum_l w_l E_l;$$
$$E_l = \frac{1}{4N_l^2} \sum_{ij} (G_l(\hat{x}) - G_l)_{ij}^2; \tag{4}$$
$$G_l = H(M(F_l(x_{S_1}), F_l(x_{S_2})...F_l(x_{S_n})), \overline{h}).$$

The function $M()$ is a element-wise max operation takes $nN_l \times H_l \times W_l$ feature maps $F(x_{S_n})$ with the nth reference image at the lth layer and outputs a $N \times N$ matrix, G_l'. Specifically, the function $M()$ computes each element g_{ij}' of G_l' as

$$g'_{ij} = max\left(F_i(x_{S_1})^T F_j(x_{S_1}), F_i(x_{S_2})^T F_j(x_{S_2}), ..., F_i(x_{S_n})^T F_j(x_{S_n})\right). \tag{5}$$

The function H is a histogram specification function to normalize the G'_l with the reference density histogram, $\bar{h}$, for numerical stabilization. $\bar{h}$ is the density histogram of a $n \times N_l \times N_l$ matrix stacked by n $N_l \times N_l$ style gram matrices.

The size of nowadays mammography is commonly bigger than 2080×2080, and may require formidably large GPU memory for any off-the-shelf NST method. In our experience, the ST for an image with the size of 512×512 could consume up to $10.8\,\text{GB}$ GPU memory for inference. For the mST with original size, it is estimated to require more than $160\,\text{GB}$ GPU memory and hence is very impractical for the clinical usage or laboratorial study. Accordingly, we here propose a multi-resolution strategy that can more efficiently use the GPU resources and still attain the goal of better consideration of local details in the mST scheme.

Referring to Fig. 2, the multi-resolution is implemented by considering the 2048×2048 original image (scale0), division of image into 4 1024×1024 patches with overlapping (scale1) as well as 16 512×512 patches with overlapping (scale2). The image of scale0 and the patches of scale1 are resized into 512×512 to fit the memory limit and support the feature learning with the middle- and large-sized receptive fields.

The image and patches of the scale0, scale1 and scale2 are transferred by taking multiple reference style images, see Fig. 2. For each patch/image of each scale, we perform the style transfer by optimizing the multi-reference style term $L_{Multi-ref}$ defined in Eq. 4. Afterward, the all transferred patches of scale1 and scale2 are further reconstructed back to the integral mammograms. The reconstructed mammograms of scale1 and scale2 as well as the transferred image of scale0 are then further resized back to the original size. For the final output, we integrate the three transferred images of scale0, scale1 and scale2 with weighted summation and further refine the summed image by a refiner network. The final style transferred mammogram can be computed as

$$M_{out} = R(S_0, S_1, S_2) = r(\sum_{n=0}^{2} w_n S_n), \tag{6}$$

where R is the refiner network and r denotes a network composed by 3 1×1 convolutional layers [9], and w_0, w_1, and w_3 are three learnable weights. The refiner network is trained with the GAN scheme, where the refiner network is treated as generator to fool a discriminator D. The discriminator D, with the backbone of ResNet18 [4], is devised to check whether the input image is of the target style. The training of the refiner GAN can be driven by minimizing the loss:

$$L_{GAN}(R, D) = \log D(Style) + \log (1 - D(R(S_0, S_1, S_2))). \tag{7}$$

3   Experiments and Results

In this study, we involved 1,380 mammograms, where 840 and 540 mammograms were collected from two distinctive hospitals, denoted as H_A and H_B, with local IRB approvals. The mammograms from H_A and H_B were acquired from the GE healthcare (GE) and United Imaging Healthcare (UIH), respectively. All mammograms are based on the unit of breast. Accordingly, there are half cranicaudal (CC) and half mediolateral oblique (MLO) views of mammograms in our dataset. For the training of the refiner GAN with the Eq. 7, we use independent 80 GE and 80 UIH mammograms, which are not included in the 1,380 images.

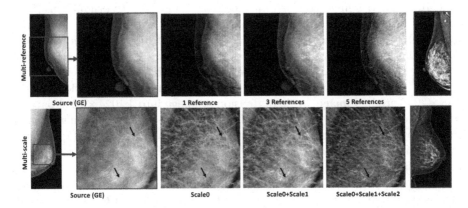

Fig. 3. The visual illustration of the multiple reference and multiple resolution effect. The red arrows suggest the calcifications or μCs in the images. (Color figure online)

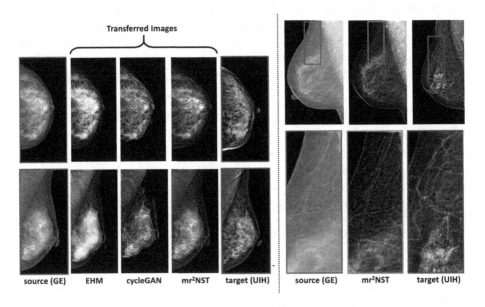

Fig. 4. Visual comparison of mST results from different methods. The right part gives zoom-in comparison in terms of vessel structures.

Throughout the experiments, we set the source and target domains as GE (H_A) and UIH (H_B), respectively. As can be found in Fig. 1 and Fig. 4, the image style of GE is relatively soft, whereas the UIH style is sharper. Accordingly, the image styles from different vendors can be very distinctive. We compare our method with the baselines of cycleGAN [11] and exact histogram matching (EHM) [1]. Since the cycleGAN requires training step, we randomly select 100 and 80 images from H_A and H_B, respectively, to train the cycleGAN. Except the refiner GAN, our mr^{2}NST doesn't need a training step. For each ST inference with mr^{2}NST, we select 5 reference images of the target UIH domain with 5 best similar images from an reference image bank of 40 UIH images, which are not included in the 1,380 images and the 80 training data of refiner GAN. The similarity for the selection is based on the area of breast. The selected reference images are of the same view (CC/MLO) with the source image to be transferred. The optimizer Adam is adopted with 400 epochs of optimization for our mr^{2}NST.

Figure 3 illustrates the efficacy of multi-reference and multi-resolution scheme for the mST from GE to UIH. The upper row in Fig. 3 shows better enhance on glandular tissues with 5 reference images on a case with high density, while the lower row suggests the calcification can be better enhanced by fusing the transferred images from all three scales. Figure 4 shows the mST results from our mr^{2}NST and the baselines of cycleGAN and EHM. From visual comparison, the quality of the transferred images from mr^{2}NST are much better. The cycleGAN requires large GPU memory and can't support mST in high resolution. Meanwhile, referring to the right part of Fig. 4, mr^{2}NST can preserve the details of vasculature after the mST.

Table 1. NIMA scores of UIH, GE and mST results.

	GE	UIH	mr2NST	cycleGAN	EHM
Score	5.16 ± 0.12	5.43 ± 0.10	5.42 ± 0.15	4.74 ± 0.22	5.29 ± 0.11

Two experiments are conducted to illustrate the efficacy of our mr^{2}NST w.r.t. the transferred image quality and detection performance. The first experiment aims to evaluate the quality of transferred images with the neural image assessment (NIMA) score [10]. Specifically, we randomly select 400 GE and 400 UIH (not overlapped with the training dataset of cycleGAN) for mST. The 400 GE images are transferred to the UIH domain with the comparing methods and the resulted NIMA scores of the transferred images are listed in Table 1. We also compare the NIMA scores between the transferred and original images at UIH domain with the student t test. The computed p-values are 0.58, 4.76×10^{-12}, and 3.34×10^{-61}, w.r.t. mr^{2}NST, EHM, and cycleGAN, suggesting that the quality of mST images from mr^{2}NST is not significantly different to the quality of original UIH images in terms of NIMA scores. On the other hand, the quality differences of mST images from EHM, and cycleGAN to the UIH images deem to be significant.

The second experiment aims to illustrate if the mST can help to mitigate the domain gap problem and improve the detection performance. The dataset of UIH (H_B) is relatively small, and therefore, we aim to illustrate if the mST from GE to UIH can assist to improve the detection results in the UIH domain. Since the baselines can't yield comparable image quality to the target UIH domain, we only perform this experiments with mr^2NST. Specifically, we conduct 5 schemes of various combination of UIH, UIH^{GE} (simulated UIH with mr^2NST from GE), and GE data for the training of Faster-RCNN [6] with the backbone of resnet50. The detection results for masses and μCs are reported in Table 2.

The testing UIH data, which is served as the testing data for all training settings in Table 2, include 120 images of 90 positive cases and 30 normal images. The 90 testing positive cases have 36 and 28 images with only masses and μC, respectively, and 26 images with both. For the training with only real UIH data, there are 420 images with 100 normal cases and 320 positive cases (131 only masses, 123 only μC, and 66 both). For the 2nd to 5th schemes in Table 2, we aim to compare the effects of adding 420 and 840 extra training data with either real GE or UIH^{GE} images. The UIH^{GE} data of the 2nd and 3rd are the mST results from the GE data of 4th and 5th schemes, respectively, and 420 GE images is the subset of 840 GE images. For systematical comparison, the 420 images GE has the same distribution of mass, μC and normal cases with the real UIH 420 images, whereas the 840 GE images are distributed in the same ratio with double size.

In Table 2, the detection performance is assessed with average precision (AP) and recall with average 0.5 ($Recall^{0.5}$) and 1 ($Recall^1$) false-positives (FP) per image. As can be observed, the adding of UIH^{GE} in the training data can better boost the detection performance, by comparing the rows of 2nd, 3rd to 1st row in Table 2. Referring to 4th and 5th rows in Table 2, the direct incorporation of GE data seems to be not helpful for the detection performance. The transferred UIH^{GE} images on the other hand are more similar to the real UIH images and can be served more informative samples for the training of detector.

Table 2. Detection performance comparison.

Training data	Masses			μCs		
	AP	$Recall^{0.5}$	$Recall^1$	AP	$Recall^{0.5}$	$Recall^1$
420 real UIH	0.656	0.761	0.869	0.515	0.459	0.567
420 real UIH + 420 UIH^{GE}	0.724	**0.823**	0.891	0.569	0.593	0.702
420 real UIH + 840 UIH^{GE}	**0.738**	0.811	**0.912**	**0.670**	**0.622**	**0.784**
420 real UIH + 420 GE	0.641	0.741	0.847	0.555	0.509	0.651
420 real UIH + 840 GE	0.654	0.738	0.869	0.632	0.604	0.738

4   Conclusion

A new style transfer method, mr^{2}NST, is proposed in this paper to normalize the image styles form different vendors on the same level. The mST results can be attained with high resolution by take multiple reference images from the target domain. The experimental results suggest that style normalization with mr^{2}NST can improve the detection results for masses and μCs.

References

1. Coltuc, D., Bolon, P., Chassery, J.M.: Exact histogram specification. IEEE Trans. Image Process. **15**(5), 1143–1152 (2006)
2. Freer, T.W., Ulissey, M.J.: Screening mammography with computer-aided detection: prospective study of 12,860 patients in a community breast center. Radiology **220**(3), 781–786 (2001)
3. Gatys, L.A., Ecker, A.S., Bethge, M.: Image style transfer using convolutional neural networks. In: Proceedings of the IEEE Conference on Computer Vision and Pattern Recognition, pp. 2414–2423 (2016)
4. He, K., Zhang, X., Ren, S., Sun, J.: Deep residual learning for image recognition. In: Proceedings of the IEEE Conference on Computer Vision and Pattern Recognition, pp. 770–778 (2016)
5. Kooi, T., et al.: Large scale deep learning for computer aided detection of mammographic lesions. Med. Image Anal. **35**, 303–312 (2017)
6. Ren, S., He, K., Girshick, R., Sun, J.: Faster R-CNN: towards real-time object detection with region proposal networks. In: Advances in Neural Information Processing Systems, pp. 91–99 (2015)
7. Rodriguez-Ruiz, A., et al.: Stand-alone artificial intelligence for breast cancer detection in mammography: Comparison with 101 radiologists. J. Nat. Cancer Inst. **111** (2019). https://doi.org/10.1093/jnci/djy222
8. Simonyan, K., Zisserman, A.: Very deep convolutional networks for large-scale image recognition. arXiv preprint arXiv:1409.1556 (2014)
9. Szegedy, C., et al.: Going deeper with convolutions. In: Proceedings of the IEEE conference on computer vision and pattern recognition, pp. 1–9 (2015)
10. Talebi, H., Milanfar, P.: NIMA: neural image assessment. IEEE Trans. Image Process. **27**(8), 3998–4011 (2018)
11. Zhu, J.Y., Park, T., Isola, P., Efros, A.A.: Unpaired image-to-image translation using cycle-consistent adversarial networks. In: Proceedings of the IEEE International Conference on Computer Vision, pp. 2223–2232 (2017)

Template-Oriented Multi-task Sparse Low-Rank Learning for Parkinson's Diseases Diagnosis

Zihao Chen[1], Haijun Lei[1], Yujia Zhao[1], Zhongwei Huang[1], Xiaohua Xiao[2], Yi Lei[2], Ee-Leng Tan[3], and Baiying Lei[4(✉)]

[1] College of Computer Science and Software Engineering, Guangdong Province Key Laboratory of Popular High-Performance Computers, Shenzhen University, Shenzhen, China
[2] First Affiliated Hospital of Shenzhen University, Health Science Center, Shenzhen University, Shenzhen, China
[3] School of Electrical and Electronic Engineering, Nanyang Technological University, Singapore, Singapore
[4] School of Biomedical Engineering, Health Science Center, Shenzhen University, Shenzhen, China
leiby@szu.edu.cn

Abstract. Parkinson's disease (PD) is a long-term degenerative disorder of the central nervous system. Early diagnosis of PD has great clinical significance as patients would be able to receive specialized treatment earlier to slow down the PD progression. Many researchers proposed various machine learning methods to classify the different stages of PD using magnetic resonance imaging (MRI). However, these methods usually extract features from MRI only using a single template. In this paper, we propose a new template-oriented multi-task sparse low-rank learning (TMSLRL) method using MRI for multi-classification of PD patients. Firstly, we extract features from MRI using different templates where each template is corresponding to a particular task. These tasks form a template-oriented multi-task learning to concurrently obtain an inner relationship of each task. Secondly, sparse low-rank learning is performed to capture the potential relationships between the inputs and the outputs and select the most class-discriminative features. Finally, we feed the selected features to train the classifier to get the final classification result. Our proposed model is evaluated by the data from the Parkinson's progression markers initiative (PPMI) dataset. Furthermore, the results of experiments we performed indicate our method have greater performance than the similar methods.

Keywords: Multi-task · Parking's disease · Low-rank learning · Multi-classification

1 Introduction

Parkinson's disease (PD) is one of the most common diseases around the world, which is a long-term degenerative disorder of the central nervous system. It is reported by the World Health Organization that the ratio of PD is between 9.7 and 13.8 per 100000 people every year [1]. What's more, the proportion is higher among older people. Thus, this proportion

I. Rekik et al. (Eds.): PRIME 2020, LNCS 12329, pp. 178–187, 2020.
https://doi.org/10.1007/978-3-030-59354-4_17

will gradually increase in the following years with the population aging. It is urgent to identify the PD patients from suspected patients, which are not only characterized by motor symptoms due to the degeneration of the dopaminergic neurons [2], but also accompanied by non-motor symptoms which contain sleep disorders, depression, and cognitive impairment [3]. Moreover, early diagnosis of PD has great clinical significance as patients would be able to receive specialized treatment earlier to slow down the PD progression and provide PD patients with valuable time to prevent the disease from worsening. The early stages of PD include the prodromal of PD (PPD) and scans without evidence for dopaminergic (SWEDD). PPD is the period from the beginning of PD to the appearance of the clinical symptoms. In addition, SWEDD means the patient is clinically diagnosed with PD but lacks an imaging abnormality. Each stage requires specialized treatment since SWEDD and PDD are different disorders of PD. Especially, chronic progression and undetectable neuropenia of PD make the diagnosis and treatment relatively difficult [4]. When the relevant biomarkers have shown the progress of the lesion, the routine clinical symptoms used for diagnosis merely begin to occur in clinical diagnosis. Therefore, it is a great challenge for doctors to detect patients with PD because the diagnosis is based on clinical scores [5].

To discriminate PD stages and monitor the disease, the neuroimaging techniques (e.g., magnetic resonance imaging (MRI)) can provide informative information for its powerful ability to reveal dying brain cells. Nowadays, machine learning techniques and algorithms also play a vital role in this field to assist the doctor for a more accurate diagnosis. However, high dimension neuroimaging data and a limited sample size can cause over-fitting problem [6]. Feature selection can be used as an effective way to overcome this issue [4, 7, 8]. When the weight of irrelevant features are set to zero, the entire weight matrix can reach a sparse state [9]. For example, when the number of feature dimensions is significantly larger than the number of samples, [10] introduce a l_1-regularizer as a sparse term for feature selection in the classification model. However, it is not enough to select the most related features in multi-classification task. In this paper, we use $l_{2,1}$-regularizers to sparse the weight matrix to discard the redundant features. Furthermore, to discover the underlying relationships between input data and output targets, we propose to select the most related features and learn a multi-classification model using low-rank structures inspired by the modular structure of the brain [11, 12]. Moreover, the important biomarkers such as gray matter (GM), white matter (WM), and cerebrospinal fluid (CSF) in the brain are also used as features [13, 14]. There are many ways to define the regions of interest (ROI) of the brain area since the structure of the brain is complex and diverse. The common way to define is 90, 116 and 200 brain region templates divided by automated anatomical labeling (AAL) atlas. The features of neural image extraction are mainly obtained based on the brain areas. Most of the existing methods are based on the single template method to obtain the brain area distribution map of the brain image, and the single template can only reflect the abnormal function of the limited brain area [15, 16]. On the contrary, multi-template-based methods provide richer brain structure information, which is more potential to discover disease states and compare differences between groups. At this point, we use multiple templates as mentioned above to extract different features from MRI where each template is corresponding to a task and we suppose that every task is interrelated and mutually reinforcing for classification performance of PD. By proposing template-oriented multi-task learning to fuse these different features, a larger feature space and a more discriminative feature model are constructed to promote the classification accuacry. The proposed method composes the low-rank constrains and the sparsity to capture their inner low-rank structure simultaneously for selecting the most disease-relevant feature for each task. Finally, we perform experiments on Parkinson's Progression Markers Initiative (PPMI) [17] datasets to evaluate our model and compare with several similar methods.

2   Method

The proposed method is designed to select the most relevant and discriminative features, which will improve the prediction of multi-class classifier (e.g., support vector machine (SVM) [18], random forest (RF) [19] and k-nearest neighboring (KNN) [20]). Firstly, we extract neuroimaging features from MRI using different templates where each template is corresponding to a particular task. These tasks form a template-oriented multi-task learning to obtain an inner relationship concurrently between these tasks. Secondly, a sparse low-rank learning is performed to capture the potential relationships between the inputs and the outputs and extract the most class-discriminative features. In our framework, the same feature selection method perform for each task. By exploring relationships from many perspectives, our method takes into account more relationship information when processing informative neuroimaging data. Finally, the selected features are fed to train the classifier to predict the final result. The flow chart of our proposed model is illustrated in Fig. 1. We will show the detail of the template-oriented multi-task low-rank learning in Sect. 2.1 and Sect. 2.2.

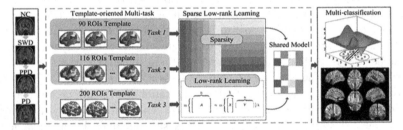

Fig. 1. The flow chart of our proposed method.

2.1   Proposed Model

For multi-task learning in the proposed model, we assume that T tasks exist and each task has data of input and output. We refer the feature matrix for input as $\mathbf{X}^{(t)} \in \mathbb{R}^{m \times n}$ that is extracted using t-th template and the target matrix for output as $\mathbf{Y}^{(t)} \in \{0, 1\}^{m \times c}$, where c, m, and n represent the number of target classes, samples, and feature dimensions respectively and t represent the t-th task. We need to compute the weight matrix $\mathbf{W}^{(t)}$

that satisfies the linear regression model $\mathbf{Y}^{(t)} = \mathbf{X}^{(t)}\mathbf{W}^{(t)}$. Solving the objective function will obtain this matrix $\mathbf{W}^{(t)}$, which is denoted as

$$\min_{\mathbf{W}^{(t)}} \sum_1^t \left\| \mathbf{Y}^{(t)} - \mathbf{X}^{(t)}\mathbf{W}^{(t)} \right\|_F^2, \tag{1}$$

where $\|\mathbf{X}\|_F = \sqrt{\sum_i \|\mathbf{X}^i\|_2^2}$ is referred to as the Frobenius norm of the matrix $\mathbf{X}$. In the multi-classification tasks, several response variables are contained. Hence, we can regard Eq. (1) as the least square regression for those variables separately. Nevertheless, Eq. (1) is just an uncomplicated and direct linear regression model that has no constrains on any variable and leads to inferior performance. An advanced approach should consider the properties of the weight matrix, which can select the most informative features and discard the redundant features. As we know, PD is related to some brain regions. Thus, the importance of features corresponding to various brain regions is different. A weight matrix is used to denote the importance of features extracted in the feature selection process.

Given these, we suppose every group of features is interrelated. To take possible factors into consideration, The low-rank constraint is introduced as $rank(\mathbf{W}^{(t)}) \leq \min(n, c)$, where $rank(\mathbf{W}^{(t)})$ means the rank of the matrix $\mathbf{W}^{(t)}$. The low-rank constrain is introduced to consider the relationships among different features and response variables. Furthermore, we can transform the low-rank constraint on $\mathbf{W}^{(t)}$ to the product of two independent matrices. The one is the low-rank part which is denoted as $\mathbf{M}^{(t)}$ and the other is the remaining part denoted as $\mathbf{N}^{(t)}$ which makes $\mathbf{W}^{(t)}$ completed. Hence $\mathbf{W}^{(t)}$ is calculated by

$$\mathbf{W}^{(t)} = \mathbf{M}^{(t)}\mathbf{N}^{(t)\mathrm{T}}, \tag{2}$$

where $\mathbf{M}^{(t)} \in \mathbb{R}^{n \times r}$ is a low-rank matrix and $\mathbf{N}^{(t)} \in \mathbb{R}^{c \times r}$ is an orthogonal matrix. Beside, $\mathbf{N}^{(t)T}$ denotes as the transpose of $\mathbf{N}^{(t)}$. The role of $\mathbf{N}^{(t)}$ is transferring the low-rank matrix into the original data space as the rotation operation. In many machine learning applications the data matrix is not balanced so that the issue of over-fitting appear frequently. In addition, this issue is more severe in neuroimaging-aid diagnosis because the number of brain images we collected is very small and yet the information they provided is extensive. Hence, we want to reduce some features which are not important. We employ the $l_{2,1}$-norm denoted as $\|\mathbf{X}\|_{2,1} = \sum_i \|\mathbf{X}\|_2 = \sum_i \sqrt{\sum_j x_{i,j}^2}$ on the low-rank framework to select the discriminative features. Using sparse representation, the objective function is formulated as

$$\min_{\mathbf{M}^{(t)}, \mathbf{N}^{(t)}} \left\| \mathbf{Y}^{(t)} - \mathbf{X}^{(t)}\mathbf{M}^{(t)}\mathbf{N}^{(t)T} \right\|_F^2 + \alpha \mathbf{M}_{2,1}^{(t)}, \tag{3}$$

where α is the tuning parameter. In predicting the clinical labels, the coefficients of $\mathbf{M}^{(t)}$ is penalized by the $l_{2,1}$-norm regularizer to select the most related features and discard unimportant ones. By learning the relationships between the response variables and the neuroimaging features, the low-rank feature learning framework can select the representative features. Thus, for every task, we suppose that features are relevant to batch of features while the relationships between these batches may be sparse. The same orthogonal constraints $\mathbf{N}^{(t)}$ and low-rank weight coefficients are shared by multiple tasks. We assume that every task is interrelated and mutually reinforcing for classification performance of PD. In the multi-task learning, we can formulate the final objective function as

$$\min_{\mathbf{M},\mathbf{N}} \sum_1^t \left\| \mathbf{Y}^{(t)} - \mathbf{X}^{(t)}\mathbf{M}^{(t)}\mathbf{N}^{(t)T} \right\|_F^2 + \alpha \mathbf{M}_{2,1}. \tag{4}$$

Then, $\mathbf{M}$ will have different row vectors filled with zeros after optimizing Eq. (4), which set the weight matrix to reach a sparse situation. Those vectors with the uncorrelated features can be discarded. Finally, we concatenate the remainder features and feed to train classifiers.

2.2 Optimization

To converge the objective function, we can use the alternating update method. With fixed values, we iterate the following two steps to solve Eq. (6): (a) fixed $\mathbf{M}$ to update $\mathbf{N}$; (b) fixed $\mathbf{N}$ to update $\mathbf{M}$. With fixed $\mathbf{M}$, the objective function can be formulated as

$$\min_{\mathbf{N}} \sum_1^t \left\| \mathbf{Y}^{(t)} - \mathbf{X}^{(t)}\mathbf{M}^{(t)}\mathbf{N}^{(t)T} \right\|_F^2. \tag{5}$$

where Eq. (5) is an orthogonal Procrustes problem or a matrix approximation problem in linear algebra. We can get the optimal solution of $\mathbf{N} = \mathbf{S}\mathbf{D}^T$, where $\mathbf{S} \in \mathbb{R}^{c \times r}$ and $\mathbf{D} \in \mathbb{R}^{r \times r}$. Among them, $\mathbf{D}$ is a diagonal matrix. We can use the singular value decomposition of $\mathbf{Y}^T\mathbf{X} = \mathbf{S}\mathbf{V}\mathbf{D}^T$ to acquire $\mathbf{S}$ and $\mathbf{D}$. Further, with fixed $\mathbf{N}$, the formula of the objective function is equivalent to

$$\min_{\mathbf{M}} \sum_1^t \left\| \mathbf{Y}^{(t)}\mathbf{N}^{(t)} - \mathbf{X}^{(t)}\mathbf{M}^{(t)T} \right\|_F^2 + \alpha tr\left(\mathbf{M}^T \mathbf{H} \mathbf{M} \right), \tag{6}$$

where $\mathbf{H} \in \mathbb{R}^{n \times n}$ is a diagonal matrix with $h_{i,j} = \frac{1}{2\|\mathbf{M}^j\|_2^2}$. By differentiating Eq. (5) and then setting it to zero, we obtain $\mathbf{M} = \left(\mathbf{X}^T\mathbf{X} + \alpha\mathbf{H} \right)^{-1}\mathbf{X}^T\mathbf{Y}\mathbf{N}$.

Accordingly, we alternately update the values of $\mathbf{M}$ and $\mathbf{N}$ until the objective function converges.

3 Experiments

3.1 Experimental Setting

The proposed method is evaluated by classifying PD subject to different stages, including normal control (NC), PPD, SWEED, and PD. We also compare with sparse learning (SL), sparse low-rank learning (SLRL), and low-rank learning (LRL) which are similar to our proposed method. Specifically, SL has a $l_{2,1}$ regularizer to sparse the weight matrix. LRL contains the low-rank constraint to select the relevant features. And SLRL contains not only the low-rank learning but also a $l_{2,1}$ regularizer to sparse the weight matrix.

We also apply multiple classifiers for each method, including logistic regression (LR), SVM, random forest (RF), KNN, GBDT, BY, Adaboost, XGBoost, DNN, and capped-norm SVM (cSVM). Thus, we can find out whether the extracted features are effective for most classifiers. For the parameters in our experiments, only one parameter is used, which is α in Eq. (4). We set the range $[2^{-5}, 2^{-4},...,2^5]$ as the initial value of α which is specified by a 5-fold cross-validation strategy. Finally, we adopted several measures to estimate the performance of methods, including accuracy (ACC), specificity (SPE), precision (PRE), sensitivity (SEN), and the receiver of curve (ROC). In addition, we adopt a 10-fold cross-validation strategy to evaluate the classification performance of TMSLRL for fair evaluation.

3.2 Data Preprocessing

We use PPMI datasets [17] for our experiments and then divide the experiments into two parts. The first part is NC vs. SWEDD vs. PD denoted as PD3. The second part is NC vs. SWEDD vs. PPD vs. PD denoted as PD4. As for the experimental subjects, there are 238 subjects including 62 NC, 34 SWEDD, and 142 PD subjects for PD3. On the other hand, we collected 347 subjects including 127 NC, 34 PPD, 56 SWEDD, and 130 PD subjects for PD4. We only collect the subject which is segmented and visualized successfully. According to this criterion, we exclude the subjects that cannot get to the final feature extraction step and get the final data.

We first preprocess the data using the anterior commissure-posterior commissure (ACPC) correction and skull-stripping [21]. Subsequently, these preprocessed data are segmented into GM, WM, and CSF using Statistical Parametric Mapping (SPM) toolbox [22]. Further, we begin to extract features from these images. In our proposed method, we collect 90, 116, and 200 regions of interest (ROI) respectively based on multiple AAL template. Finally, we extract features by calculating the average tissue density of each region. As the number of ROIs increases, the feature dimension also increases. However, as the information increases in detail, the difficulty to select feature also increases. Fortunately, we can learn more information from features using the template-oriented multi-task learning, such as the inner relation of features from multiple templates. Then, we can also select the most discriminate features to promote the classification performance by the sparse low-rank learning.

3.3 Classification Performance for PD

We conduct the comparative experiments in accordance with the experimental setting. The classification results are shown in Fig. 2 and Fig. 3 for PD3 and PD4. As we can see from the classification results, the ACC of our proposed method is higher than that of SLRL in PD3 and PD4 respectively with certain classifier cSVM, which shows that the relationships between multiple template help to improve the classification performance. It prove that we use multiple template to extract more feature to provide more information. Furthermore, by comparing the classification accuracy of SLRL with SL and LRL in PD3 and PD4, we can conclude that the sparse low-rank learning has selected the most discriminate feature and discarded the redundant features to improve the classification accuracy. By comparing these methods in other performance measures such as PRE,

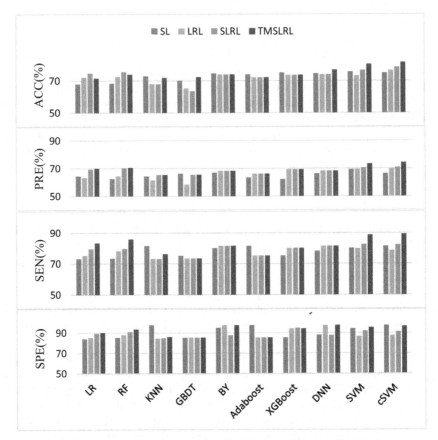

Fig. 2. Classification results of PD3 (NC vs. SWEDD vs. PD).

SEN, SPE and AUC, we can also find out the performance of our proposed method is better than others. It can prove that our proposed method is robust.

Then we perform these four methods with numbers of classifiers, such as LR, RF, SVM, cSVM and so on. Indeed, our proposed method proved to be more efficient than SL, LRL, and SLRL with each classifier, which proves that our proposed method can discover the intrinsic relation within features effectively.

We also draw the receiver of curve (ROC) of our proposed method and other methods to compare, where we use cSVM as classifier for these four methods. Figure 4 shows the ROC results of methods comparison. Undoubtedly, the ROC performance of our proposed method is better than other comparative methods with the selected classifier whether it is in PD3 or PD4.

3.4 Potential Disease-Related Brain Regions

When the related biomarkers indicate the progress of PD, clinical symptoms for PD diagnosis would begin to emerge. Therefore, the recognition and monitoring of biomarkers

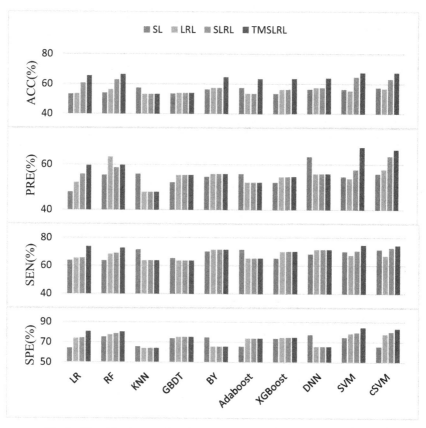

Fig. 3. Classification results of PD4 (NC vs. SWEDD vs. PPD vs. PD).

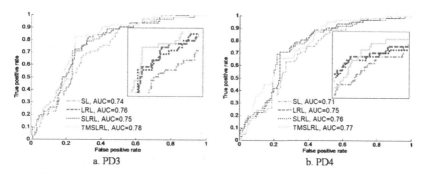

Fig. 4. ROC plots of several similar methods with certain classifier cSVM.

play a meaningful role in early diagnosis. In view of this, we further intend to find out the most distinguished and related brain regions of PD.

By using our feature selection method we choose the top 10 related ROIs within potential disease-related ROIs. These ROIs are displayed in Fig. 5. Each of the ROIs is shown in different views such as from left to right, sagittal left hemisphere, coronal, sagittal right hemisphere, and axial views. We also use different color to indicate the top 10 ROIs which are most disease-related in each figure. When multiple prodromal stages are taken into consideration, some areas require special attention.

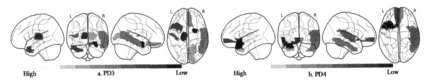

Fig. 5. Top 10 selected ROIs most-related with PD. Each color indicates one ROI. High indicates higher relevance with the disease classification

4   Conclusion

This paper introduce a template-oriented multi-task sparse low-rank learning method for a multi-stage diagnosis of PD. Every task is added a low-rank regularization and sparsity to the weight coefficient in our framework, which exposes the basic relationship in the data, and then finds the underlying inner relationship between these tasks. With the correlation dependence of disease-related brain features and the dimensionality reduction of neuroimaging feature matrices, our method can discover the most representative features. With the selected neuroimaging data from the PPMI dataset, a large number of experiments show that our method perform best in multi-classification task compared with other similar methods.

References

1. Neurological disorders report, public health challenge (2016). https://www.who.int/mental_health/neurology/neurological_disorders_report_web.pdf
2. Emrani, S., McGuirk, A., Xiao, W.: Prognosis and diagnosis of Parkinson's disease using multi-task learning. In: Proceedings of the 23rd ACM SIGKDD International Conference on Knowledge Discovery and Data Mining, pp. 1457–1466 (2017)
3. Dickson, D.W.: Neuropathology of Parkinson disease. Parkinsonism Relat. Disord. **46**(Suppl 1), S30–S33 (2018)
4. Lei, B., Yang, P., Wang, T., Chen, S., Ni, D.: Relational-regularized discriminative sparse learning for Alzheimer's disease diagnosis. IEEE Trans. Cybern. **47**(4), 1102–1113 (2017)
5. Zhu, X., Suk, H.-I., Lee, S.-W., Shen, D.: Subspace regularized sparse multitask learning for multiclass neurodegenerative disease identification. IEEE Trans. Biomed. Eng. **63**(3), 607–618 (2015)
6. Kong, Y., Deng, Y., Dai, Q.: Discriminative clustering and feature selection for brain MRI segmentation. IEEE Signal Process. Lett. **22**(5), 573–577 (2014)
7. Lei, B., et al.: Adaptive sparse learning using multi-template for neurodegenerative disease diagnosis. Med. Image Anal. **61**, 101632 (2020)

8. Lei, H., Zhao, Y., Huang, Z., Zhou, F., Huang, L., Lei, B.: Multi-classification of Parkinson's disease via sparse low-rank learning. In: 2018 24th International Conference on Pattern Recognition (ICPR), pp. 3268–3272 (2018)
9. Chen, X., Pan, W., Kwok, J.T., Carbonell, J.G.: Accelerated gradient method for multi-task sparse learning problem. In: 2009 Ninth IEEE International Conference on Data Mining, pp. 746–751 (2009)
10. Jothi, G., Hannah, I.H.: Hybrid Tolerance Rough Set-Firefly based supervised feature selection for MRI brain tumor image classification. Appl. Soft Comput. **46**, 639–651 (2016)
11. Zhang, D., Shen, D.: Alzheimer's disease neuroimaging initiative: multi-modal multi-task learning for joint prediction of multiple regression and classification variables in Alzheimer's disease. NeuroImage **59**(2), 895–907 (2012)
12. Zhu, X., Suk, H.-I., Shen, D.: Low-rank dimensionality reduction for multi-modality neurodegenerative disease identification. World Wide Web **22**(2), 907–925 (2018). https://doi.org/10.1007/s11280-018-0645-3
13. Chaudhuri, K.R., Healy, D.G., Schapira, A.H.: Non-motor symptoms of Parkinson's disease: diagnosis and management. Lancet Neurol. **5**(3), 235–245 (2006)
14. Fung, G., Stoeckel, J.: SVM feature selection for classification of SPECT images of Alzheimer's disease using spatial information. Knowl. Inf. Syst. **11**(2), 243–258 (2007). https://doi.org/10.1007/s10115-006-0043-5
15. Spadoto, A.A., Guido, R.C., Carnevali, F.L., Pagnin, A.F., Falcão, A.X., Papa, J.P.: Improving Parkinson's disease identification through evolutionary-based feature selection. In: 2011 Annual International Conference of the IEEE Engineering in Medicine and Biology Society, pp. 7857–7860 (2011)
16. Caesarendra, W., Putri, F.T., Ariyanto, M., Setiawan, J.D.: Pattern recognition methods for multi stage classification of Parkinson's disease utilizing voice features. In: 2015 IEEE International Conference on Advanced Intelligent Mechatronics (AIM), pp. 802–807 (2015)
17. Marek, K., et al.: The Parkinson progression marker initiative (PPMI). Prog. Neurobiol. **95**(4), 629–635 (2011)
18. Suykens, J.A., Vandewalle, J.: Least squares support vector machine classifiers. Neural Process. Lett. **9**, 293–300 (1999). https://doi.org/10.1023/A:1018628609742
19. Liaw, A., Wiener, M.: Classification and regression by randomForest. R news **2**(3), 18–22 (2002)
20. Keller, J.M., Gray, M.R., Givens, J.A.: A fuzzy k-nearest neighbor algorithm. IEEE Trans. Syst. Man Cybern. SMC **15**(4), 580–585 (1985)
21. Sadananthan, S.A., Zheng, W., Chee, M.W.L., Zagorodnov, V.: Skull stripping using graph cuts. NeuroImage **49**(1), 225–239 (2010)
22. Penny, W.D., Friston, K.J., Ashburner, J.T., Kiebel, S.J., Nichols, T.E.: Statistical Parametric Mapping: The Analysis of Functional Brain Images. Elsevier, Amsterdam (2011)

Multimodal Prediction of Breast Cancer Relapse Prior to Neoadjuvant Chemotherapy Treatment

Simona Rabinovici-Cohen[1]([⊠]), Ami Abutbul[1], Xosé M. Fernández[2] [iD],
Oliver Hijano Cubelos[2], Shaked Perek[1], and Tal Tlusty[1]

[1] IBM Research – Haifa, Mount Carmel, 3498825 Haifa, Israel
simona@il.ibm.com
[2] Institut Curie, 26 Rue d'Ulm, 75005 Paris, France

Abstract. Neoadjuvant chemotherapy (NAC) is one of the treatment options for women diagnosed with breast cancer, in which chemotherapy is administered prior to surgery. In current clinical practice, it is not possible to predict whether the patient is likely to encounter a relapse after treatment and have the breast cancer reoccur in the same place. If this outcome could be predicted prior to the start of NAC, it could inform therapeutic options. We explore the use of multi-modal imaging and clinical features to predict the risk of relapse following NAC treatment. We performed a retrospective study on a cohort of 1738 patients who were administered with NAC. Of these patients, 567 patients also had magnetic resonance imaging (MRI) taken before the treatment started. We analyzed the data using deep learning and traditional machine learning algorithms to increase the set of discriminating features and create effective models. Our results demonstrate the ability to predict relapse prior to NAC treatment initiation, using each modality alone. We then show the possible improvement achieved by combining MRI and clinical data, as measured by the AUC, sensitivity, and specificity. When evaluated on holdout data, the overall combined model achieved 0.735 AUC and 0.438 specificity at a sensitivity operation point of 0.95. This means that almost every patient encountering relapse will also be correctly classified by our model, enabling the reassessment of this treatment prior to its start. Additionally, the same model was able to correctly predict in advance 44% of the patients that would not encounter relapse.

Keywords: Breast MRI · Convolutional neural networks · Neoadjuvant chemotherapy treatment

1 Introduction

Neoadjuvant chemotherapy (NAC), in which chemotherapy treatment is administered prior to surgical therapy, is one of the approaches available in treating locally advanced breast cancer. The potential clinical advantages of NAC have been largely studied and include improved success of breast-conserving therapy, minimized nodal surgery, and more accurate *in-vivo* observation of tumor sensitivity [1]. Today, the clinical parameters used to select the NAC option are based on breast cancer subtype, tumor size, disease

© Springer Nature Switzerland AG 2020
I. Rekik et al. (Eds.): PRIME 2020, LNCS 12329, pp. 188–199, 2020.
https://doi.org/10.1007/978-3-030-59354-4_18

grade, number of affected nodes, age, and tumor growth amongst others. Imaging is used to evaluate the position of the tumor and its size, but not to predict the outcome of the treatment. Moreover, quantitative models based on clinical and imaging features are not considered when evaluating the potential success of the treatment.

Predicting a relapse after NAC, essentially determining whether the breast cancer is likely to recur in the same location, is an important clinical question. If this future outcome could be predicted based on data available prior to the initiation of NAC treatment, it could impact the treatment selection. Because administering chemotherapy may weaken or even prevent other treatments, it is vital to correctly assess the contribution of NAC treatment in advance.

About 10% of NAC treated patients will suffer a relapse, but clinicians have difficulty estimating who is at risk for this outcome. Artificial intelligence models that predict relapse can empower clinicians in their treatment selection and decision-making. Specifically, predicting treatment outcome using medical imaging is an emerging area of interest in the medical community. It aims to extract large numbers of quantitative features from the patient's own medical images, and thus is an important enabler of precision medicine.

In this paper, we describe methods to improve relapse prediction using multi-modal data of different types. We describe a deep learning (DL) model for magnetic resonance imaging (MRI) data, a traditional machine learning (ML) model for clinical data, and an ensemble model of the individual clinical and MRI models. For the imaging modality, we use Dynamic Contrast Enhanced MRI (DCE-MRI) of the breast. DCE-MRI imaging acquires T1 changes in tissues before and after injection of gadolinium-based contrast agents at several points in time. We trained and evaluated our models on a cohort of 1738 patients, out of which 567 have MRI data. The results show that our approach is able to identify those patients likely to encounter relapse.

The paper is organized as follows. In Sect. 2, we describe the work related to this topic. We present the methods used to develop our multimodal predictor in Sect. 3 and the evaluation of our models in Sect. 4. We then discuss our results and conclusions in Sect. 5.

2   Related Work

Recent studies have explored various methods to predict cancer repetition after chemotherapy treatment. There are three types of cancer repetition: (i) relapse, the tumor redevelops at the same location where it was diagnosed before treatment; (ii) metastasis, the spread of cancer from the original tumor where it first formed to other areas in the body; (iii) recurrence, the cancer may come back to the same place as the original tumor or to another place in the body. Previous work can be divided into two major methods: predicting repetition using clinical features [2–6] and prediction using features that are extracted from imaging modalities [7–11].

Abreuet et al. [2] present a comprehensive review of 17 published studies done between 1997 and 2014, which predict the recurrence of breast cancer from clinical data using different machine learning techniques. The work shows the gaps in current studies, such as the lack of data. Most of the works use very small datasets for training and evaluation, imbalanced cohorts, and problematic feature selection. Recent work by Chen et al. [3] present a comparison study for the evaluation of a single classifier to predict recurrence from clinical data features. Different ML methods are used to evaluate a public set of 286 patients, and the results are compared using different metrics. Other works fuse the predictions of more than one classifier to achieve more accurate results [4, 5]. Tseng et al. [6] use ML techniques on a cohort of 148 patients to predict metastasis from clinical features, such as demographic data, tumor information, pathology data, and laboratory data.

The use of MRI data to predict the repetition of cancer has not been widely explored. Hylton at el. [7] and Drukker at el. [8] use tumor volume approximations, as extracted from DCE-MRI modality, to predict recurrence. A significant correlation between approximated volumes and recurrence is presented in both works for tumor volumes extracted at different times during neoadjuvant chemotherapy treatment. In an extension to [8], Drukker at el. [9] add 7 kinetic curve features extracted from within the tumor area of MRI, in addition to the approximated tumor volume. The extracted features were used to train their Long Short Term Memory (LSTM) model. This model was then evaluated on the ISPY1 publicly published dataset, which contains 222 patients [10], of which 157 patients were selected for the analysis. Another approach for using the MRI modality extracts texture features, which indicate the tumor's heterogeneity in addition to its size feature [11]. This work shows a significant correlation between these features and the ability to predict recurrence.

There are other works related to our problem that predict NAC therapy response using imaging modality. Hyunjong et al. [12] use radiomic features extracted from ROI PET/CT volumes as well as clinical and pathological features to train a logistic regression model to predict NAC treatment response. Rabinovici-Cohen at el. [13] explore features extracted from mammography and clinical data for response prediction, and present possible improvements by fusing mammograms and clinical features. Most of the works for response prediction use features extracted from the MRI modality [14–18]. Eben et al. [14] created a multi-representation-based prediction of response to NAC therapy in breast cancer. They use both CNN and radiomics on DCE-MRI volumes to extract features from within the tumor area and from the peritumoral region outside the tumor. Work by Haarburger et al. [15] uses radiomic texture features extracted from the DCE-MRI tumor area of 38 patients. A retrospective study by Ravichandran et al. [16] on 42 patients, examined the ability to predict response using a two-branch CNN with cropped DCE-MRI images around a lesion, from before and after chemotherapy is administered. Ha et al. [17] used the open dataset of ISPY1 [10] for the task. Here, a CNN was applied to MRI-DCE tumor slices with consideration of pre and post contrast via the input channel of the images. He et al. [18] applied a VGG-like network to predict the response on lesion patches extracted from a 3D voxel segmentation.

Our work differs from previous methods in four main aspects: (i) We focus on the prediction of relapse that has its own clinical importance, rather than the prediction of recurrence or response to treatment. (ii) We work specifically on patient data before NAC treatment, allowing us to focus on a more defined task. (iii) Compared to previous works, we use a relatively large set of imaging data and train our end-to-end neural network using full images extracted from the MRI volume. In addition, we evaluate the results on a large holdout set of 100 patients (iv) We perform multimodal analysis that includes both imaging and clinical features.

3   Methods

Our dataset was collected from patients prior to NAC treatment, and contains data from several modalities, including MRI, mammography, ultrasound, and clinical data. Because our work is focused on MRI and clinical data modalities, our model consists of two branches. Each branch was trained using one of the modalities. We then combined the two branches into one final ensemble model. In this section, we elaborate on each of these components. We present our dataset, describe the MRI model branch and the clinical model branch, and then detail the final ensemble model that combines the two branches.

3.1   Dataset and Annotations

Our dataset is from Institut Curie in France and includes a cohort of 1738 breast cancer patients that received NAC treatment between 2012 and 2018. For each patient, the data includes a label marking whether this patient encountered a relapse since her treatment ended. From this cohort, we excluded 100 patients that had clinical and MRI data, for holdout evaluation. The remaining 1638 patients were considered for our cross-validation experiments.

We used two data subsets in our experiments because some patients had only clinical data while other patients had clinical and MRI data. The first data subset is a large cohort of 1638 patients for clinical data evaluation. The clinical data included demographics such as age, weight, height, and tumor properties such as breast cancer histology, grade of the tumor, Ki67, and molecular subtypes based on estrogen, progesterone, and HER2. The second data subset was a small cohort of 467 patients who, in addition to the clinical data, also had MRI scans taken prior to NAC treatment. The small cohort is a subset of the larger cohort.

A DCE-MRI scan of a patient with breast cancer includes multiple volumes. The volumes are taken before a contrast agent is injected, and at several intervals after the injection. For our analysis, we used a digital subtraction of the volume acquired after injection of the contrast agent and the baseline volume acquired before the injection. We chose to use the subtraction volumes because this type of imaging is used by radiologists for medical diagnosis and was likely to contain the information relevant for our analysis.

As mentioned, we held out the data for a cohort of 100 patients that included clinical and MRI data. The inherent distribution between negative and positive samples for the holdout set was similar to the cross-validation set. This holdout data was annotated by expert radiologists. They annotated the most important subtraction volume in which the tumor appeared to be the brightest in terms of relative illumination. In the selected volume, they also annotated the significant slice in which the tumor was the largest.

The rest of the MRI volumes were used for cross-validation. The most important subtraction as well as the significant slice were annotated by non-expert researchers. Data distribution in the cross-validation cohorts and the holdout cohort is presented in Table 1.

Table 1. Number of patients for relapse predication

	Total number of patients	Relapse	Relapse-free
Large cohort	1638	187	1451
Small cohort	467	46	421
Holdout cohort	100	10	90

3.2 MRI Model

Our MRI model branch consists of two components. The first component is a CNN model that produces embedding features containing the CNN output score, together with 32 features taken from the previous CNN layer. These features are then used as input to the second component, which includes a logistic regression classifier. In this section, we begin by describing the pre-processing steps we applied to the raw MRI subtractions and continue with a description of each model.

Pre-processing: The input to the CNN is the significant slice and the two pre and post adjacent slices (i.e., three slices in total) that are extracted from the selected MRI subtraction volume. The significant slice is the slice in which the tumor is most visible and appears to be largest. This slice is not well-defined and different clinicians may select different slices as the significant slice.

The selected slices undergo a cropping and resizing process. Our data consisted of axial MRI volumes, which contain both sides of the breast. Hence, we cropped the image vertically and continued processing only the relevant side in which the tumor was located. Then, we cropped the image horizontally to exclude non-breast parts that appeared in the image. This process was done automatically using a sliding window, where we searched the most enhanced organs within the first slice in the MRI volume, and found a cut line above them that was used for our three selected slices. Each of the vertically and horizontally cropped slices was then resized to 512×256 pixels to bring them all to the same size.

The last two steps of the pre-processing included rotating the slices, so the breast was facing in the same direction for all slices. We also under sampled the slices where there was overlap between slices in the volume.

CNN Model: Our CNN model is a modification of ResNet [18] as a classifier. We specifically used ResNet18 formulation, but reduced the number of filters per layer to speed up training and avoid over-fitting. The original Resnet18 consists of blocks of convolutions, with residual connections between the blocks. Each convolution layer is followed by a batch normalization layer and ReLU activation. For our network, we used 7 residual blocks with [32, 64, 128, 128, 256, 256] filters per convolutional layer. This 2D-CNN model was applied simultaneously to the 3 slices, i.e., the same 2D-CNN model with the same weights was applied to each slice. Next, a 4D-tensor was used to aggregate features produced from the 3 input slices. Finally, a 3D convolution layer was applied, followed by a 3D average global pooling layer. The output of the pooling layer was treated as an embedding vector $v \in \mathbb{R}^{32}$. On top of this embedding layer, we added a simple sigmoid-activated linear layer as an output layer. A detailed diagram of the CNN model is depicted in Fig. 1.

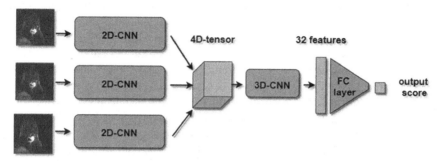

Fig. 1. MRI CNN Architecture. Three adjacent MRI slices (pre-significant, significant, post-significant) form the input to three 2D-CNN that have the same weights. The features are aggregated into a 3D-CNN followed by an average global pooling layer and a fully connected layer that outputs the probability of a patient having a relapse.

CNN Training: we split the small cohort of 467 patients with MRI scans into 5 folds with equally distributed positive and negative samples among folds. We implemented our ResNet model in Keras with TensorFlow as backend [19]. We trained from scratch using the ADAM optimizer with binary cross-entropy as a loss function. We used a batch size of 24 samples and an initial learning rate of 10^{-4} with 'reduce on plateau' scheduler. With the training limited to 150 epochs using an early stopping protocol, we then selected the best epoch weights based on the AUC on validation set. For each volume (3 selected slices), we applied a standardization of zero mean and unit variance independently from other volumes. Also, as part of the practice for small datasets, we applied several regularization methods to prevent over-fitting. These included L_2 regularization and augmentation, which included shifts, zoom, rotation, and horizontal flip.

We refer to the model that outputs the CNN scores as the "MRI-scores" model. We also used the CNN as a feature extractor. For each subtraction volume, it produced a feature vector of size 33, which was a concatenation of the output score and the 32 features from the output of the pooling layer.

Embeddings Model: We used 33 embedding features coming from the CNN and applied a scaler that scales all features to the [0,1] range. We then trained the embeddings with logistic regression and created a model that we refer to as "MRI-embeddings".

In summary, we produced two models: MRI-scores and MRI-embeddings. MRI-scores is based on the CNN scores without the logistic regression step and MRI-embeddings is the output after the logistic regression step. We performed cross-validation and computed the receiver operating characteristic (ROC) area under the curve (AUC) with a confidence interval, specificity at sensitivity for each fold, as well as the mean values. We then selected the best model and used it to evaluate the holdout data AUC and specificity at several sensitivity operation points.

3.3 Clinical Model

We split the large cohort of 1638 patients with clinical information into 5 folds with equally distributed positive and negative samples among folds; this covered approximately 90% negative relapse and 10% positive relapse patients. The folds were created in correlation with the folds of the small cohort that includes the patients with MRI; namely, a patient remains in the same fold in both datasets.

We created our model using the 26 pre-treatment features per patient, described in Sect. 3.1. The features have values in different ranges and some values are missing; thus, we preprocessed the data by applying a scaler that scales all features to the [0,1] range. An imputation process replaced missing values with the mean value. One feature that suffers from a lot of missing values is lymph node involvement. This weakened our model as this feature was found to be a strong predictor of relapse [20].

To select the best classifier for our task, we trained the data with three known ML algorithms: Random Forest, Logistic Regression, and XGBoost. We performed cross-validation and computed the ROC, AUC with confidence interval, specificity at sensitivity for each fold, and the mean values across folds. We then selected the best model, found to be Random Forest, and used it to evaluate the holdout data AUC and specificity at several sensitivity operation points. We also examined the features of importance produced by our models.

3.4 Ensemble Model

The ensemble model depicted in Fig. 2 receives six scores per patient: three scores based on clinical data and three scores based on the MRI data. To improve generalization, we created multiple variations of each model where each different variation started its train from a different initialization. Thus, the three scores for clinical data are produced from three variations of the clinical model that differ in their training initialization. Likewise, the three scores for MRI data are produced from three variations of the MRI model that differ in their training initialization.

We tried both options of the MRI model, namely MRI-scores and MRI-embeddings. We created an ensemble of the MRI-scores model with the clinical model, and then compared it to an ensemble of MRI-embeddings model with the clinical model.

We examined several strategies for combining the models and evaluated the cross-validation AUC and specificity at sensitivity for each option. We first tried the stacking classifier, in which we trained a meta model on top of the six models' scores using the small cohort folds. We also tried several voting strategies. However, we found that the most effective strategy used the average value of all available scores per patient.

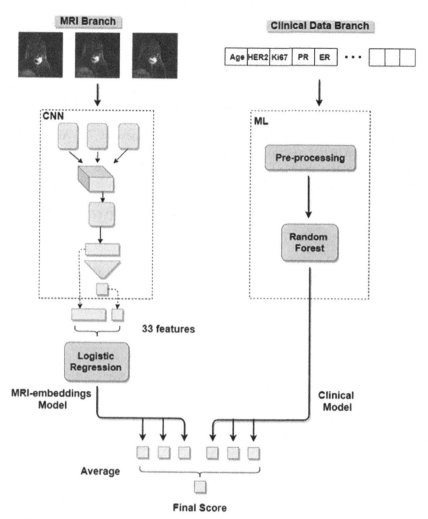

Fig. 2. Ensemble Model Architecture. (left) MRI model branch with three slices as input, (right) clinical model branch with 26 clinical features as input, and (bottom) merge of the two branches into one ensemble. The final score is the average of three scores from MRI-embeddings model variations and three scores from clinical model variations.

4   Results

For each modality, we evaluated the individual models, as well as the final ensemble model. Each model was trained on the largest dataset it could use. For example, the MRI was trained on the small cohort while the clinical model was trained on the large cohort. We evaluated the final ensemble model on the small cohort since it included both MRI and clinical data, and we could compare the contribution of each modality.

As part of our evaluation, we performed a 5-fold cross-validation as well as test on a holdout dataset of 100 patients. For both, cross-validation and holdout test, we report

AUC with 95% confidence interval and specificity at a sensitivity operation point of 0.95. For the holdout evaluation, the patient score was the average of the scores of the 5 models selected from the 5-fold cross-validation.

Table 2 below summarizes the results for the cross-validation and holdout test. In the MRI-only models branch, we evaluated two models: the MRI-scores model whose score is the output of the CNN (row 1) and the MRI-embeddings model, in which the score is the output of the logistic regression applied on the CNN embedding features (row 2). In the cross-validation, the MRI-scores model achieved 0.716 AUC with 95% confidence interval [0.672, 0.756] and specificity 0.363 at sensitivity operation point of 0.95. In the holdout test, the MRI-scores model achieved 0.682 [0.639, 0.722] AUC and 0.409 specificity. For the second MRI-embeddings model, the cross-validation achieved a slightly worse result with AUC of 0.708 [0.665, 0.749] and the same specificity. In the holdout data, the MRI-embeddings model achieved 0.704 [0.661, 0.743] AUC and specificity 0.424.

Table 2. Evaluation of the models on cross-validation and holdout test

	Cross-validation		Holdout test	
	AUC	Spec at Sens = 0.95	AUC	Spec at Sens = 0.95
MRI-scores	0.716	0.363	0.682	0.409
MRI-embeddings	0.709	0.363	0.704	0.424
Clinical	0.687	0.321	0.671	0.2
MRI-scores with Clinical	0.737	0.385	0.716	0.233
MRI-embeddings with Clinical (final model)	**0.745**	**0.442**	**0.735**	**0.438**

In the clinical-only model branch, similar results were achieved using either XGBoost or Random Forest classifiers, but Random Forest was slightly better and thus selected. It is possible that further hyperparameters tuning is needed when using XGBoost. In cross-validation, we obtained 0.687 [0.642, 0.728] AUC and 0.321 specificity. In the holdout test, we obtained 0.671 [0.627, 0.711] AUC and 0.2 specificity (row 3). The important features found by the model were age, BMI, Ki67, tumor grade, and molecular subtypes HER2, estrogen, and progesterone.

In the MRI with clinical ensemble model, we evaluated both MRI-scores with clinical (row 4) and MRI-embeddings with clinical (row 5). The second option achieved better AUC and specificity in the cross-validation evaluation and thus was selected as our final model. In the cross-validation, the final model achieved 0.745 [0.702, 0.784] and 0.442 specificity, while the holdout test achieved 0.735 [0.694, 0.773] and 0.438 specificity.

Figure 3 below shows the cross-validation and the holdout test ROC curves. They exhibit similar trends. In both, the MRI model shows promise in predicting relapse after NAC treatment with good specificity for above 0.95 sensitivity. The clinical model shows the ability to predict relapse with higher specificity around the 0.5 sensitivity but lower specificity around the 0.95 sensitivity. The ensemble of MRI and clinical leveraged both modalities and improved the AUC and specificity at various operation points.

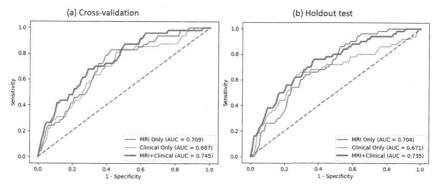

Fig. 3. Cross-validation and holdout ROC Curves. (a) Cross-validation evaluation with MRI+Clinical ensemble mean AUC of 0.745 (b) Holdout evaluation with MRI+Clinical ensemble mean AUC of 0.735.

5   Discussion and Conclusion

We demonstrated our ability to predict relapse using multimodal algorithms that include features extracted from MRI images and clinical data prior to neoadjuvant chemotherapy treatment. Each modality alone shows the ability to offer predictions in this problem setting, but the multimodal model offers better results.

We used deep learning algorithms to analyze our MRI models and traditional machine learning algorithms to analyze the clinical data. Then, we combined the two branches to create an ensemble model that produced the final prediction. Using two branches enabled us to use the best method per modality and utilize the maximum available data for each data type. After excluding the data of 100 patients for holdout, we had a cohort of 1638 patients with clinical information, out of which 467 patients also had MRI data. We were able to use the large cohort to train the clinical model and the small subset cohort to train the MRI model. Moreover, experimental training of a clinical model on the small cohort obtained an almost random model, so using the large cohort for the clinical model training was essential.

In the MRI branch, we examined two models: MRI-scores and MRI-embeddings. The cross-validation MRI-scores produced results that were slightly better in AUC than the MRI-embeddings but slightly worse in specificity. When we examined the cross-validation of these models ensembled with the clinical model, the MRI-embeddings seemed to be more calibrated and it outperformed in both AUC and specificity. Thus, the MRI-embeddings was selected for the final model.

While our MRI data for predicting relapse after NAC treatment is one of the largest compared to those reported in prior art, it is relatively small for deep learning networks. Moreover, MRI has no standardized protocol for scan acquisition and high variance of image resolution, voxel size, and image contrast dynamics. We selected special MRI preprocessing and neural network to adjust for these limitations, and the major contribution of this modality to our prediction is clear. Yet, to get robust models that are not sensitive to fold partitions and generalize better, we need to retrain our models on much larger datasets.

We used a holdout of 100 patients, which is relatively large when compared to our train set of 467 patients with MRI. However, comparing the results on the holdout with the results on the cross-validation shows that there isn't a significant decrease in performance, and we still have good generalization in the holdout cohort. This holds the promise that our models may be able to generalize to unseen but similar datasets.

High sensitivity was important in our problem setting since we wanted almost all patients that encountered relapse to be correctly classified by our model and enable NAC treatment options to be reassessed in advance. It is also important to know the specificity in these high sensitivity operation points. A false negative could potentially turn into a life-threatening situation if the patient thinks she may be cured, while in fact the cancer will come back. Adding the MRI modality enabled us to improve the specificity at high sensitivity operation points.

A future direction we intend to follow lies in improving our imaging-based model by using additional imaging data, professional annotations, and different advanced methods. In addition, using a larger cohort from additional sites is expected to help produce more generalized models.

Acknowledgements. We thank Prof. Fabien Reyal and Dr. Beatriz Grandal Rejo of Institut Curie for defining the clinical use case. We thank Chani Sacharen from IBM Research - Haifa for her help in editing the manuscript.

Research reported in this publication was partially supported by European Union's Horizon 2020 research and innovation program under grant agreement No 780495. The authors are solely responsible for the content of this paper. It does not represent the opinion of the European Union, and the European Union is not responsible for any use that might be made of data appearing therein.

References

1. Teshome, M., Hunt, K.K.: Neoadjuvant therapy in the treatment of breast cancer. Surg. Oncol. Clin. N. Am. **23**(3), 505–523 (2014)
2. Abreu, P.H., et al.: Predicting breast cancer recurrence using machine learning techniques: a systematic review. ACM Comput. Surv. (CSUR) **49**(3), 1–40 (2016)
3. Goyal, K., Aggarwal, P., Kumar, M.: Prediction of breast cancer recurrence: a machine learning approach. In: Behera, H.S., Nayak, J., Naik, B., Pelusi, D. (eds.) Computational Intelligence in Data Mining. AISC, vol. 990, pp. 101–113. Springer, Singapore (2020). https://doi.org/10.1007/978-981-13-8676-3_10
4. Chen, X., et al.: A reliable multi-classifier multi-objective model for predicting recurrence in triple negative breast cancer. In: 2019 41st Annual International Conference of the IEEE Engineering in Medicine and Biology Society (EMBC). IEEE (2019).
5. Al-Quraishi, T., Abawajy, J.H., Chowdhury, M.U., Rajasegarar, S., Abdalrada, A.S.: Breast cancer recurrence prediction using random forest model. In: Ghazali, R., Deris, M.M., Nawi,

N.M., Abawajy, J.H. (eds.) SCDM 2018. AISC, vol. 700, pp. 318–329. Springer, Cham (2018). https://doi.org/10.1007/978-3-319-72550-5_31

6. Tseng, Y.-J., et al.: Predicting breast cancer metastasis by using serum biomarkers and clinicopathological data with machine learning technologies. Int. J. Med. Inf. **128**, 79–86 (2019)

7. Hylton, N.M., et al.: Neoadjuvant chemotherapy for breast cancer: functional tumor volume by MR imaging predicts recurrence-free survival—results from the ACRIN 6657/CALGB 150007 I-SPY 1 TRIAL. Radiology **279**(1), 44–55 (2016)

8. Drukker, K., et al.: Most-enhancing tumor volume by MRI radiomics predicts recurrence-free survival "early on" in neoadjuvant treatment of breast cancer. Cancer Imaging **18**(1), 12 (2018). https://doi.org/10.1186/s40644-018-0145-9

9. Drukker, K., et al.: Deep learning predicts breast cancer recurrence in analysis of consecutive MRIs acquired during the course of neoadjuvant chemotherapy. In: Medical Imaging 2020: Computer-Aided Diagnosis, vol. 11314. International Society for Optics and Photonics (2020).

10. ISPY1. https://wiki.cancerimagingarchive.net/display/Public/ISPY1

11. Li, H., et al.: MR imaging radiomics signatures for predicting the risk of breast cancer recurrence as given by research versions of MammaPrint, Oncotype DX, and PAM50 gene assays. Radiology **281**(2), 382–391 (2016)

12. Lee, H., et al.: Predicting response to neoadjuvant chemotherapy in patients with breast cancer: combined statistical modeling using clinicopathological factors and FDG PET/CT texture parameters. Clin. Nucl. Med. **44**(1), 21–29 (2019)

13. Rabinovici-Cohen, S., et al.: Radiomics for predicting response to neoadjuvant chemotherapy treatment in breast cancer. In: Medical Imaging 2020: Imaging Informatics for Healthcare, Research, and Applications, vol. 11318. International Society for Optics and Photonics (2020)

14. Eben, J.E., Braman, N., Madabhushi, A.: Response estimation through spatially oriented neural network and texture ensemble (RESONATE). In: Shen, D., et al. (eds.) MICCAI 2019. LNCS, vol. 11767, pp. 602–610. Springer, Cham (2019). https://doi.org/10.1007/978-3-030-32251-9_66

15. Haarburger, C., et al.: Multi scale curriculum cnn for context-aware breast MRI malignancy classification. In: Shen, D., et al. (eds.) MICCAI 2019. LNCS, vol. 11767, pp. 495–503. Springer, Cham (2019). https://doi.org/10.1007/978-3-030-32251-9_54

16. Ravichandran, K., et al.: A deep learning classifier for prediction of pathological complete response to neoadjuvant chemotherapy from baseline breast DCE-MRI. In: Medical Imaging 2018: Computer-Aided Diagnosis, vol. 10575. International Society for Optics and Photonics (2018).

17. Ha, R., et al.: Prior to initiation of chemotherapy, can we predict breast tumor response? Deep learning convolutional neural networks approach using a breast MRI tumor dataset. J. Digit. Imaging **32**(5), 693–701 (2018). https://doi.org/10.1007/s10278-018-0144-1

18. He, K., et al.: Deep residual learning for image recognition. In: Proceedings of the IEEE Conference on Computer Vision and Pattern Recognition (2016)

19. TensorFlow. https://www.tensorflow.org. Accessed 5 July 2020

20. Klein, J., et al.: Locally advanced breast cancer treated with neoadjuvant chemotherapy and adjuvant radiotherapy: a retrospective cohort analysis. BMC Cancer **19**, 306 (2019). https://doi.org/10.1186/s12885-019-5499-2

A Self-ensembling Framework for Semi-supervised Knee Cartilage Defects Assessment with Dual-Consistency

Jiayu Huo[1,2], Liping Si[3], Xi Ouyang[1,2], Kai Xuan[1], Weiwu Yao[3], Zhong Xue[2], Qian Wang[1], Dinggang Shen[2], and Lichi Zhang[1(✉)]

[1] Institute for Medical Imaging Technology, School of Biomedical Engineering, Shanghai Jiao Tong University, Shanghai, China
`lichizhang@sjtu.edu.cn`
[2] Shanghai United Imaging Intelligence Co., Ltd., Shanghai, China
[3] Department of Imaging, Tongren Hospital, Shanghai Jiao Tong University School of Medicine, Shanghai, China

Abstract. Knee osteoarthritis (OA) is one of the most common musculoskeletal disorders and requires early-stage diagnosis. Nowadays, the deep convolutional neural networks have achieved greatly in the computer-aided diagnosis field. However, the construction of the deep learning models usually requires great amounts of annotated data, which is generally high-cost. In this paper, we propose a novel approach for knee cartilage defects assessment, including severity classification and lesion localization. This can be treated as a subtask of knee OA diagnosis. Particularly, we design a self-ensembling framework, which is composed of a student network and a teacher network with the same structure. The student network learns from both labeled data and unlabeled data and the teacher network averages the student model weights through the training course. A novel attention loss function is developed to obtain accurate attention masks. With dual-consistency checking of the attention in the lesion classification and localization, the two networks can gradually optimize the attention distribution and improve the performance of each other, whereas the training relies on partially labeled data only and follows the semi-supervised manner. Experiments show that the proposed method can significantly improve the self-ensembling performance in both knee cartilage defects classification and localization, and also greatly reduce the needs of annotated data.

Keywords: Knee osteoarthritis · Self-ensembling model · Semi-supervised learning

1 Introduction

Osteoarthritis (OA) is one of the most common joint diseases, which is characterized by a lack of articular cartilage integrity, as well as prevalent changes

© Springer Nature Switzerland AG 2020
I. Rekik et al. (Eds.): PRIME 2020, LNCS 12329, pp. 200–209, 2020.
https://doi.org/10.1007/978-3-030-59354-4_19

associated with the underlying bone and articular structures. OA can lead to joint necrosis or even disability if it is not intervened at an early stage [4]. Knee cartilage defects assessment is highly correlated to knee OA diagnosis [9], so that it can be treated as a subtask. Magnetic resonance imaging (MRI) is a powerful tool for OA diagnosis. Compared with X-ray, MRI has a better imaging quality for cartilage and edema areas, which makes it practical for the early-stage clinical diagnosis.

Computer-aided diagnosis (CAD) based on MRI have achieved greatly for diagnosing OA, since it can reduce the subjective influences from the radiologists, and also greatly release the burdens of their works. A number of contributions have been achieved in the field of CAD using deep learning techniques [1,2,7]. For example, Antony et al. [1] used a CNN model pretrained from ImageNet [2] dataset to automatically quantify the knee OA severity from CT scans. Liu et al. [7] implemented a U-Net [10] for the knee cartilage segmentation, and fine-tuned the encoder to evaluate structural abnormalities within the segmented cartilage tissue. However, the good performance achieved by the supervised deep neural networks highly relies on the manually annotated data with extensive amount, which is generally high-cost. In order to alleviate the needs of huge amount manual annotations, several semi-supervised methods were developed. Laine et al. [5] designed a temporal ensembling model for the natural image classification. Yu et al. [12] proposed an uncertainty-aware framework for the left atrium segmentation. But, the semi-supervised framework for knee joint disease diagnosis has not been proposed yet.

In this paper, we propose a self-ensembling semi-supervised learning approach, named as dual-consistency mean teacher framework (DC-MT), to resolve the high demand of annotated data. Our DC-MT framework aims to quantify the severity of knee cartilage defects simultaneously, to provide informative attention masks for lesion localization. This quantification task can be treated as a subtask of knee OA diagnosis. The attention masks highlight regions that related to knee cartilage defects and its severity can be used as the basis to interpret the diagnosis results in clinical practice. On the other hand, such attention-based localization tasks could improve the performance of knee cartilage defects classification.

In summary, the main contributions are listed as follows: 1) DC-MT consists of a student model and a teacher model, which share the same architecture. Two additional attention mining branches are added into the two models respectively to obtain the attention masks, which can be considered as the basis for classification. 2) We define an attention loss function to constrain the attention mask generation, which can yield more accurate attention masks. It could also let the classification results more credible if the corresponding attention masks are precise. 3) We propose novel dual-consistency loss functions to penalize the inconsistency of output classification probability and attention mask. It can help the whole framework achieve consistency between the student and teacher models in both attention and classification probability level, so that the two networks support each other to improve performance interactively.

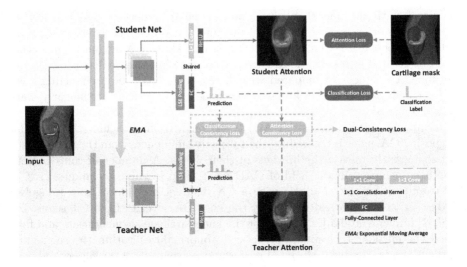

Fig. 1. The pipeline of our DC-MT framework for semi-supervised classification and localization of knee cartilage defects. Two dark green round rectangles denote the supervised loss functions, and two pink round rectangles denote the dual-consistency loss functions. (Color figure online)

2   Methodology

The proposed DC-MT framework for knee cartilage defects diagnosis is illustrated in Fig. 1, which consists of a teacher model and a student model with the same architecture. Both models generate the classification probabilities for knee cartilage defects severity and provide the attention masks for lesion localization simultaneously. The dual-consistency loss functions are proposed to ensure improved classification and localization performance.

2.1   Mean Teacher Mechanism

Mean teacher model [11] is a self-ensembling model which is designed for the classification task of the natural image. It typically contains two models (i.e., student model and teacher model) with the same network structure. As shown in Fig. 1, a knee joint image is input to the student and teacher networks respectively. The output includes both the knee cartilage defects severity probabilities and the corresponding attention masks. Specifically, the student network is optimized by both the supervised and the unsupervised loss functions, and the teacher model is updated by *exponential moving average* (EMA) [5]. The EMA updating strategy is used to merge network weights effectively through optimization. The weight of the teacher model θ'_τ at training step τ is updated by:

$$\theta'_\tau = \alpha \theta'_{\tau-1} + (1 - \alpha)\,\theta_\tau, \tag{1}$$

where α is a decay factor that controls the weight decay speed, and θ_τ is the student model's weight. It can be seen that the student network is more adaptive to training data and the teacher network is more stable. By using the two models, we hope that the final trained networks can demonstrate a combined advantage of the networks.

2.2   Attention Mining

The goal of attention mining is to generate attention masks while performing localization and classification tasks. In this work, the attention mining strategy is based on guided attention inference network [6,8]. It shows that the generated attention masks will be more accurate if the segmentation results of the targets are added as the supervision. Here we apply a U-Net-based model to firstly segment the femur cartilage region and utilize it for attention supervision. Since the lesions are generally located in the cartilage region, it is indicated that our cartilage segmentation results can help refine the attention masks and improve their corresponding classification performance. In this way, we add an attention loss to constrain the attention mask generation. Besides, a regularization term is also added so that the attention mask which is small and within the segmented cartilage region is also acceptable. The entire attention loss is therefore defined as:

$$L_a = \lambda_a \frac{\sum_k |f_\theta(x_i)_k - S(x_i)_k|^2}{\sum_k f_\theta(x_i)_k + \sum_k S(x_i)_k} + \lambda_r \left(1 - \frac{\sum_k (f_\theta(x_i)_k \cdot S(x_i)_k)}{\sum_k f_\theta(x_i)_k} \right), \quad (2)$$

where $f_\theta(x_i)_k$ denotes the attention masks generated by the student model with input x_i at the k-th pixel, and $S(x_i)_k$ denotes the corresponding femur cartilage segmentation result. The U-Net-based model is denoted as S, and λ_a and λ_r are the loss weighting factors. With the help of the attention loss, the network can generate more accurate attention masks, which further improve the classification performance.

2.3   Dual Consistency Loss

Using the additional attention mining branch, the student model and teacher model yield a classification probability and an attention mask at the same time. To better coordinate the two networks, we need to ensure the consistency between output probabilities, and also between the attention masks. Hence, we propose the novel attention consistency loss to meet the requirement. When a batch of images are treated as input, the two models yield the probability and the attention mask, respectively. The student model is optimized by the supervision loss and the dual consistency loss, as a result the whole framework achieve a better performance. In this work, we design the dual-consistency loss functions as mean squared error (MSE) regards of probability and attention maps. Specifically, the dual-consistency loss functions are defined as:

$$L_{cc} = \frac{1}{n} \sum_n |p_\theta(x_i)_n - p_{\theta'}(x_i)_n|^2, \quad (3)$$

$$L_{ac} = \frac{\sum_k |f_\theta(x_i)_k - f_{\theta'}(x_i)_k|^2}{\sum_k f_\theta(x_i)_k + \sum_k f_{\theta'}(x_i)_k}, \tag{4}$$

where θ and θ' represent parameters of the student and teacher models, respectively. $p_\theta(x_i)$ and $p'_\theta(x_i)$ are probabilities of the models with respect to input x_i. n represents the number of classification categories. With our proposed dual-consistency loss, the DC-MT framework can learn structure consistency and probabilistic distribution consistency synchronously, which is essential for the two models to support each other to improve the performance.

The overall loss function consists of classification loss, attention loss and dual-consistency loss, which is shown as:

$$L_{total} = L_c + L_a + w_c(\tau)L_{cc} + w_a(\tau)L_{ac}, \tag{5}$$

where L_c denotes the cross-entropy loss. $w_c(\tau)$ and $w_a(\tau)$ represent a ramp-up function of training step τ respectively, which can adjust the weighting factors of dual consistency loss functions dynamically. During the training procedure, the values of $w_c(\tau)$ and $w_a(\tau)$ will increase as the training procedure goes on. In our work, $w_c(\tau)$ and $w_a(\tau)$ are the same and set to $w(\tau)$. Here we define $w(\tau)$ as an exponential function, which is $w(\tau) = e^{-5 \cdot (1-\tau/\tau_{\max})^2}$. τ_{max} is the maximum training step. By this design setting, the network training procedure can be guided by the supervised loss at the beginning, so that the whole framework can be better trained, preventing the network sink into a degenerate condition.

3   Experiments

3.1   Dataset

In the experiments, we used 1408 knee T2 weighted MR images collected from Shanghai Jiao Tong University Affiliated Sixth People's Hospital to conduct the knee cartilage defects assessment task. The images were categorized into three classes according to whole-organ magnetic resonance imaging score (WORMS) [9]: normal thickness cartilage (WORMS 0 and 1), partial-thickness defect cartilage (WORMS 2, 2.5, 3 and 4) and full-thickness defect cartilage (WORMS 5 and 6). An experienced radiologist selected and classified 6025 2D slices to generate the ground-truth, and the three categories are mostly balanced among them. Cartilage segmentation for all images was obtained through an inhouse U-Net toolkit, which was also validated by the radiologist. A dilation operation was applied to enlarge the segmentation results, which can reduce the difficulty of the localization task. We then randomly selected 90% images of each class to form the training set, and the rest as the testing set. Particularly, the data selection was conducted according to subject, which can avoid slices from the same person were put into both the training and testing set.

3.2   Experimental Settings

The proposed algorithm was implemented using PyTorch. The backbone of the framework is the Se-ResNeXt50 model [3]. We changed the convolution stride in the fourth block so that a bigger feature map of the final convolution layer can be obtained. The size of the feature map is 1/16 of the input image size, which is necessary for accurate attention mask generation. Adam optimizer was employed and the value of weight decay was set to 0.0001. The learning rate was initialized with 0.001. The input image size of the network is 256 × 256, and data augmentation techniques were utilized to prevent over-fitting. The batch size was 30, including 20 labeled images and 10 unlabeled images. The loss weighting factors λ_a and λ_r in the attention loss were set to 0.5 and 0.001, respectively.

3.3   Experimental Results

Efficacy of Attention Loss. We use four metrics to quantitatively evaluate the effect of the newly defined attention loss, including Recall, F1-Score, area under the ROC curve (AUC) and threshold intersection over union ratio (TIoU). TIoU means the ratio of the number of cases with correct localization against the total number of cases. If the intersection over union (IoU) ratio between the attention mask and the segmentation result is bigger than a prescribed threshold, the corresponding localization result is considered as correct. We set different thresholds T (T = {0.1, 0.2, 0.3, 0.4, 0.5, 0.6, 0.7}) and calculated IoU for evaluation. These values of IoU were then averaged to get TIoU. The first three metrics are used to evaluate the classification performance, and the last one for analyze the localization performance. We only use 10% labeled training data to learn the student network.

A quantitative experiment of attention loss was conducted by setting the different values of λ_a and λ_r. The part of attention loss would not be calculated if the loss factor was set to 0. Table 1 shows the result of the classification and localization performance under the different settings of the two attention loss factors. If λ_a and λ_r were both equal to 0, which means there is no supervision in attention mask generation, the network obtained a poor localization performance. However, if we only set the regularization item factor λ_r to 0 and λ_a to 0.5, the localization performance improved dramatically, also the classification performance was benefited and enhanced. With the help of the two penalties (λ_a equals to 0.5 and λ_r equals to 0.001), the network can achieve the highest performance in both classification and localization task. It also demonstrates the importance of attention loss when annotations are limited.

Evaluation of the Proposed Mechanism. This experiment illustrates the efficacy of our proposed mechanism. We trained the fully-supervised student network using all and 10% labeled training data, which can be regarded as the upper-line and base-line performance, respectively. The proposed semi-supervised method also used all the training data, while certain percentage

Table 1. Attention loss ablation using the metrics of Recall, F1-Score, AUC and TIoU.

Metrics	$\lambda_a = 0, \lambda_r = 0$	$\lambda_a = 0.5, \lambda_r = 0$	$\lambda_a = 0.5, \lambda_r = 0.001$
Recall	68.3%	74.4%	**75.8%**
F1-Score	68.2%	74.7%	**75.3%**
AUC	82.1%	86.0%	**89.4%**
TIoU	7.5%	62.0%	**71.3%**

Table 2. Comparison of Recall, F1-Score, AUC and TIoU between the fully supervised method and our proposed method. FS means full supervision and DC-MT is our proposed method.

Metrics	FS (10% labels)	FS (100% labels)	DC-MT (10% labels)
Recall	75.8%	85.0%	79.3%
F1-Score	75.3%	84.6%	79.1%
AUC	89.4%	93.7%	90.1%
TIoU	71.3%	90.3%	87.3%

had their classification and segmentation information hidden. The experimental results are shown in Table 2. It can be observed that the fully-supervised method achieved an average F1-Score of 75.3% and TIoU of 71.3% with only 10% labeled data. By considering the feature consistency and structure consistency simultaneously and efficiently utilizing unlabeled data, our proposed mechanism further improved the performance by achieve 79.1%, F1- score and 87.3% TIoU. For the localization task, our method's performance can reach the fully-supervised ones with all labeled data.

We conducted another quantitative evaluation to analyze the importance of the attention consistency loss by adjusting the ratio of labeled data in the training set to obtain the labeled data contribution. The ratio of labeled data was set to 10%, 30% and 50%, respectively. Moreover, we compared it with the original mean teacher model (MT) [11] to prove the necessity of our proposed loss functions. Because the MT model was designed for semi-supervised classification tasks, we only compared the classification metrics for fair comparison. As shown in Table 3, an apparent improvement of the performance was observed as the ratio of labeled data increased. Here DC-MT (NAC) means that the attention consistency loss was not added into the proposed mechanism, and NAC stands for no attention consistency. Compared with the MT model, DC-MT (NAC) improved by 3.4% Recall, 3.9% F1-Score and 3.0% AUC, respectively, when only 10% labeled data were used for training. This demonstrates that the attention loss can help to improve the classification performance. When the attention consistency loss was added into the whole framework, DC-MT achieved 79.3% Recall, 79.1% F1-Score and 90.1% AUC, which was the highest performance among all the methods. As the number of labeled data increases (e.g. from

Table 3. Quantitative analysis of all methods. DC-MT (NAC) means the attention consistency loss was not added into the proposed mechanism.

Metrics		MT	DC-MT (NAC)	DC-MT
Recall	10% labels	73.4%	76.8%	**79.3%**
	30% labels	78.0%	81.5%	**83.1%**
	50% labels	81.0%	81.3%	**84.3%**
F1-Score	10% labels	72.7%	76.6%	**79.1%**
	30% labels	78.0%	81.5%	**83.2%**
	50% labels	81.0%	81.4%	**83.8%**
AUC	10% labels	86.2%	89.2%	**90.1%**
	30% labels	87.9%	**92.7%**	91.9%
	50% labels	90.9%	92.7%	**92.8%**

30% to 50%), DC-MT (NAC) seemed to have reached a bottleneck. However, compared with DC-MT (NAC), DC-MT is still able to maintain stable growth in all these metrics. Although DC-MT achieved 91.9% AUC when 30% labeled data was used for training, which was lower than 92.7% achieved by DC-MT (NAC), 83.1% Recall and 83.2% F1-Score of DC-MT were still higher than DC-MT (NAC). This also proved the importance of the novel attention consistency loss and the necessity of the combination between two attention related losses.

Visualization Results. Figure 2 shows three visualized results of our method when the model weight is used to make predictions on the testing set. The yel-

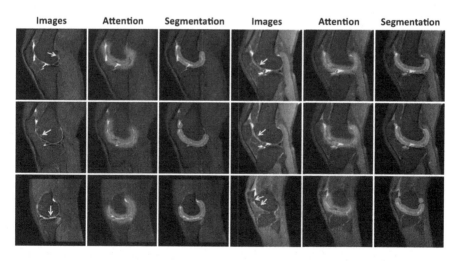

Fig. 2. Visualization of attention maps with the segmentation results from the knee cartilage defects diagnosis.

low arrows on the images indicate the specific location of knee cartilage defects, which was labeled by the experienced radiologist. It shows that the areas indicated by arrows are also highlighted by the corresponding attentions maps. More importantly, these conspicuous area in attention maps are similar to the segmentation results. Which shows that the network can classify correctly according to the accurate localization results.

4   Conclusion

We developed a self-enssembling semi-supervisesd network for knee cartilage defects classification and localization and proposed a dual consistency learning mechanism to coordinate the learning procedure of the student and teacher networks. Attention loss is used to not only encourage the network to yield the correct classification result, but also to provide the basis (accurate attention maps) for correct classification. Furthermore, we presented the attention consistency loss to make the general frame be consistent in the structure level. With the help of two supervised losses and dual consistency losses, our mechanism can achieve the best performance in both classification and localization tasks. The ablation experiments also confirmed the effectiveness of our method. The future works include conducting experiments in other knee datasets (*e.g..*, OAI dataset) and investigating the effect of our method to other knee joint problems.

Acknowledgement. This work was supported by the National Key Research and Development Program of China (2018YFC0116400), STCSM (19QC1400600, 17411953300, 18JC1420305), Shanghai Pujiang Program (19PJ1406800), and Interdisciplinary Program of Shanghai Jiao Tong University.

References

1. Antony, J., McGuinness, K., O'Connor, N.E., Moran, K.: Quantifying radiographic knee osteoarthritis severity using deep convolutional neural networks. In: 2016 23rd International Conference on Pattern Recognition (ICPR), pp. 1195–1200. IEEE (2016)
2. Deng, J., Dong, W., Socher, R., Li, L.J., Li, K., Fei-Fei, L.: ImageNet: a large-scale hierarchical image database. In: 2009 IEEE Conference on Computer Vision and Pattern Recognition, pp. 248–255. IEEE (2009)
3. Hu, J., Shen, L., Sun, G.: Squeeze-and-excitation networks. In: Proceedings of the IEEE Conference on Computer Vision and Pattern Recognition, pp. 7132–7141 (2018)
4. Karsdal, M., et al.: Disease-modifying treatments for osteoarthritis (DMOADs) of the knee and hip: lessons learned from failures and opportunities for the future. Osteoarthr. Cartil. **24**(12), 2013–2021 (2016)
5. Laine, S., Aila, T.: Temporal ensembling for semi-supervised learning. arXiv preprint arXiv:1610.02242 (2016)
6. Li, K., Wu, Z., Peng, K.C., Ernst, J., Fu, Y.: Tell me where to look: guided attention inference network. In: Proceedings of the IEEE Conference on Computer Vision and Pattern Recognition, pp. 9215–9223 (2018)

7. Liu, F., et al.: Deep learning approach for evaluating knee MR images: achieving high diagnostic performance for cartilage lesion detection. Radiology **289**(1), 160–169 (2018)
8. Ouyang, X., et al.: Weakly supervised segmentation framework with uncertainty: a study on pneumothorax segmentation in chest x-ray. In: Shen, D., et al. (eds.) MICCAI 2019. LNCS, vol. 11769, pp. 613–621. Springer, Cham (2019). https://doi.org/10.1007/978-3-030-32226-7_68
9. Peterfy, C., et al.: Whole-organ magnetic resonance imaging score (WORMS) of the knee in osteoarthritis. Osteoarthr. Cartil. **12**(3), 177–190 (2004)
10. Ronneberger, O., Fischer, P., Brox, T.: U-Net: convolutional networks for biomedical image segmentation. In: Navab, N., Hornegger, J., Wells, W.M., Frangi, A.F. (eds.) MICCAI 2015. LNCS, vol. 9351, pp. 234–241. Springer, Cham (2015). https://doi.org/10.1007/978-3-319-24574-4_28
11. Tarvainen, A., Valpola, H.: Mean teachers are better role models: weight-averaged consistency targets improve semi-supervised deep learning results. In: Advances in Neural Information Processing Systems, pp. 1195–1204 (2017)
12. Yu, L., Wang, S., Li, X., Fu, C.-W., Heng, P.-A.: Uncertainty-aware self-ensembling model for semi-supervised 3D left atrium segmentation. In: Shen, D., et al. (eds.) MICCAI 2019. LNCS, vol. 11765, pp. 605–613. Springer, Cham (2019). https://doi.org/10.1007/978-3-030-32245-8_67

Author Index

Printed in the United States
By Bookmasters